2nd Edition

MAKING SENSE OF IT ALL

An Introduction
to Philosophical Inquiry

DAVID H. LUND

Bemidji State University

Prentice
Hall

Upper Saddle River, New Jersey 07458

Library of Congress Cataloging-in-Publication Data

Lund, David H.
   Making sense of it all : an introduction to philosophical inquiry /
   David H. Lund.—2nd ed.
      p. cm.
   Includes bibliographical references and index.
   ISBN 0–13–098891–X
   1. Philosophy—Introductions. I. Title.

BD21 .L86 2003
100—dc21   2002023150

Editor-in-Chief: Charlyce Jones Owen
Acquisitions Editor: Ross Miller
Editorial Assistant: Carla Worner
Editorial/Production Supervision: B. Christenberry
Manufacturing Buyer: Brian Mackey
Cover Designer: Bruce Kenselaar
Art Director: Jayne Conte

© 2003, 1999 by Pearson Education, Inc
Upper Saddle River, New Jersey 07458

This book was set in 10/12 Baskerville by DM Cradle Associates
and was printed and bound by RR Donnelley/Harrisonburg.
The cover was printed by Phoenix Color Corp.

Printed in the United States of America

10 9 8 7 6 5 4 3 2 1

ISBN   0-13-098891-X

PEARSON EDUCATION LTD., *London*
PEARSON EDUCATION Australia PTY. Limited, *Sydney*
PEARSON EDUCATION Singapore, Pte. Ltd.
PEARSON EDUCATION North Asia Ltd., *Hong Kong*
PEARSON EDUCATION Canada, Ltd., *Toronto*
PEARSON EDUCATION de Mexico, S.A. de C.V.
PEARSON EDUCATION —*Japan, Tokyo*
PEARSON EDUCATION Malaysia, Pte. Ltd.
PEARSON EDUCATION, *Upper Saddle River, New Jersey*

To Rose and John

CONTENTS

PREFACE to the SECOND EDITION

Though this edition preserves the basic structure, the participatory approach, the ultimate aims, and the problem-centered focus of the first edition (features that are discussed in the preface to that edition), alterations have been made in each of the ten chapters. Most of the alterations are additions to the content, the most substantial of which occur in chapters 2, 3, 4, 6, 8, and 10. The most important additions to chapter 2 consist in a more extensive treatment of truth and a more detailed attempt to specify what knowledge is. Chapter 3 now includes discussion of the problem of universals. What has been added to chapter 4 is an expanded treatment of functionalism, an argument for viewing causation as an irreducible relation, and an explanation of how mind-body interaction may be understood in such a view of causation. The most important addition to chapter 5 is a brief discussion of the futility of attempting to ground personal identity in genetic identity.

Chapter 6 now contains a much more extensive treatment of the problem of natural evil and of plausible theistic responses to it. A more extensive (though still comparatively brief) defense of the agency theory is now part of chapter 7. Chapter 8 now includes a more explicit specification of deontological moral concerns along with an attempt to bring them into balance with the concerns of the utilitarian. Chapter 9 now makes more explicit how the tentative conclusions reached in earlier chapters, particularly the chapter on the self, are relevant to the issue of whether our survival of bodily death is conceivable. Finally, the manner in which and the extent to which the foregoing reflections and tentative conclusions may affect our quest for meaning is made much more explicit in chapter 10. The remaining alterations consist primarily in various minor changes intended to provide the text with a higher level of cohesiveness than it already had.

PREFACE to the FIRST EDITION

Philosophic inquiry can be an intellectually exciting, mind-transforming activity. This book is intended to introduce you to it, if you are encountering it for the first time. If you have already been exposed to such inquiry, I hope to heighten your appreciation of its power to enrich our lives and to enlarge your understanding of it, partly by showing how it may be of great help to us in "thinking things through." In either case, I hope to entice you to grapple with some of the most fundamental intellectual problems known to us. I invite you to think along with me in a searching examination of these philosophical problems, not only to see precisely what they are, why they pose as obstacles to our understanding, and how we might respond to them, but to do so with the ultimate aim of arriving at a vision of reality as a whole. But I also wish to suggest that such an examination is quite unavoidable if we are to live our lives in even a modestly thoughtful, reflective way, that is, unavoidable if we are intent on pursuing the good life. It has long been recognized by those who have managed to attain some wisdom that an unreflective, unexamined life is a diminished one. Indeed, the great Greek philosopher Socrates went so far as to proclaim that the unexamined life is not worth living. That may seem disputable. What is beyond dispute, however, is that an unexamined life is a diminished form of existence for anyone capable of exercising critical, independent thought in a quest for truth and understanding. To leave unexercised such a potentially ennobling capacity is to live a life unworthy of us.

I provide a treatment of nine fundamentally important problems or issues, each of which must be addressed if our aim is to arrive at an adequate understanding of ourselves and of our relation to the whole of reality. Taken together they are sufficiently comprehensive to justify the claim that anyone who has come to grips with them may well have succeeded in "making sense of it all," that is, in arriving at a philosophically informed world-view. What we understand these problems to be and how we might go about resolving them are inseparable from our quest for a philosophically informed understanding of ourselves and our place in the world.

Many works in philosophy take a historical approach, focusing on introducing the reader to the thought of the great philosophers, and assuming (often quite justifiably) that this is what would interest the reader. If this would interest you, you are to be commended. Interest in this is a precious possession. But perhaps you presently have no such interest. Perhaps you know little of Plato and have never heard of Hume or Descartes. If this is true of you, then you may have little interest in finding out what great thinkers such as these have said. But chances are you *would* be interested if you came to see that the concerns of these philosophers were essentially those of all reflective persons trying to attain a more carefully reasoned and more synoptic understanding of the world and their existence in it.

These concerns (or problems) will be our focus here—the concerns that naturally lead us into philosophic inquiry. Because of them, my approach here is not historical, but problem-centered. By adopting this approach, I do not intend to suggest that the views of the great philosophers are of lesser value than we may have thought, but only that a focus on them may be more effective later than at the outset. You need not be motivated to explore them now. I try not to assume, or rely on, any initial interest in either the subject matter or the methods of philosophic study. I will attempt to draw you into philosophic inquiry, largely by exposing you to the gripping effect of the most important questions we can raise, and by showing that raising fundamental philosophic questions is natural for us, if not something we inevitably do at some time. For these questions arise quite naturally, given the conditions under which we must live, along with our need to understand the world within and around us. By focusing on such questions, I hope to engage at the outset your capacity for critical thought and then hold your attention as we proceed. But in philosophic study there is really no substitute for natural intellectual curiosity and a robust desire to understand, and I would be somewhat remiss if I did not caution you about what an intellectually strenuous undertaking any serious attempt to grapple with the problems of philosophy must be. As we descend into the depths and complexity of the study, the terrain inevitably becomes difficult, and it will not always be easy to find our way. Indeed, there may be times when we seem to be caught up in a veritable labyrinth, unable to find a way out. Full awareness of this at the outset is important, enabling us to brace ourselves for what we will encounter. Not only will we find ourselves struggling to attain clarity, but we may be led to call into question some of our basic and most cherished beliefs. It is, perhaps, at this point that philosophic inquiry becomes most trying, demanding of us an emotional strength to seriously question beliefs that may be of great importance to us, while maintaining a resolve to understand and the conviction that truth is good even when it turns out not to be what we had hoped. The pursuit of a difficult and elusive truth, which may turn out to be painful as well, is probably not for the faint-hearted or weak of spirit.

But we should not find this intimidating or disheartening. Rather, we should see it as a challenge to which we can rise. The intellectual honesty and the toughness of spirit which philosophic study requires of us will serve us well. However, a strenuous and sometimes unsettling undertaking is only the more somber part of what we should anticipate. Though philosophy challenges and disturbs, it also calms and consoles. And, if we give it free rein, it would take us on an exciting adventure of the mind. Nothing liberates the mind like philosophic thought. In leading us to apply our critical intelligence and think things out for ourselves, it frees us from the confines of uncritically acquired and unreflectively held belief; it loosens the grip of prejudice, custom, and provincial thought. It can be revolutionary when it radically transforms our entire perspective—of what is real, of what is possible, and of what we should seek or take to be of central importance. Those who are deeply moved by it end up marching to a different drummer.

I have tried to employ the problem-centered approach in more or less the following way: I attempt to make the problem under consideration "come alive," so to speak, in the hope that you will be pulled into it sufficiently to feel its grip; I will show how it arises quite naturally or unavoidably in our attempt to attain a fundamental understanding of ourselves and our place in the world; I will encourage you to "join forces" with me as we wrestle with it; and I will give you at least a glimpse (if not a greater view) of its depths and the intellectual challenge it presents. We will apply our best efforts to resolve it; and then, after having been led to a full appreciation of its difficulty and of our inability as reflective persons to simply ignore it, we will be poised to consider the insights of the great philosophers to see if those insights may be of help to us. However, we will not focus on such consideration here.

As I have already indicated, we will work at resolving the problems that we have brought to light. We will take note of the lines along which a satisfactory resolution might be attained and even arrive at tentative solutions or conclusions. Of course, we will do this with full appreciation of the formidable difficulty of the problem and the great unlikelihood that we have reached a definitive or conclusive answer. Perhaps our tentative "answer" is more accurately construed as our best guess in the light of our current understanding. But that we venture an answer anyway is, I think, important. We may find ourselves frustrated with philosophy when it raises deep, unsettling questions without attempting to provide answers. Of course, we must realize that we may have unrealistic expectations about what philosophy should be able to provide. Philosophy ordinarily cannot satisfy a demand for certainty; and when people learn this, they learn something important about philosophy and its problems. Nevertheless, tentative answers based upon the evidence currently available to us and expressing our present level of understanding are quite appropriate to provide, when possible, and may be of considerable value to us even if they are only temporary vantage points in an ongoing quest that has no end in sight. Even if they turn out to have little value as answers, they may prove to be interesting targets for critical examination and ultimately the stepping stones to a better view.

These answers, however, are not left isolated from one another. My aim is not merely to encourage you to apply your critical intelligence to a number of the fundamentally important problems of phiiosophy (and, if philosophic study is new to you, to thereby introduce you to the method and content of philosophic thought as well), but to provide the elements of a world-view, i.e., to fit the various considerations together in a way that enables you to do what philosophic thought has traditionally been regarded as helping us to do—to "make sense of it all." We inevitably do this to some degree. Philosophic study should make us much more proficient at doing this. It should help us arrive at a better informed, a more carefully reasoned, and a more synoptic understanding of our experience. One of my central aims in this work is to have you proceed a considerable distance along the route to becoming a philosopher in your own right—probably a nonprofessional one, but a philosopher just the same. With respect to this aim, I hope to show rather than merely tell how philosophic thought can have a transforming effect upon our lives.

Though the problems and issues we shall consider are certainly worth studying for their own sake and indeed cannot be ignored by thoughtful people, I should emphasize the importance and the type of intellectual activity in which we must engage as we study them. This is an activity of great value, not only because of the role it must play in any serious quest for truth and understanding but because of the manner in which it exercises the mind—an exercise whose benefits are a significant bonus that we should not overlook. I will be encouraging you to engage in critical and independent thought—a type of thinking whose value cannot be overestimated. Though I will present concepts, issues, and arguments (as I must), I intend my implicit approach to be, as I indicated earlier, one of "let's think about this together." Your participation in the effort to resolve the problems under consideration, rather than a passive assimilation of the subject matter, is what I will be encouraging. We will examine basic concepts, test beliefs and propositions in an effort to determine their truth, and construct arguments in which we will reason carefully from premises to conclusion. In this process, you will be exposed to both analytic and synthetic thought. Since my own orientation in philosophy is analytical, you will encounter a good deal of analysis. But you will also be called upon to think synthetically, as I will encourage you to weave the considerations and conclusions of the various chapters into a single coherent world-view. I will show you what the problems are, indicate what must be taken into account to provide an adequate treatment of them, and even offer tentative conclusions. But I hope to always leave you vividly aware of the importance of your own involvement in resolving them and of how much more there is left to do if we are finally to "make sense of it all."

ACKNOWLEDGMENTS

I wish to thank Michael Field, Matthew Lund, and Bowen Johnson for reading the entire manuscript and making helpful suggestions. I would also like to express my appreciation to my reviewers: G. John M. Abbarno, D'Youville College; David B. Annis, Ball State University; Theodore M. Drange, West Virginia University; Charles F. Kielkopf, Ohio State University; John Knox, Jr., Drew University; Alexander T. Levine, Lehigh University; Timothy Shanahan, Loyola Marymount University; and Richard L. Wilson, Towson State University. Finally, I wish to thank my wife, Elaine, for the long hours spent in word-processing the manuscript.

1

INTRODUCTION

PHILOSOPHY AND THE NEED TO UNDERSTAND

Philosophy is a quest for fundamental truth and understanding—for that which would enable us to explain the world, to make sense out of our experience, and to determine how we ought to live. It is the study of the most fundamental and most broadly important questions that there are. Its central goal is to help us attain a broad understanding of the world, both within and without—a vision of the whole of reality and of our place in it. The goal is to develop in us a coherent, adequate world-view, as we try to answer the fundamental questions and come to understand the problems of human experience out of which they emerge. This book is intended to engage you in philosophic study and thereby to show you what great benefit such study can have in our efforts to live as wisely and as well as possible.

Although philosophy is widely regarded as a highly abstract, specialized study remote from the lives of most people, in fact it is intimately involved in many of our deepest concerns. For it arises out of a need that is intensely felt at some time or other by almost everyone, however inchoate or unacknowledged that need may remain for the ordinary person. When we think of human needs, what comes first to mind are physical needs for food and shelter, and the emotional need for love. We share many of these needs with other members of the animal kingdom, but we also have a uniquely human need—an intellectual need to understand, to make sense out of our existence in the world. Some of the other animals undoubtedly have experiences of various kinds, but only we are conscious of *ourselves as having experience*. We are *reflectively* aware of our own states and of a world distinct from us. Out of this unique characteristic arises a unique need. Our self-conscious nature—which proves to be both a blessing and a burden—enables us to reflect upon our experience; and when we do so, as we inevitably do at some time, we feel a need to make sense of it, to see it in a larger context or framework. We may direct our reflective gaze upon ourselves in an effort to understand our own nature and to determine how we ought to live. We may reflect upon the nature of the world around us, upon how we fit into it, and on what is happening there. We may reflect upon what we might do to improve the conditions of our existence. And we may reflect upon how all of this fits together into a larger framework in which each item has its place.

As we do so, we may find much that is puzzling. Quite obviously, neither our being in the world nor the world itself is *self*-explanatory. It is up to us to provide some interpretation or explanation, and we are prompted by a *need* to do so—by a need to understand. Philosophy makes its appearance in this context as an unusually disciplined and persistent attempt to understand ourselves and our place in the world. Its traditional and primary concern is with the great questions of life, which ordinary people might pose to themselves in their reflective moments. In brief, philosophizing is thinking hard about life's most fundamental questions.

Philosophy is distinguished from other attempts to answer such questions by its relentless use of reason. It prods us to critically examine our beliefs, not only to see if they are based on evidence and consistent with each other, but to become clearer about precisely what we are believing in holding them. To engage in it is to engage in an intellectual activity that sharpens our wit as it liberates us from the tyranny of custom and provincial thought. It exposes us to a diversity of views and issues we have never considered, and it demands of us that we think things out for ourselves in a manner that is both critical and constructive. It helps us to reason better and to argue more effectively. It stretches our imagination, opening up new worlds for us to explore, as it develops our capacity for analytical and abstract thought. It can enrich our lives in ways that nothing else can. But the motivation to engage in it at all is entirely dependent, initially at least, upon our natural curiosity and our need to understand.

It seems undeniable that everyone capable of reflective thought has such a need, at least to some degree, even if in many it has remained unrecognized and unappreciated. Gaining an understanding—or at least a feeling of understanding, of having figured things out to some degree or in some respect—is something we seem to desire for its own sake, quite apart from the significant practical benefits that may result. For many of us, to have reached a state of mental clarity and understanding in thinking through the large questions of life is deeply satisfying. Indeed, one might argue that the extent to which some gain in understanding strikes a deep responsive chord in us is a measure of our mental or intellectual health and thus of something of intrinsic worth to us. Our intellectual health, like our physical health, is a good worth valuing for its own sake. These forms of health or well-being are also alike in that each is developed and nurtured by the appropriate exercise, physical or intellectual as the case may be. And just as we seem fitted by nature to enjoy physical activity when we have physical well-being, we seem similarly fitted to enjoy intellectual activity, and the gain in understanding it may yield, when we are intellectually healthy—that is, when we are prompted by a natural curiosity and the boldness to apply our own critical powers instead of simply taking over the opinions of others. That we should find some gratification in the mental state of understanding, in and of itself, should not seem at all unnatural or surprising in creatures having the cognitive and linguistic powers that we possess, even if their limitations are frequently apparent.

If this characterization of the universality and the strength of the desire to understand should seem more ideal than real, we should note that on a less lofty level there can be no question of the universality of the need to make some degree of sense of one's experience. For every human being endowed with self-consciousness has some concept or other of herself and of the world she experiences, however dimly formed or unsophisticated these concepts may be. She has, in other words, a world-view—that larger, or even all-encompassing, view of reality within which her experience makes sense to her. Using such tools of the intellect she comes to believe, at least in an implicit way, that she has a general understanding of reality and of how she fits into it.

If there is an issue here, it is not whether we have intellectual needs which lead us to a world-view (or, more precisely, an interpretive framework within which our experience makes sense to us), but whether we should be content to leave this view unacknowledged and unexamined. If we fail to examine it, our world-view will nevertheless remain implicit in what we say and do. On the other hand, if we manage to expose it and then subject it to critical examination, we will not only transform it into something much more defensible, but we will be engaging in an activity that hones the mind to a keen edge. The philosophic enterprise may be seen in this context as a sustained attempt to understand—an undertaking prompted by a tenacious spirit that would not allow us to become content with a view until it had been well thought out and shown to be capable of withstanding critical scrutiny.

Of course, the need to understand is much more clearly displayed, and difficult to satisfy, in some rather than others. Perhaps this is so not because some people lack such a need but because they require very little for its satisfaction. For these people, a world-view that is totally unfounded or even incoherent will suffice, especially if it was foisted upon them by authority figures when they were too young to examine it critically. Having had no significant role in the formation of their world-view, they have in effect allowed others to do what should have been their thinking about the fundamental questions. Philosophy, on the other hand, would have us do our own thinking. It requires that we achieve some level of intellectual independence. Although the insights, encouragement, and stimulation provided by others may be invaluable, others cannot do our philosophizing for us. We may secure the services of others to satisfy many of our needs, but what we should come to see, at least when the philosophic spirit moves us, is that grappling with the fundamental problems of human experience is something we must do for ourselves.

FUNDAMENTAL PHILOSOPHICAL QUESTIONS

The quest for philosophic understanding begins in curiosity and wonder. Unfortunately, our natural curiosity may have faded sufficiently to require rekindling. We become quite accustomed to being in the world after having been in it for some time. It comes to seem quite familiar to us. We get into our daily routines, immersed in our various concerns, and uncritically assume that we have our own existence and our place in the world fairly well understood, at least in broad outline. This familiarity provides security, but it also effectively insulates us from the profound mystery of existence—a mystery that comes into view when we manage to disengage ourselves momentarily from our ordinary commonsensical interpretation of reality. As we step back and gaze at the world as though it were something we had just encountered, we will have placed ourselves in a good position to call into question the web of beliefs that poses as the foundation of our understanding. This fresh perspective may be likened to that which we probably had as little children, when everything was new to us and we looked upon the world with a sense of excitement and wonder. Not having yet acquired that complex network of beliefs about self and world that we now employ to make sense out of our experience, we were fully exposed to the sheer mystery and wonder of existence. What we should strive to do is re-enter that condition, for then the fundamental questions which naturally arise out of it will again have the power to move us. Let us consider some of these questions.

Why are we in the world at all? How is the fact that you exist (or that I exist) to be understood? The world need not have included *any* persons. But beyond this, it seems clear that someone else could have existed in your place, that is, *instead* of you. But if so, then why *you* rather than another? Also, *what* are you—what is that to which you refer with the word *I*? Are you an entirely material being, a non-material soul, a collection of experiences, a psychophysical unity, or (incredibly) nothing at all? As we shall see, even the last alternative has been taken seriously. Perhaps no question has greater philosophical ramifications or significance than this one.

Turning to the world around us, in addition to having questions about its nature or composition and the natural laws that reign there, we might wonder if the natural realm is all there is. More specifically, does the world include a supernatural dimension? Is there a God—a supernatural being with personal attributes?

This question invites others. Do our lives have a purpose or a destiny beyond anything disclosed to us through our scientific study of the natural world? Can our lives be meaningful even if we have no higher destiny—if our existence comes to an absolute end when we die? What *makes* them meaningful, if they are? If it is up to us to make them meaningful, how should we go about doing that? What might we do to mitigate our suffering? How should we conduct our lives? What should we seek? What is of highest worth, or of greatest value? And finally, how does the inevitability and possible finality of death bear upon these questions? If it should turn out that upon death we simply cease to exist, never to exist again, how might our acceptance of this affect our assessment of the value and meaningfulness of our lives?

Can we come to know the answers to such questions? What can we know for sure? Our common sense leads us to assume that the world really is as it appears to be, and it appears to contain billions of human beings as well as an enormous number of other material things. Furthermore, we uncritically assume that human organisms other than our own are conscious beings like ourselves. These assumptions are fundamental and may be very well grounded, but are they really beyond question? Could it be that your life is really a long continuous dream? If it were, then almost everything you now believe about the world would be false. Of course, the suggestion that your life may be a dream may seem quite preposterous. You would claim to know (perhaps with complete certitude) that it is *not* a dream. But such conviction does not answer the question of *how* you know this, assuming that in fact you do. And it is this question which turns out to be the focus of our concern—the question of *how* (not whether) you know this and how this knowledge should be understood. With this turn we have moved to another fundamental question or problem of philosophy: the problem of knowledge. What, if anything, can we know with such bedrock certainty that no reasonable person could doubt it?

Knowing is a relation—a relation between ourselves as knowers and that which we come to know. Thus our concern about knowing and what we can know is the flip side of our concern about the nature of reality—that which is known when we know. The philosophic study of knowledge is epistemology, and the philosophic inquiry into the nature of ultimate reality is metaphysics (or ontology). Such study is unavoidable as we attempt to answer fundamental questions about ourselves and the nature of our world. It is also an appropriate starting point for us as we attempt to answer these fundamental questions.

OVERVIEW OF THE BOOK

We will begin, then, with an investigation of knowledge itself—of what we can know and how we can know it—for all the other fundamental questions that concern us are implicit requests for knowledge and understanding. Our concern is not about acquiring specific information but with that foundational knowledge which forms the basis of our understanding of ourselves and the world around us. That we have *some* such knowledge may seem beyond question; but, as we shall see, there is very little, if anything, which has not been questioned in the course of philosophical inquiry. There are skeptics who deny that we have *any* knowledge of a world external to us, and they back up their denial with compelling arguments. They present a challenge that we cannot avoid without simply ignoring the possibility that our most fundamental beliefs have no rational foundation.

Since we rely very heavily upon our senses for our knowledge of the world, we shall devote some of our attention to what our senses reveal about the nature of reality and to how our sense perception brings us into relation with the external world. As we examine our perceptual experience, we will be led to the conclusion that only a part of it is contributed by the things in the external world which are affecting our senses. The other portion is "experience-dependent" or "consciousness-dependent"; that is to say, it is contributed by us, or by our nervous systems. This fact, among others, leads us to distinguish between the mental and the physical—a distinction whose basis and implications we shall examine in chapter 4. There we shall inquire about whether our minds are something distinct from our brains and the rest of our bodies, and, if they are, how we should conceive of them and their relation to our bodies.

If, as it seems, our minds are different from our bodies, then the question as to what we are becomes even more pressing. Are we our bodies? Are we our minds? Or are we some combination of the two, some psychophysical complex? In what (if anything) does our deep identity consist—that to which we refer when we use the word *I* to refer to ourselves? Chapter 5 is an exploration of the territory that these questions bring to mind. However, the results of this exploration are not only important in themselves but are highly relevant to the central topic of chapter 6—the nature and existence of God. At this point we turn from our investigation of the natural realm to inquire about whether there is a supernatural dimension, which includes a supernatural being with personal attributes. If there is a supernatural personal being (i.e., if there is a God) and we can know that there is, this knowledge would have profound implications for our broader understanding of reality and of how we fit into it.

In chapter 7 we examine a concept that is central to our view of ourselves as morally responsible beings—the concept of free will. Here we will examine our deep-seated conviction that we are in control of what we do, that there are times when we could have chosen to do something other than what we actually did, and that, consequently, we can make free choices for which we can be justifiably held responsible. We will take a careful look at the determinist view of human nature, try to specify the conditions that must be met if we are ever to act freely, and then see if those conditions ever obtain.

So far we will have been primarily concerned to find out what is *true* of us and of the world in which we find ourselves. We will have been trying to approach the world in a value-neutral way. But our experience of the world is *not* value-neutral. We commonly make value judgments in addition to judgments about what the facts are. We judge things to be right or wrong, good or bad, or better or worse than something else—judgments which, though of great importance, may appear to be *neither true nor false*. In chapter 8 we will try to arrive at an understanding of what value is, and of what we are doing when we make value judgments. We will pay special attention to judgments of moral value, that is, to *morality*; for concerns about how we should treat others are some of the most important concerns we have.

Chapter 9 is about death and how we should think about it. Our awareness of the fact that we must die may have a profound effect upon our lives. We shall be concerned with how we might come to grips with that awareness, and also with what death itself is. This is important, for how we ultimately come to terms with death is deeply affected by what we take death to be. The question about the nature of death is not, of course, about what *biological* death is, but about whether our nature as persons is such that our survival of biological death is possible. At this juncture our earlier investigations into our own nature become highly relevant. A good deal of our effort here will be spent in an attempt to see how strong a case we have for thinking that our existence does not end with biological death. Perhaps this case is strong enough to make the belief in existence after death a rational one to hold. On the other hand, this case may be so weak that the only rational position is to brace ourselves for extinction upon death. In any event, the question of what happens to us when we die strikes us as of the highest importance. We would likely not know what to make of someone who genuinely felt indifferent to it.

What we believe death to bring may deeply affect our feelings about whether or how life can be meaningful. In chapter 10, the final chapter, we shall focus on what may be the ultimate problem of philosophy—the problem of the meaning of life. We will take a careful look at what the problem about the meaning of life is supposed to be, and, in doing so, try to get clear about what might be troubling to us when we raise questions about life's meaning. We will examine what the word *meaning* itself means when we use it to talk about the meaning of life, and we will try to answer the question of what makes a life meaningful. We will attempt to uncover the source of meaning and to identify what it is about the world that may make our quest for meaning a quite difficult one.

Our concerns about the meaningfulness of our lives seem urgent and of ultimate importance. Fortunately, by the time we address them we will have at our disposal the insights gained from our previous investigations. This we will need, for the question of life's meaning is too large and multifaceted to be adequately addressed in isolation from our deliberations about the other fundamental questions. With this in mind, let us embark upon our study.

2

KNOWLEDGE

Central to any philosophical study is a concern about what we can know and how we are able to know it. An inquiry into the nature of knowledge is in any case an appropriate way to begin since it has implications for all the other questions.

As we think about what it is to know something, we note that we use the words *knowing* and *knowledge* in several different ways. We speak of *knowing how* to do something (e.g., to swim or to ride a bicycle). This knowledge consists of the possession of skills. We may also speak of knowing something (e.g., the call of the loon or the taste of peppermint) simply in virtue of having experienced it. Such knowledge consists in the mere having of the experience, rather than in any thoughts about the experience or any inferences drawn from it. This knowledge is sometimes called knowledge "by acquaintance," though there is controversy about whether it should be considered knowledge at all.

We need not enter this controversy, however, for our concern is with knowledge of another kind—with what is usually called *knowing that* something is the case. This is called propositional knowledge since a proposition makes an assertion about what is or is not the case, and it is what is expressed by a clause beginning with the word *that*. And so your knowledge *that* you are now awake and *that* you are reading these words is propositional knowledge. Whether aware of it or not, this is the kind of knowledge we are claiming to have whenever we claim to know that something or other is the case. But propositions are either true or false, and thus to claim that something is the case is to claim that a certain proposition is *true*. Because of its connection to truth, this kind of knowledge is of great concern to us, at least when we are engaged in philosophical inquiry. Let us examine it in more detail.

TRUTH AND BELIEF

As we have noted, to have propositional knowledge is to have knowledge of truth. Truth alone, however, does not constitute such knowledge, for a proposition can be true even though its truth is unknown to us.

Certainly the proposition that the earth is a sphere was true even during those times when nearly everyone believed the earth to be flat. To have such knowledge, the proposition known must not only be true but one must *believe* it to be true as well. In short, knowledge includes belief—a belief that is true. Of course, a belief may be false rather than true (as it will be if the proposition one believes is false), and a false proposition may be what a person believes when making a knowledge claim. But such a claim would be false, even if the person believes, with great conviction, that it is true. And so, this would not be a case of knowing, for one can know only what is true. Though false belief is all too common, there can be no false knowledge.

Clarity about truth and its relation to belief are crucially important in our understanding of what knowledge is. Although true belief is necessary for knowledge to exist, what makes the belief true lies outside the belief itself. A belief is true if the proposition believed is true, but what *makes* a proposition true is *not* our believing it. Rather, the proposition is true if (and only if) what it asserts or claims to be the case is in fact the case. To illustrate, the proposition expressed by the sentence "Snow is white" is true if and only if snow really *is* white. Belief is the subjective element of knowledge; it is our contribution. Unlike truth, it may vary from person to person. But knowledge also has an objective element, independent of personal belief, for it is grounded in the objectivity of truth. All truths are objective, even truths about our beliefs and our other subjective states. For the truths about these states are (like all other states) dependent upon what these states actually are, rather than upon our beliefs or opinions about them. The crucially important point here is that truth depends upon what *is*; and so unless our beliefs conform to it they will not be true, and thus will be of little philosophic interest to us in our quest for truth and understanding.

THEORIES OF TRUTH

It may be that this view of the relation between truth and belief commits us to a certain theory about what it is for a belief to be true, namely, a *correspondence* theory: A belief is true if, and only if, it corresponds to what it is about. If we are so committed, then we are, in effect, assuming that an adequate theory of the correspondence type can be worked out, despite the formidable challenges that must be met if such a theory (or any other theory of truth) is to be entirely satisfactory.

According to one version of the correspondence theory, a true belief corresponds to a fact that obtains objectively, i.e., independently of the belief. More generally, facts obtain independently of the mind, unless, of course, they are facts *about* the mind. But even if they are, they are objective in that they obtain independently of beliefs about them. Even beliefs about the existence or character of some belief are true only if they depict the belief as it independently is. Thus true beliefs, in virtue of corresponding to a reality outside them, depict the world (or, more precisely, some part or aspect of it) as it is in itself, i.e., independently of any perspective or point of view from which it is apprehended, whether the perspective is that of an individual or a society. As such, this theory stands opposed to subjectivist and relativist conceptions of truth, according to which what *is* true (rather than merely what is *believed* to be true) varies from individual to individual or from society to society.

This theory also stands in opposition to coherence and pragmatic theories of truth. According to the coherence theory, a belief is true if and only if it fits or coheres with a large system of other beliefs, which taken together constitute a comprehensive view of reality. In short, truth is to be understood in terms of a relation among beliefs rather than as a relation between beliefs and the world. The pragmatic theory, as it occurs in the pioneering work of William James and John Dewey, is best understood as an account of the criteria to be used to determine whether a belief is true, that is, best understood as a theory of *justification*—a theory about when one is justified in taking a belief to be true.[1] Roughly speaking, a belief may be deemed true if it "works." A concern to explain the nature of truth—of what it is for a belief to be true—gets overshadowed by a concern with the problem of justification. Indeed, the contemporary American pragmatist Richard Rorty, whose work in the area has been quite influential, maintains that truth does not stand in need of explanation, arguing that talk about the truth of a belief is nothing more than a way of praising a belief we currently regard as so well established that we are entirely justified in accepting it.[2] Beliefs are reduced to devices for coping with particular concrete problems; and any concern about whether they connect with an extralinguistic reality, if intelligible at all, can be justifiably put aside. Truth loses the crucially important theoretical role that we are naturally inclined to give it.

We should note that the correspondence theory, despite the difficulties with it, fares quite well when compared with the alternative views. Not only does it appear to provide the best fit with our pre-analytic commonsensical assumptions about truth and reality, but it seems to remain the most plausible theory after examination. The other theories owe much of their appeal to their effect of paring philosophy down to our size, so to speak. At least one of the notoriously difficult problems of philosophy would become much more tractable if we could come to view as fundamentally misguided our belief that our quest for truth must include an effort to establish epistemic contact with an extralinguistic reality—a reality as it is in itself, independently of our talk and belief about it. This paring down effect is evident in the pragmatic theory, especially that of Richard Rorty, who apparently holds that the idea of a reality as it is in itself, independently of our language and of the standpoint from which it is viewed, is unintelligible. But such an extreme linguistic skepticism seems unacceptable. Perhaps we cannot know conclusively anything about an external world as it independently is. But it is quite another matter to claim that we cannot even *conceive* or *coherently think* of a reality as it might be in itself, independently of one's language and perspective on it. If, as seems undeniable, we do have epistemic access to at least some of our own conscious states as they are in themselves, then we can hardly deny that we have a conception of *something* real as it is in itself—a conception that would be applicable to an external reality as well, even if we were unable to know in a conclusive sense anything about the character of that reality.

The coherence theory also has a paring down effect. In it too we need not concern ourselves with the idea of a reality as it is in itself, independently of our belief systems. But the difficulties with it seem at least as serious as those plaguing the correspondence theory. The correspondence theory is often criticized on the grounds that we are apparently unable to provide an adequate specification of what it is for a belief to correspond to a fact or to any other reality as that reality may be in itself. We do not understand, or understand adequately, how a true belief might "hook on" to reality. But the coherence theory must confront a similar challenge: What is it for a system of beliefs to *cohere*? Beliefs in a coherent system must, of course, be logically consistent with one another, but the required relations must bind the system more tightly than what is entailed by mere logical consistency; and what else is required seems very difficult to specify.

Beyond this difficulty is the one arising from the possibility of there being more than one internally coherent system of beliefs. What grounds could we have for preferring one over another if there is more than one? We would have such grounds if we could show that only one system is connected to a reality external to the systems, but then we would have to face difficulties similar to those confronting the correspondence theory. If, on the other hand, the idea of a connection to an external reality is not supposed to arise, then how could one choose among systems if there were many? Indeed, what would guarantee the *truth* of an *entire system* even if there were only one?

Though this is hardly the occasion to try to formulate a detailed statement and defense of the correspondence theory, we have pursued the issue far enough to see grounds for two conclusions: (1) the correspondence theory is at least no more problematic than each of the alternative views, and (2) even if it were more problematic we might wish to embrace it anyway on the grounds that it does not diminish the significance of truth or succumb to the temptation to make the quest for truth less difficult by lowering its aim. That we should be so tempted is quite understandable. The problem of truth, like so many of the main problems of philosophy, may seem hopelessly difficult at times; and when it does, we may welcome the suggestion that any effort to obtain knowledge of a reality as it is in itself is misguided. But we should resist such a temptation, at least if we are reluctant to abandon the fundamental assumption (which seems unrelinquishable) that there is an objectively existing reality, a way things are in themselves, apart from the language we use to think and talk about them, and from any beliefs about them that we may come to hold. For we cannot continue to assume that there is such a reality and yet maintain that, because of the (possibly insuperable) difficulties involved in coming to know about it, any legitimate philosophical concern should be directed elsewhere. If we were to allow difficulties, even apparently insuperable ones, to determine what our philosophical concerns should be, our philosophical aspirations would wither, and our interest in philosophic inquiry would likely suffer as well. The stakes would no longer seem so high, nor would the inquiry seem so eminently worth carrying out. Diminished aims do not serve us well in our philosophical undertakings, even though they may be what guides the prudent course of action in many other affairs.

KNOWLEDGE AND JUSTIFIED TRUE BELIEF

We have noted that if our view of the truth-belief relation commits us to the adequacy of a correspondence theory of truth, our position is not rendered less satisfactory on that account. But we have not yet determined whether more than truth and belief are needed for knowledge. Though truth and belief are necessary for knowledge to exist, there is a third element or condition which must be present as well—the evidence condition. A belief might just happen to be true, perhaps the result of a lucky guess; and this we would surely not count as knowledge. Suppose that I have a few (unloaded) dice in my hand and announce, prior to my tossing them, that a five will turn up on every one. You are skeptical, as you should be; but, lo and behold, each does turn up a five. I then gleefully exclaim, "I knew it." Clearly, I would be mistaken. For it would have been impossible for me to have had evidence sufficient to know that each die would turn up a five. My being correct would have been the result of a lucky guess, and that cannot be considered knowledge. To have knowledge, one must have not only a true belief but adequate evidence that the belief is true.

But what is adequate evidence? This is a difficult question. Until rather recently, there was widespread agreement among epistemologists that the evidence for the truth of the belief would be adequate if and only if the belief were "justified," and that, consequently, knowledge could be defined more or less as *justified true belief.* Since justification for holding a belief consists in having good reason to hold it, the matter of what constitutes a sufficiently good reason for believing must be given some precision. But a major problem for this definition of knowledge became clear when it was pointed out (by Edmund Gettier in 1963)[3] that there can be cases in which we would agree that a person is justified in holding a certain belief that turns out to be true even though the person's justified true belief falls short of being knowledge.

Gettier provides an example. Imagine that you and some other person, Smith, are applying for the same job and that you have good reason to believe the conjunctive proposition (a)—"Smith is the person who will get the job and there are ten coins in Smith's pocket." You also (and with equally good reason) believe (b)—"There are ten coins in the pocket of the person who will get the job." For you see that (b) is entailed by (a). But now suppose that, though unknown to you at the time, *you* will get the job and you happen to have ten coins in your pocket. Though (a) is false, (b) is true; and you are justified in believing (b). In virtue of believing (b) you have a justified true belief. Yet we would not wish to say that you *know* that there are ten coins in the pocket of the person who will get the job. For you do not know that you will get the job or that you have ten coins in your pocket.

Though the example may seem unduly contrived and unlikely to play out in an actual situation, it does show (along with many other examples like it) that justified true belief is insufficient for knowledge. There have been many attempts to specify what must be added to justified true belief if the resulting complex is to be sufficient for knowledge, but none have gained universal acceptance. Perhaps the most promising strategy consists in distinguishing between different kinds of justification and arguing that justified true belief amounts to knowledge only if the justification is of a certain kind. More specifically, knowledge obtains only if the state of affairs that justifies one in accepting a belief as true is evidentially related to the state of affairs that makes the belief true. If there is an evidential relation, then we might call the justification *relevant*, as contrasted with irrelevant justification or with simple insufficient justification. Armed with the concept of relevant justification, we can define knowledge as *relevantly justified* true belief.[4]

What needs to be specified in some detail, however, is how the evidential relation is to be understood, since there can be no relevant justification unless it is present. Let us say that one is relevantly justified in accepting a true belief only if the epistemic conditions are such that the state of affairs making the belief true is providing sufficient evidence to justify one in accepting the belief as true. The conditions are such that the state of affairs making the belief true is epistemically available, and epistemically linked, to the knower.

When we apply this analysis of the concept of knowledge to our Gettier-type case, we see that although you are justified in accepting the true belief, (b), your justification is not of the relevant kind. For the state of affairs that makes (b) true is that state consisting in there being ten coins in *your* pocket, and *that* state is not providing you with sufficient evidence to justify your belief that (b) is true. Indeed, you are not even aware of *that* state of affairs. However, when we apply this analysis to the ordinary cases of justified true belief that qualify as knowledge, such as my present justified true belief that my computer is turned on, we see that they are unproblematic because the required evidential relation is present: The state of affairs constituted by my computer being on is epistemically available to me and is providing evidence sufficient to justify my true belief that my computer is on.

It seems, then, that the concept of relevant justification that we have articulated can serve as our concept of adequate evidence. But even if it should prove to be unacceptable (and that the other proposals are no more helpful), we would not be in a position of never being able to determine whether the evidence *is* adequate. In some cases, the evidence is nonexistent (as in the dice-tossing case). In others, such as your knowing that you are now having an experience of reading these words, it is undoubtedly adequate. Here the evidence seems conclusive: There can be no additional information, which, if we had it, would lead us to conclude that your belief is false. But the demand that the evidence be conclusive is too strong. It can rarely be satisfied and is beyond our reach in nearly all of the circumstances of ordinary life. But we now have in our service a weakened standard of adequacy—the concept of relevant justification. Such justification is sometime called *defeasible* justification, as it is always subject to the possibility of being overturned or defeated by contrary facts. It makes possible a conception of knowledge rooted in evidence that is not complete or absolutely conclusive, and promises to serve quite well for ordinary purposes. Still, we might keep in mind the conception of complete or conclusive evidence and of *non-defeasible* justification as we proceed with our philosophical inquiry into what we can know about ourselves and our experience of the world, as well as about the world as it is, independently of our experience. For it would be interesting to find out what knowledge, if any, we have about these matters that can satisfy even the most austere of standards.

DIRECT AND INDIRECT KNOWLEDGE

We have been trying to determine the conditions that must be met for knowledge to exist. But we should also note that we can distinguish two kinds of knowledge—direct and indirect. This distinction comes into view when we see that some of our knowledge (viz., indirect knowledge) is grounded in other things we know. Indirect knowledge is knowledge we have only in virtue of knowing something else. Direct knowledge, on the other hand, is not mediated by other knowledge; it is possessed directly or immediately, that is, not in virtue of knowing something else. For example, your knowledge that you are now having an experience of reading these words is direct or immediate, for it is not inferred on the basis of something else you know—something you know in a more direct fashion.[5] But you are also able to draw some well-grounded inferences on the basis of your present experience. Suppose that you are now seated on a chair and resting this book on a table in front of you. You do not see or feel the legs of the chair. Yet you can infer that they are still intact. If they were not, you would not be in the position you are in and having the experience you are now having. But your knowledge that they are still intact is indirect; for it is mediated by your (direct) knowledge of your present experience.

Of course, you could acquire direct knowledge of their presence by looking at them or touching them. But much of what we know indirectly at any given time is about things we cannot perceive or directly experience in any other way. Examples of such things are the conscious states of others and all physical things as they exist in themselves, independently of our perceptions. Our (indirect) knowledge of such things is based upon what we might call an "inference to the best explanation"—inferring their existence provides us with the best explanation as to why we have the experience we do have, and thereby accounts for the existence of that which we know directly. As we shall see, most of our knowledge is only indirect. Nevertheless, much of this knowledge is of fundamental importance.

KNOWING VERSUS FEELING CERTAIN

It should be clear that knowing must be distinguished from feeling certain. For we can feel certain and yet be mistaken, whereas we cannot be mistaken about that which we actually know. How certain we feel is a measure of the strength of our belief; but, as we have noted, even a strongly held belief may be false. Thus a feeling of certitude or conviction, even one of great conviction, may be misleading. Yet the question of when feeling certain is justified and of how certain we are entitled to feel are questions that we cannot avoid in our deliberations about knowledge. For though we realize that when we know we then have knowledge of truth, we may nevertheless feel uncertain, in any given case, about whether we do have knowledge. In other words, we may actually have knowledge and yet feel uncertain that we have it.

As we have seen, we have knowledge when we have a relevantly justified true belief. If we have a relevantly justified belief, then we have adequate evidence that the belief is true. But unless the evidence is conclusive, the belief supported by it could be false; and if the belief were false, it could not, of course, be the true belief that is held in a case of knowing. If the possibility that it is false cannot be eliminated, then complete certitude or confidence that it is true is not rationally justifiable. Now, if the belief is false we cannot have knowledge. Thus our degree of confidence that we have knowledge should match our degree of confidence that the belief is true. And our confidence that the belief is true should depend on the strength or amount of evidence of its truth. Consequently, if the degree of confidence we feel is to be rational (or reason-based), it should depend upon the quality and quantity of evidence for the truth of the belief.

BELIEF AND THE INFLUENCE OF EVIDENCE

We should be forewarned, however, that the goal of having the amount of confidence we have that a belief is true (or that it is false) appropriately fit the available evidence of its truth (or falsity) is far from easy to attain. The truth-tracking method of effective philosophic inquiry would lead us to believe a proposition when the evidence available to us justifies our believing it, to reject a proposition when our evidence disconfirms it, and to suspend judgment about it when our evidence neither confirms nor disconfirms it. Unfortunately, what people believe is often a result of factors that are irrelevant to the evidence for or against their belief. Psychological studies have shown that (1) we tend to persevere in maintaining our present beliefs even when we become aware of evidence that discredits them, that (2) our feelings of self-worth tend to get entangled in our beliefs, with the result that our self-opinion tends to suffer if we acknowledge error or inconsistency in them, and that (3) we tend to engage in wishful thinking—to hold those beliefs we wish were true, even when all the evidence available to us indicates that they are false.

Moreover, there are social factors that influence us to hold beliefs without considering, or considering sufficiently, the evidence that discredits them. Having one's beliefs conform to those of others promotes acceptance by the group and removes a source of conflict. Sensing this, we are inclined to succumb to the pressures of peers, friends, relatives, and the broader community to accept uncritically the beliefs they would have us hold. Additional pressure to accept beliefs without looking for evidence that might discredit them results from the widespread tendency to believe the testimony of people we take uncritically to be authorities. Though we are justified in relying on the testimony of genuine authorities who are testifying in the area of their expertise, we should not be persuaded by that fact to accept uncritically the proclamations of advertisers, sports heroes, movie stars, and other celebrities who bring gain to themselves or their sponsors by bringing about certain beliefs in us. In general, we should always be prepared to rely on our own critical intelligence, especially when in the presence of those whose motivation to persuade us is something other than a concern for the truth.

When we reflect upon the various and virtually constant pressures to accept and to hold beliefs with little or no concern about the possibility of discrediting evidence, we may wonder how we can proceed in the truth-tracking manner that effective philosophic inquiry requires. Fortunately, there is a course of action we can take and an attitude we can foster that will prove to be enormously helpful. The course of action consists in doing what we can to sharpen our intellectual skills—to hone them to a keen edge. We need to have some proficiency in collecting, organizing, and analyzing data with an eye to how they bear upon the truth of a claim. We need to become proficient not only in weighing evidence and drawing correct inferences but in recognizing the logical relations between beliefs or the propositions they express, that is, in recognizing what a proposition follows from, what is consistent with it, and what it implies. Clearly, at least a general knowledge of a broad range of subjects will be very helpful as well.

The attitude to be fostered is characterized by an abiding desire to find out—a resolve to know the truth, insofar as one can, even though one's most cherished beliefs may be placed in jeopardy. Perhaps the cultivation of such an attitude is even more important to a truth-seeking endeavor than well-honed intellectual skills. For without the will to use one's skills in a truth-seeking effort to determine what beliefs are justified, the skills are of limited value. They might be used simply to defend what one already believes or wishes to believe and to obscure the truth, rather than to search for and then consider in an impartial way the evidence that would indicate whether or not these beliefs are justified.

Clearly, the attitude we have been considering involves a high level of open-mindedness—being open to alternative views of reality and to evidence that might weigh against our own beliefs. It also requires a resolve to be intellectually honest with ourselves—to see little merit in deceiving ourselves or others, at least with respect to the matters that concern us when we are motivated to engage in philosophic inquiry. Finally, it requires a tolerance for ambiguity and uncertainty. Given our limitations in conjunction with the complexity of the world, we must often be content with far less understanding than what we might have hoped to gain and with answers that may strike us as little more than informed guesses, especially if what is concerning us are the fundamental problems of philosophy. Perhaps the character traits we have described can be possessed to a very high degree only by a few, and only intermittently manifested even by them. But fortunately for the rest of us, these traits admit of degrees; and so, in their highest degree or purest manifestations, may serve as ideals to which we may aspire even if we cannot fully realize them.

THE SOURCES OF KNOWLEDGE

Before turning to the question of *what* we know, there is another question that merits some attention as we get started—the question about the sources of our knowledge. Out of what does our knowledge arise? Many answers have been offered, but all seem consistent with there being two broad sources: experience and reason. We experience a world and we reason about what we experience. Out of these activities much of our knowledge arises. However, since this way of expressing the matter implies that "reason" is to be equated with "reasoning," we should note that reason is often understood to include our concept and judgment-forming capacities. Reason, broadly viewed, may be understood to include our capacity to acquire and use language, to understand propositions and to form beliefs about the world, and not only to form concepts but to recognize items in the world to which they apply. Also, some philosophers have argued that reason by itself, independently of experience, can yield knowledge of the world.[6] But (while acknowledging that reason, broadly understood, includes much more than reasoning) we will focus our attention on two of the least controversial and most important sources of knowledge: our experience and our reasoning from it.

LOGIC AND REASONING

Some further discussion of reasoning will be helpful, as we will be engaging in it throughout our inquiry. We shall understand it as a process of drawing inferences—of reaching a conclusion from a set of premises. A set of one or more premises plus a conclusion drawn from them is called an argument. There are two kinds of arguments (or, we might say, two kinds of reasoning): inductive and deductive. As we shall see, they differ in the way in which the conclusion is thought to be linked to the premises.

Unfortunately, people sometimes reason badly, and we will be especially concerned to avoid doing that. Thus we will focus on what it is to reason correctly. As we do so, we will be studying the fundamentals of logic. Logic may be defined as the study of the methods and the principles by which we distinguish correct from incorrect reasoning (or good arguments from bad ones). If an argument is deductive and the reasoning in it is correct, the argument is valid. A valid deductive argument is one whose conclusion follows *necessarily* from the premises. Thus if in a valid deductive argument the premises are true, the conclusion *must* be true as well. In other words, a valid deductive argument is *necessarily truth-preserving*. This is why such arguments are important. They give us assurance that if we begin with truth (that is, if all the premises are true), we must end up with truth as well (that is, the conclusion must also be true).

Of course, the premises may not be true. If even one is false, we lose the assurance that the conclusion is true, even if the argument is valid. Consider, for example, the following argument:

Premise: All cats are mammals.
Premise: All mammals are herbivores.
Conclusion: Therefore all cats are herbivores.

This argument *is* valid, for the conclusion is correctly drawn from the premises. If they were true, it would have to be true as well. Clearly, *if* all mammals were herbivores, then since all cats are mammals it would have to be true that all cats are herbivores. But, of course, cats are carnivores, not herbivores, and so the conclusion is false. Thus we see that even a valid argument can have a false conclusion if at least one premise is false.

Now consider a somewhat different argument:

Premise: All cats are mammals.
Premise: All mammals are animals.
Conclusion: Therefore all cats are animals

Like the previous argument, this one is deductive. For the conclusion is intended to follow necessarily from the premises. And it really does follow as intended—it *must* be true if the premises are true. In other words, this argument is valid, or *necessarily truth-preserving*. But, unlike the earlier argument, this one has truth to preserve; for both premises are true. Since the premises are true and the argument preserves or carries that truth into the conclusion, the conclusion must be true as well. Such arguments—valid arguments having only true premises—are said to be *sound*. Sound arguments are especially important because they guarantee the truth of their conclusions. And so, we will try to engage in sound argumentation as we reason deductively. However, as we shall see, in our investigations the truth of our premises is sometimes very difficult to determine. But we can mitigate this problem somewhat by always doing our best to reason validly whenever we reason deductively. For then we will have the assurance that *if* all our premises *are* true, then our conclusion must be true as well.

Once we have the character of deductive reasoning firmly in mind, inductive reasoning or inductive argumentation is relatively easy to understand. In an inductive argument, even a good one, the truth of all the premises does not guarantee the truth of the conclusion. This is because the conclusion of an inductive argument always goes beyond the premises—it describes or refers to a new case not included in the premises. The following is a very good inductive argument:

Premise: The sun has risen in the east each morning for about five billion years.
Conclusion: Therefore, (probably) the sun will rise in the east tomorrow morning.

But note that the conclusion goes beyond the premises in mentioning a new case, viz., *tomorrow* morning. Because this case is not included in the premise, it is possible for the premise to be true and the conclusion false. Indeed, we can easily imagine the sun exploding tonight, in which case there would be no sun to rise in the east tomorrow morning. Still, the truth of the premise makes very probable the truth of the conclusion, and this is what makes the argument a good inductive one. Though such an argument cannot be necessarily truth-preserving (and thus, unlike a deductive argument, should not be thought of as either valid or invalid), it can be *probably* truth-preserving. It is probably truth-preserving if the truth of its premises makes probable the truth of its conclusion. If it does this, it is ordinarily called a *strong* inductive argument.

On the other hand, an inductive argument may be weak, rather than strong. Consider this weak inductive argument:

Premise: I have just tossed this penny ten times and have had "heads" turn up every time.

Conclusion: Therefore, it is extremely unlikely that I will have "heads" turn up the next time I toss it.

This is a weak inductive argument because the truth of the premise does not make probable the truth of the conclusion. The chances of my getting "heads" is one-half (not extremely unlikely), just as it was on each previous toss. To accept this argument as strong is to commit a version of the gambler's fallacy.

Now, if an inductive argument is strong and has only true premises, it is usually said to be *cogent*. Since all of the premises of a cogent inductive argument are true and since (being a strong argument) it is probably truth-preserving, its conclusion is probably true. Obviously, we shall strive for cogent arguments when we reason inductively. But as we noted in our discussion of deduction, the truth of our premises is often difficult to determine, at least those premises about the subject matter we will deal with here. Still, if we can make sure that our inductive arguments are strong, then we will at least have the assurance that if our premises are true, our conclusions are probably true.

THE DREAM HYPOTHESIS

So far we have been trying to answer questions about what knowledge is (i.e., what conditions must be satisfied for it to exist), about the degree of certitude that may be appropriate in relation to a knowledge claim, about the influence a consideration of evidence should have upon our beliefs, and about what kinds and sources of knowledge will be of special concern to us. We will now turn to the question of what we have knowledge *of*, or *what* we know. More precisely, we will examine some beliefs we feel certain about—we feel certain that they are true and that their truth is known to us.

We believe that we know a great deal. You are now reading this book and know that you are reading. Perhaps you are seated on a chair in a library, holding this book in your hands or resting it on a table in front of you. Looking around, you may see several tables, computers, shelves of books, and other people reading or browsing—people who would describe your surroundings more or less as you would. As you gaze out the window, you may see other buildings, a few trees, and some fleecy clouds moving slowly through the blue sky. All of this is immediately apparent to you because it is part of what you presently observe. But it comprises only a very small fraction of what you, like almost everyone else, would claim to know. Beyond this room, you would insist, is a city which is part of a nation located on a continent which, together with oceans and other continents, cover the surface of our globe—a planet we share with countless other living things. And beyond our planet is our solar system, our galaxy, other galaxies, and clusters of galaxies—in short, the rest of the physical universe.

You may add that the universe has a history, indeed, that it is very old. Even the earth, though of rather recent origin by cosmological standards, has (according to scientific theory) been in existence about five billion years. And you too have a history, albeit a relatively brief one. You know that you were born at a certain time and place to certain parents, attended an elementary school, later graduated from high school, and eventually came to the university. Not only do you know a great deal about your own past, but you have knowledge of many historical events, e.g., that Washington became the first U.S. president and that the North won the Civil War. And all of this knowledge of the past is, of course, in addition to your knowledge of what presently exists or is occurring now.

You might also claim that we now know a lot about the compositions of things, mainly because of the advance of modern science. You know that you have a brain and other bodily organs composed of a great many cells, each of which is constituted by an enormous number of molecules. You may claim to know that these molecules and indeed all physical things, whether organic or inorganic, are composed of atoms which are also composite entities. They are comprised of sub-atomic particles which, in turn, may be made up of extremely tiny and largely unknown entities called quarks.

Science has also, you may add, disclosed to us much about the way nature behaves, the natural laws that reign there—the laws in accordance with which bodies fall, glaciers form, diseases come about, hurricanes build, and the atomic elements combine with one another. Then too, there are the laws of social science, of psychology, economics, and sociology. Because of science we now possess a much better understanding of ourselves, of the causal factors that bear upon how we think, feel, and behave, both as individuals and as members of groups.

This list of items that you believe you know is, of course, only a beginning and could go on indefinitely. You would agree that you do not know all of these things with the same degree of certitude. But what we must now ask is whether you have conclusive evidence for any of this, or know it with such certitude that no reasonable person could doubt it. It may appear silly to question something that you seem to know directly, such as that you are now reading this book. The conditions for knowing this could not be better, you say. If your sense experience cannot give you certainty in this case, then it cannot provide you with certainty at all. But consider the speculation that you are dreaming or hallucinating (a speculation seriously entertained, and made famous, by the great French philosopher, Rene Descartes).[7] If this were true, your experience of reading this book would not be brought about by a real physical book reflecting light to your eyes. Yet it would nevertheless *seem* to you that you are reading a book—a book that you believe to be a physical thing existing independently of you. But if your experience would be the same on either hypothesis, that is, the same whether or not you are seeing your physical hands holding a physical book, then how do you know which hypothesis is correct? How do you know that you really are doing what you believe you are doing—holding and reading a physical book which is part of a world that exists independently of you? And if you don't know *that*, or don't know how you know it, can you be sure that you know anything about a world outside your mind?

Let us consider the dream hypothesis more carefully to see if it really is as preposterous as it may seem when we first encounter it. According to this hypothesis, the experience you are now having is part of a gigantic dream (i.e., a "mega-dream"). You have never awakened from it, and, for all you know, you never will. Awakening from it may not even be possible. You believe you have had many ordinary dreams from which you have later awakened. But both these dreams and what we call your waking states are parts of your mega-dream. Could this hypothesis be true?

The answer certainly seems to be no. You feel absolutely certain that you are not dreaming now. You remember having awakened this morning, and, let us suppose, haven't slept since then. But this really doesn't support a negative answer. You have had the experience of awakening and of being awake in ordinary dreams, and so your experience of being awake now does nothing to support your belief that this experience cannot be part of a mega-dream. You obviously can dream that you are awake, and may be doing so at this moment.

It may be tempting simply to declare that, although in a dream you may sometimes be deceived about being awake, you clearly *do* know that you are awake *when* you are. But, again, this takes you nowhere. For you could be dreaming that you are making this declaration. The epistemic problem that the dream hypothesis raises comes into full view when you become convinced that there is nothing which you could experience while awake which you could not experience in a dream. For then you see that any test you could apply (e.g., pinching yourself, checking to see if glass will break when struck with a hammer, or talking to someone else about this matter) would not rule out the possibility that you are merely dreaming that you are applying this test, and any circumstance or feature of your experience that you could observe (e.g., that your experience seems too detailed, vivid, and intense, or that your level of consciousness seems too high) would not eliminate the possibility that you are dreaming of observing this.

THE SKEPTIC'S CHALLENGE

Clearly, it will be difficult if not impossible to eliminate absolutely and conclusively the possibility that you are dreaming. But now let us consider the claim of a skeptic who doubts that there is an external world, more specifically, the claim that you cannot know anything of a world around you (viz., an external world) unless you know that you are not dreaming. If this claim is true, then any test that you could apply to your experience, or any observation you could make, would fail to provide you with any knowledge of an external world, unless you *already* knew that you were not dreaming. Consequently, we again reach the conclusion that no such test or observation could rule out the possibility that you are dreaming. If knowing conclusively or indubitably that you are not dreaming is necessary for you to have *any* knowledge of a world around you, as the skeptic claims, then, paradoxically, you know nothing of such a world. All of your experiences that you believe are of an external world fail to show that you are not dreaming and thereby fail to provide any support for your belief.

But is this claim true? Well, let us note how very plausible it can seem to be. Suppose that you are and always have been dreaming. It could nevertheless be true that there is a world external to you and that it happens to be just like your dream. This would be a most remarkable and fortunate correspondence. But because you are dreaming you would have no evidence of this correspondence and thus no *knowledge* of it. Though your beliefs about a world around you would be true, they could not count as knowledge of that world. But then, if you don't have indubitable knowledge that you are not dreaming, can you know conclusively that your experience is of an external world? It seems very plausible to say that you cannot—that you can have no such knowledge if you cannot rule out the possibility that you are dreaming.

Somehow, then, you must be able to eliminate the possibility that you are dreaming if you are to meet the skeptic's challenge. The possibility that you are dreaming implies not only the possibility that you have no knowledge of an existing external world but also the possibility that there is no such world for you to know. Thus, it appears, you must be able to rule out the possibility that you are dreaming if you are to have any indubitable knowledge (i.e., anything that the *skeptic* would count as knowledge) of an external world. But *if* you must, you must somehow do so independently of any appeal to what you have been supposing is knowledge of a world around you. Such an appeal would be going in a circle and would get you nowhere. Another way to see this problem is to remind yourself that you can experience in a dream anything that you can experience while awake. Thus all of your sensory experience is compatible with the possibility that you are dreaming and, consequently, can be of no use whatsoever in your attempt to eliminate that possibility.

Any knowledge you have of a world around you is based entirely upon your sensory experience. You have nothing else to go on. That basis initially seemed more than sufficient. But now, when what philosophers call "the problem of the external world" has come into full view, you may find yourself wondering how your sensory experience can provide *any* rational basis for your belief that you are immersed in a world existing independently of you. Since you cannot tell, conclusively, by means of your sensory experience whether or not you are dreaming, all of your sensory experience is compatible with the possibility that you *are* dreaming and thus fails to eliminate the possibility that there is no world around you. If this possibility is incompatible with your having knowledge of an external world, then it would seem that the problem of the external world is unsolvable—that if there is such a world you cannot have knowledge of it.

This is the conclusion reached by the skeptic about the external world—that knowledge of an external world is impossible. Since other people are, of course, part of the world external to him, he ends up denying knowledge of any concrete thing other than himself and his experiences.[8] This position is called solipsism, and there are two forms of it: the dogmatic solipsist asserts that only he and his experiences exist, while the skeptical solipsist maintains that he can have *knowledge* of only himself and his experiences. The dogmatic solipsist has no basis for his claim to *know* that nothing lies beyond his own experience. But the skeptical solipsist presents a serious challenge to our knowledge claims. Though you will very likely never encounter a genuine believer in solipsism or have any inclination to become one yourself, the position itself is important because it forces us to reflect upon our epistemic condition (i.e., our condition with respect to what we can know) and challenges us to show that this condition is not as unfortunate as the solipsist believes. Can we meet this challenge?

It may seem at this point that we have been overlooking an obvious consideration that would show the dream hypothesis to be false. You may point out that you have a brain and eyes and a physical body, and, indeed, that without a body and brain you could not possibly be dreaming. But how, the skeptic will ask, do you know *that*? You have never seen your brain. You have seen your eyes in mirrors and most of the rest of your body without such visual aids. And, of course, you have felt it via the sense of touch, and have experienced innumerable sensations in it. But the proper conclusion to draw from this, the skeptic may say, is that you have had a great many visual, tactile, and other experiences of (or arising from, or pertaining to) what you take to be your physical body—experiences exactly like those you could be having if you were dreaming or hallucinating. The skeptic may remind you that even in ordinary dreams you have experiences of a body which you take to be your own during the dream. Clearly, you can experience a body while dreaming. Consequently, your experiences of a body fail to show that you are not dreaming all of this. Thus these experiences, like all others that you believe are of a world external to your own mind, fail to eliminate the possibility that you are merely dreaming and that there is no world whatsoever around you.

What the dream speculation seems to show is that the only *direct* (sensory) knowledge you have is knowledge of what is in your own mind. For it shows that this knowledge, apparently unlike knowledge of anything independent of your mind, is something you possess whether or not you are dreaming. In other words, you know about the contents of your mind with a directness or an immediacy that you fail to have in the case of anything external. Everything else you know is known by you only *indirectly*, that is, by way of your direct knowledge of the experience you are having.

The distinction between direct and indirect knowledge enables us to see in a somewhat different way why the common-sense appeal to one's brain and body would not impress the skeptic. Your knowledge of your brain is clearly not direct. But, the skeptic may argue, the dream experience shows that your knowledge of your body is also only indirect. This knowledge is based entirely upon your sensory experience, which includes bodily sensations. But since it is possible for you to have exactly similar sensory experiences when you are dreaming, your claim that you are having experience of your physical body apparently belongs to your *interpretation* or *account* of your sensory experience rather than to the experience itself. For you would place an entirely different interpretation upon exactly similar sensory experiences you remember having had in a dream. Suppose you have a dream in which you are looking at yourself in a mirror. As you later recall the dream, you would not interpret it as a case of viewing your physical body. Yet the dream may be exactly like an experience you do interpret in that way. Thus your belief that you are now viewing your physical body is an interpretation of your sensory experience which goes beyond the experience itself. But knowledge based upon an interpretation which reaches beyond your sensory experience cannot be direct. Your sensory experience, on the other hand, is directly known to you; and so your knowledge of it, unlike your indirect knowledge of your physical body, is not jeopardized by the possibility that you are dreaming. But any knowledge claim that *is* jeopardized by that possibility would not impress the skeptic.

You may admit that your brain, and perhaps even your entire physical body, are not directly known to you, and yet insist that your knowledge of them is nevertheless secure because without them you couldn't have any experience at all and therefore couldn't even be dreaming. But again the skeptic would be unimpressed. He would point out that your belief that your brain is causally responsible for all of your experience is based upon a theory—a theory which is supposed to *account for* the fact that you have experience and thus makes appeal to entities which lie beyond your experience. Your belief that this theory is true is certainly put in jeopardy by the possibility that you are dreaming. Since you could be dreaming that you have a brain which is the cause of your experience, an appeal to this theory does nothing to eliminate that possibility.

SCIENCE AND THE EXTERNAL WORLD

It may now be clear how the skeptic would respond to the claim that science has established the existence of a world external to your mind or experiences. Science, it may seem, provides a path that leads you from what is in your mind to an objective, external world. It not only reveals that you are linked to an external world but is continuously filling in more of the details of this linkage. The skeptic, however, would argue that the link science appears to provide is an illusion. Science may be seen as an elaborate and systematic attempt to explain and predict our experiences by appeal to something beyond them. It is an attempt to account for the way things appear to us (that is, the subjective realm of experience) in terms that refer to an underlying objective reality. This is clearly what physics may be seen as trying to do in describing an underlying realm of objectively existing atoms and sub-atomic entities. But, the skeptic will contend, science has merely presupposed, rather than established, that there is an external realm. If you cannot establish the existence of an external world by appeal to your sense experience, scientific theories will be no help to you; for they must ultimately rely on sense experience for their support. Even if you insist on referring to the findings of science as knowledge, the skeptic will point out that it is only indirect. For, he will add, everything that you claim to know via the authority of science is compatible with the possibility that you are only dreaming. You could be dreaming that you are studying science and that you or others are engaged in scientific investigation. Since your appeal to science, like your appeal to your sensory experiences, cannot eliminate that possibility, it leaves the skeptic's position untouched.

There is another reason why science cannot establish a link between the subjective realm of your experience and an objective external world. Not only does it fail to establish the existence of an external world but it doesn't even begin in the right place to link such things. For it really doesn't begin with our subjective states, though it may seem to do so. Such terms as *consciousness, subjectivity,* and *mental states* are unknown to science. If, for example, you look at a book on the physiology of the human visual system, you will find detailed physicalistic descriptions of the activity that takes place in the eyes, the optic nerves, and the occipital lobes of the brain. But there will be no mention of the subjective experience of seeing. The descriptions may include reports people have made of their visual experience when their visual systems have been stimulated in certain ways. But reports of experiences are physical phenomena that must be distinguished from the experiences themselves. And one simply doesn't come upon any mention of experience in the descriptions of the physiology involved. This is not to deny that subjective experiences are thought to be explained in the sense that kinds of experiences are found to be correlated with certain kinds of brain activity. But the point is that the descriptions of the physiology could be complete without including any reference to experiences or mental states. Nothing would need to be removed from a complete physiological account of vision (or any of the other senses) if the associated mental states should cease to exist. The physiology of vision *is* linked to the underlying physics in that descriptions of the physiology involved could, at least in a more advanced science, be replaced by descriptions of what is occurring on the micro-physical level. But there is no such link on the other end: The mental is not fitted in but left dangling.

Science and the common-sense framework are attempts to make sense out of our experience by providing a setting in which it occurs along with a causal explanation of it. In the most general terms, they do this by assuming the existence of a world that lies beyond our experience—an external world in which we and our experiences arise and have a place. If successful, they provide an explanation of our existence and of what is happening in our lives, and this is something the skeptic appears unable to do. Perhaps we have finally uncovered something that can be fashioned into a crushing argument against the skeptic.

Surely, you would contend, your own existence along with your various experiences must admit of *some* explanation. But the dream hypothesis, if true, not only rules out our ordinary explanations but seems to leave us with none at all. We believe that an ordinary dream is brought about, and thus explained, by brain activity, but that wouldn't be the explanation of your dreaming if the dream hypothesis is true. For in that case you have been merely dreaming that you have a brain and that it is causally responsible for your ordinary dreams. You have been only dreaming that you have explanations for your ordinary dreams and for your other experiences. But if that is so, you would be left without any explanation of your condition. For if your condition does admit of any explanation, it is either self-explanatory or it is causally explained by something outside it. However, the fact that you exist and are having experiences is certainly not self-explanatory. Even if you could somehow be the cause of your experience, you could not have caused *yourself* to exist. And since you would be unable to know of anything outside the dream, your condition would be inexplicable; for any explanation would appeal to something outside it. Perhaps your condition wouldn't have any explanation; but even if it did, you couldn't possibly know what that explanation was. Thus we are left with only the first of the three alternatives: The skeptic's view implies that you are left without any explanation of your condition. And this fact, it would seem, must weigh heavily against his view.

But even to this the skeptic has a reply. He would challenge the assumption that everything must admit of some explanation. His view implies that you and your dream would have no explanation if there is no world outside you. But since you and your dream would then be all there is, or, in other words, the entire world, the implication would be that the entire world considered as a whole has no explanation. And this implication, he may contend, is not at all implausible, whatever extent the entire world turns out to have. For it could have no explanation which lies outside it. Since the whole of reality is everything there is, there could be nothing beyond it to cite as its explanation. And the alternative that it is self-explanatory is highly implausible. When we wonder why there is anything at all, rather than simply nothing, we have in mind a question that certainly seems to make sense, even if it is unanswerable. A state of nothingness not only appears to be a state of affairs that we can conceive, but we seem to regard it as less in need of explanation than the fact that something does exist. But if this is so, then how can the fact that something does exist be self-explanatory? Thus only one alternative remains—that reality considered as a whole does not admit of explanation. And so the fact that the skeptic's view implies this certainly does not damage his position.

At this point, the skeptic's objections to our ordinary beliefs about what we know may seem unanswerable. There are, however, some other lines of attack which, if successful, would demolish his position. For these strategies attempt to show either that the skeptic's position, when carefully examined, is seen not to make any sense, or that it is incoherent in presupposing the truth of that whose truth is also called into question. Obviously, no position could survive a successful attack of this sort. Let us see how the skeptic fares.

THE COHERENCE OF SKEPTICISM

One strategy consists in arguing that the skeptic's position is actually meaningless, or makes no sense, because of the way it undermines the concept of dreaming—a concept which he obviously cannot do without. We form the concept of a dream by experiencing ordinary dreams and distinguishing them from (what we assume to be) our waking experience. We awaken and then discover that we have been dreaming. This discovery enables us to form the concept of a dream. But the skeptic pulls this concept out of the context in which it was formed and employs it in describing a scenario in which we could never find out whether we were awake or dreaming. You could never find out because any experience of awakening that you could have would be compatible with the possibility that you are only dreaming that you have awakened. Nor could anyone else be of help to you in discovering what condition you are in, not only because you could not know of their existence without already knowing that you are awake, but because everyone else would be in the same boat—unable to tell whether or not they were dreaming. And so there is no discoverable difference between dreaming and being awake. But a so-called difference that cannot possibly be discovered is no difference at all. The skeptic has covertly erased the difference that must be retained for his suggestion to make any sense. The suggestion that you may be dreaming only *seems* to make sense because you have been led to assume (illegitimately) that there is a viewpoint from which it could be discovered what is really going on. But there isn't, and so the skeptic's suggestion makes no sense.

What should we make of this reply to the skeptic? Is it nonsensical to speak of a dream that cannot be discovered to be a dream? It is only if reality cannot transcend what can possibly be discovered. But the skeptic would draw a sharp distinction between *being* and *knowing*, and would insist that what may exist is not reducible to what is knowable. More specifically, he would maintain that the meaningfulness of the dream hypothesis is not threatened by the fact that there is no viewpoint from which it could be discovered what is really happening. For how things really *are* is one matter; whether or not this can be *known* is another. It could be true that you are dreaming even if that truth could never be discovered. For whether or not you are dreaming is simply a matter of what state you are in and not a matter of whether anyone can know what state that is.

Does the skeptic successfully meet the objection? Well, he does if there is nothing wrong with our conception of a completely objective reality—a reality that exists independently of us and of any knowledge we may have of it. Perhaps this conception is fundamentally mistaken, but it is very difficult to see how or why it is. We seem to have no difficulty making very good sense of it. Thus again the skeptic appears to emerge unscathed.

The second, and more recent, attempt to show that the skeptic's position is fundamentally confused or incoherent arises out of a consideration of what is needed for language to be possible. The skeptic couldn't formulate, or even think about, his dream hypothesis without a language. But language, according to his critic, is essentially a public phenomenon. One can acquire a language only through interacting with others. There cannot be a language without rules for the usage of words, and, so the argument goes, training in rule-following essentially involves the activity of others since there must be a public check that one is following the rules. Thus others must exist for the skeptic to have arrived at his view in the first place, and so he must acknowledge the truth of what he also tries to call into question.

But the skeptic would see no force in this argument. He may remain unconvinced that a public check is needed, for this matter is highly controversial. In any case, even if he agrees that the activity of others is needed for one to learn a language, he would argue that these others need not be anything more than the appearances of others which one might encounter in a dream. He would remind you that if you cannot eliminate the possibility that you are dreaming, then you cannot distinguish mere appearances of others from actual others. But if you cannot tell them apart, then whatever role actual others are thought to play in teaching you a language could be equally well performed by the mere appearances of others, i.e., by what "others" would turn out to be if the dream hypothesis were true. In other words, since you know of others only by way of how they appear to you (that is, only indirectly), and since you cannot distinguish mere appearances of others from appearances of actual others if it is possible that you are dreaming, then what these appearances are appearances *of*, if anything at all, makes no difference to the way they behave and therefore cannot affect whatever role they may play in your learning a language. Thus, the skeptic would conclude, you cannot establish the existence of others by appealing to what must be true for you to have a language.

Perhaps it has seemed odd all along that a skeptic would even bother to express his views to others, given his doubts about their existence. But he has a ready reply to this too. He may say that he finds conversation with others interesting and informative, even though this activity may be nothing more than the mere play of appearances, representing nothing that exists apart from him. And if you were a skeptic, you might nevertheless be interested in reading this, even though I would be unable to refute your view that you may be only dreaming that you are doing so.

So what is there left to say to the skeptic? His view seems unimpeachable, but also impossible to believe. Can you really believe that you have no knowledge of an external world containing other people? Even if you thought you could, you would quickly change your mind when you realize that, in the skeptic's view, your epistemic condition is even worse than I have been suggesting. Not only can you know nothing of a world beyond your own experiences or mental states, but you can know nothing beyond your *present* experiences. Your conviction that you have a past is at least as strong as your belief in a world around you. But note that you have no direct access to the past. Any evidence of a past lies in the present. Your conviction that you have a past is based primarily on your own memory impressions, but they are in the *present*. All of your evidence of a past is consistent with the possibility that you just now came into existence, but with a whole set of memory impressions which lead you to falsely believe that you have a past. You cannot eliminate this possibility any more than you can eliminate the possibility that you are dreaming. And so, if you wish to be a consistent or thoroughgoing skeptic, you must deny knowledge of a past as well as of a world around you.

This, however, *is* intolerable if not simply incredible. You would insist that you *do* know more than merely what mental states you are presently having. Fair enough, but the problem is to justify this conviction and show how skepticism can be avoided. That is the point in considering the skeptic's challenge in the first place. Because his position is unacceptable, this challenge is one that must somehow be met. But it cannot be met if all knowledge must be direct. This becomes evident when we consider what must be true for us to know that other people exist.

KNOWLEDGE OF OTHER MINDS

Let us assume that you do know that you are not dreaming and that there is a world external to you. You know that there is a material universe containing planets, stars, plants, animals, etc. You also know that it contains human organisms other than your own body. But unless you knew more than this, you wouldn't know that they have minds. You could observe their behavior, but nothing you could observe "from the outside" would rule out the possibility that they are mindless automatons without any inner conscious life. Though they act and speak as you do, they could be totally devoid of thoughts, feelings, sensations, and other mental states.

A consideration of this possibility shows that there is a further problem in knowing about other minds; for you cannot observe them as you can observe the bodies of other people. It also shows that your knowledge of other minds cannot be direct. You have direct knowledge of, or direct access to, your own states of consciousness. But you cannot possibly have such access to the conscious states of others. What would it be for you to have direct knowledge of an experience of mine—that is, to know of it *in the way* I know of it? Listening to what I say about it or observing what I do would certainly not give you *that*. Even if you could observe what is going on in my brain at the time I am having the experience you would be no closer to having such knowledge. You would have to *have* the experience to know of it in the way I do. But then it would be an experience of your own, and not one of mine after all. For your having an experience *makes* it yours. You cannot have an experience of mine without being me, and you cannot be me and yet be you. For you are you, and I am someone else. No one can be partly you and partly me. What distinguishes one person from another seems absolute: There can be no genuine blending or merging of persons. No experience can be only *partly* yours. Thus you cannot have my experience, and so any knowledge of it that you may have must be indirect.

COUNTERING THE SKEPTIC

We are now in a position to offer a counterargument to the skeptic. The case for thinking that we have indirect knowledge provides the basis for it. But first, let us remind ourselves why we should take seriously a skepticism that may seem wildly implausible and impossible to believe. As we have seen, to embrace it is to concede that there is no rationally defensible way to break out of the enclosure of one's own mind. This presents no practical problem, however, since embracing it seems to be psychologically impossible for virtually all of us. Perhaps our powerful disposition to find it incredible is genetically based and thus well protected from the relatively weak sway of the intellect. Though we might well count this as good fortune, we should nevertheless be troubled if we have no reply to the skeptic. For it is surely a matter of intellectual importance to us that our belief in an external world be not entirely without foundation. So although this epistemic problem is purely theoretical, it is nonetheless a highly significant one; for it is a threat to our conception of ourselves as rational beings.

Perhaps the only way to counter the skeptic is to try to show that we have genuine knowledge that is indirect. For he regards all knowledge as direct; and, if we accept *that*, his position is unassailable. But although we must concede that all of our knowledge is *based upon* what we know directly, we need not agree that nothing counts as knowledge unless it is direct. Suppose we say to the skeptic that although his experience may not require explanation, he certainly does not *know* that it does not; and that maintaining that it does is certainly not implausible. Assuming that it does, we may appeal to a "best explanation" argument, maintaining that the most plausible explanation of the content of one's own mind is one which interprets that content as influenced or caused by material things and other people. Though we know of such entities only indirectly, we nevertheless have genuine knowledge of them.

Of course, the skeptic would reject this, perhaps by pointing out that since one has no direct knowledge of anything existing independently of one's own mind, our best explanation may be mistaken. But if we do not *know* that it is correct, the skeptic does not *know* that it is mistaken; and with this reply we may have achieved at least a standoff. He may argue that we should not believe in the existence of anything for which we lack adequate evidence, and that his position is preferable because it does not require him to do this. But we can respond with the rejoinder that he is not counting our *indirect* knowledge of things external to us as *knowledge* at all, and that this is to set the standards for knowledge too high—so high that we are not only unable to meet them but cannot even conceive of what it would be to do so. Consider again our knowledge of other minds. As we have seen, direct knowledge of the mind of another is inconceivable. Thus the demand that any such knowledge be direct is certainly peculiar if defensible at all.

However, the skeptic may concede that the satisfaction of his standard *is* inconceivable, at least when this standard is employed to evaluate claims to knowledge of other minds, and yet insist that this fact does not affect the conceivability of his view or even indicate that it is false. With this we can agree. We understand what he is asserting, and even how someone might be tempted to hold such a view. For we have certainly not refuted it. And though his standard for determining what will count as knowledge seems unreasonably or even ridiculously high, he will likely reply that this is a matter about which equally rational people may disagree. Perhaps so. But, on the other hand, there can be no rational *directive* to employ a standard so high that should certain kinds of things actually exist, the standard itself would rule out any knowledge of their existence, and, indeed, would render such knowledge inconceivable. Here the non-skeptic has the edge. If the nature of mind is such that direct knowledge of the mind of another is inconceivable, it would seem more rational to employ a standard which renders knowledge of other minds to be at least a possibility. Only with such a standard would an inquiry into whether one actually has such knowledge make any sense.

Still, this reply to the skeptic may seem rather weak. One would have thought that much more damaging blows could have been dealt a position that is so much at odds with common sense. We commonsensically suppose that we have direct knowledge of physical things and other people. But the skeptic would force us to the conclusion that if we know of the existence of such things at all, we know of them only indirectly, and that our claim to indirect knowledge of them is not so well founded that it cannot be denied by a reasonable person.

What the skeptic's challenge makes clear to us is that our indirect knowledge is *much* less secure than that which we know directly. We can feel the force of his declaration that it isn't knowledge at all. But without it there is no epistemic reach beyond the confines of one's own mind. The propositions that we claim to know indirectly (e.g., that there is an external world containing other people) could be false, in which case we would be mistaken in believing that they constitute knowledge. But if they *are* true, then we may *know* that they are true (i.e., our belief that they are true may be relevantly justified), even if we cannot be sure that we know this. Even though such propositions are only indirectly known, this fact would not prevent the states of affairs making our beliefs about these propositions true from being epistemically available to us if, contra the skeptic, we acknowledge that something less that a direct epistemic link can justify a claim to knowledge. Given this acknowledgement, we can have indirect knowledge of an external world even though we have no guarantee that we have it. Some uncertainty on this level (of feeling certain that we know) is apparently something we must learn to accept.

Our examination of skepticism leads us then to the conclusion that our beliefs about the external world are much less secure than we would have thought or hoped. Though these beliefs remain virtually unshaken in almost all of us, it is important for us to establish that they are not entirely without rational foundation. And if you doubt that we have succeeded in establishing even that much in our attempt to meet the skeptic's challenge, then you realize how much there is left to do.

QUESTIONS FOR FURTHER THOUGHT

1. What is truth? Is it as important as the text suggests? Why should we want to know it?
2. When is the evidence adequate to justify our belief that we have knowledge? Can't we make our work easier simply by lowering our standard of adequacy?

3. Though the skeptic is mistaken if we have indirect knowledge of an external world, how *certain* should we feel that we have such knowledge? Should we conclude that we are not rationally justified in having a high degree of confidence about this—about something we never thought of doubting before philosophical investigation? How important should we consider such confidence to be?

4. In speaking of truth, some people say, "What is true for me is true for me, and what is true for you is true for you." Is such a claim acceptable? Is it true? If you were to accept it as true, would you also have to accept as true the opinions of those who believe that you are mistaken? Would it be coherent to maintain that both your belief and their (opposing) beliefs are true?

5. How seriously should we take the dream hypothesis? Since it strikes us as an outlandish hypothesis, can we simply dismiss it as such, without further consideration?

6. What is a relevantly justified belief? What makes a justified belief (e.g., your belief that you are now reading) a *relevantly* justified belief?

7. To what extent do we have the power to adjust our beliefs to what the evidence justifies? Does our having such power imply that what beliefs we hold is something we *choose*, that is, something under our direct control? Or is this power more accurately characterized as one of *indirect* influence?

3

REALITY

So far we have raised questions about how we know that there is an external world containing other people. Now, setting that concern aside (even if we haven't laid it to rest), let us proceed to inquire about the ultimate nature or composition of this world. As we do so, we move into that area of philosophic study called *ontology* or the theory of reality.

THE SCOPE AND PROBLEMS OF ONTOLOGY

Perhaps the first point to note is that although we are able to use the words *real* and *reality* with no difficulty, it is quite difficult, if possible at all, to come up with satisfactory verbal definitions of them. What is it for something to be real? Consider the suggestion that to be real is to be "in the world," in the broadest sense of that phrase. The world in its entirety is everything there is. Something may be "in the world" in this broad sense without being in the *external* world. Clearly, your mental states are in the world, for they do exist even though they are not part of the world external to you. Our ordinary use of the word *real* may mislead us here, for we frequently say or imply that what is unreal exists only in the mind. We may, for example, say of an unreal dagger—an imaginary or hallucinatory dagger, or a dagger which appears in a dream—that it exists only in the mind. But we surely cannot equate the unreal with what exists only in the mind, for that would imply that our mental states too are unreal. Furthermore, what we wish to say of the unreal dagger is that it is not in the world at all and thus does not exist even in the mind. What does exist is the mental experience of a dagger, and this includes a certain set of hallucinatory or dream images. These images are obviously in the world even though they may exist only in the mind.

Though the concept of reality seems to be inaccessible by way of verbal definition (a definition which defines by appeal to other non-synonymous words), examples which provide access to it are easy to come by. Horses are real, but unicorns are not: There are no unicorns. However, pictures of unicorns, dream images and other mental images of them, thoughts about them, and concepts of them, are surely real. It is what such images or concepts are *of* which is not. But already a difficulty arises. Can we really think of what is *not* in the world—of that which has no being whatsoever? Though it seems clear enough that there are no unicorns, our assertion that they are not real appears to imply that they must have some sort of reality after all. For we surely do have *something* in mind when we say of unicorns that they do not exist (i.e., are not real), and this "something" apparently has to exist in some sense to be distinct from nothing at all. That it is not nothing whatsoever seems clear when we see that to think about a unicorn is certainly not to think about nothing, nor is it not to think at all. The answer cannot be that this "something" is an *image* or *concept* or *thought* of a unicorn, for these things obviously *do* exist, whereas a unicorn does not. Rather, it is what the concept of a unicorn is a concept *of*; and this, although apparently not nothing, is precisely what is asserted not to exist. Clearly, the concept of a unicorn is *not* of a *concept* of a unicorn; it is of a *unicorn*. In other words, the object of thought here is a unicorn, rather than some other *thought* of something, and thus it would seem that a unicorn must have some being or reality after all to be an object of thought. But doesn't this imply that, paradoxically, we *cannot* think of what is *not* in the world?

Although the right answer seems to be that unicorns have no being at all, and that an "object" of thought need not have any being whatsoever, it may still seem puzzling as to how such "nonexistent objects" are to be understood. Perhaps we should think of them as possible but non-actual objects. We need not pursue the matter here, however. It will be sufficient for our purposes to note in passing that we have encountered an important and difficult ontological problem: the problem of whether nonexistent objects should be deemed to have any reality of any kind, and, if they do have, what that reality should be understood to be.

Another ontological problem (or pair of related problems) consists in the difficulty in determining whether all objects are concrete particular things, or, more specifically, whether some objects are non-concrete or abstract, and, if so, whether some of them are non-particulars. If a nonexistent object such as a unicorn did exist, it would exist as a concrete particular thing, just as a horse actually does. Like a horse, it would exist in both space and time. But some putative objects are *abstract*, in that (if they are real) they are timeless and unchangeable. Numbers (e.g., the number five) and sets or classes of things might be deemed abstract, as it seems senseless to inquire about whether they might undergo change, or about when they came into existence or will cease to be. Yet they seem to be particulars in that each seems to be such that there can be only *one* of it. There can be only *one* number five (though there may be many groups of five things) and only *one* class of *all* dogs. Unlike a shade of color, such as navy blue, of which there are many instances, an abstract particular cannot have many instances. Indeed, it cannot have even one *instance*, if having one implies at least the possibility of having another.

A shade of color, as distinct from an instance of that shade in a colored thing, seems to be something that is both abstract and *non-particular*. Unlike a particular, it can have many instances; and it is abstract in that its relation to time is not that of a concrete thing. Unlike a concrete thing, it is not capable of change. A concrete thing that is navy blue in color may undergo a color change, but the navy blue color quality cannot become some *other* color. Moreover, it seems to be timeless in that its existence is not, or not obviously, dependent upon the coming into existence or ceasing to exist of navy blue things. Indeed, its existence may seem to be logically prior (and thus time-lessly related) to their existence, in that there could be no such things unless there already (or timelessly) were the navy blue color for them to have.

Entities or objects, such as color qualities, that can have many instances in particular things have been termed "universals." The ontological issue of whether there are such objects as universals is a long-standing and important one. If they exist, there are a great many of them. General words, e.g., "person," "tree," "blue," and "pen," would denote them. They would be denoted not only by nouns, but by verbs and adjectives as well. Activities such as running and thinking have many instances, just as there are many instances of being a person—one in the case of each person.

The universals we have considered so far are such that no more than a single particular is needed for them to have an instance, i.e., to be instantiated. A single particular can be blue and thus provide an instance of the blue color quality or "blueness." But other universals—the relational universals—require two or more particulars for their instantiation. Such words or phrases as "to the north of," "taller than," "between," and "under" denote relations that have many instances and thus would count as universals.

The theory that universals are real (the realist position with respect to the existence of universals) is a theory intended to account for the sameness or generality that we encounter in our experience. Of course, both sameness and difference show up in our experience. Suppose you are looking at five blue balls—five different particular things of exactly the same color. The difference you see is grounded in particularity, in the fact that each ball differs from every other in virtue of being a different particular thing. But, the realist would argue, sameness is as undeniably real as difference and thus must be equally well grounded—a grounding it would have only if a single entity (viz., blueness) had an instance in each ball.

If the realist is correct, then reality includes not only particular things but also general things or universals, such as the blue color quality. However, a nominalist would argue that realism is *not* correct, that there are no universals. A nominalist would argue that the sameness of color exhibited by the five balls is not due to a single entity having an instance in each ball but to nothing more than the fact that each ball *resembles* the others in color. Of course, the fact that the balls resemble each other in color must be acknowledged on any account. But whereas the realist contends that the resemblance is to be explained by the presence of a single entity having an instance in each particular, the nominalist contends that the resemblance is basic, that is, not explicable by appeal to anything more fundamental.

Though nominalism offers a more parsimonious account of what exists and has in this respect an advantage over realism, it faces the formidable problems of having to show not only how resemblance *can* be basic but also how a nominalist can avoid any implicit appeal to *relational* universals. Can two of the blue balls, A and B, resemble each other in color without their resemblance being due to or grounded in the *colors* of A and B? Clearly, resemblance must be grounded in qualities or characteristics possessed by the things that resemble each other. Things that are alike must be alike *in some respect*, i.e., alike in virtue of sharing some characteristic or quality, such as color. Thus to say that resemblance or likeness is basic (not grounded in anything about the things that are alike) is to imply that things that are alike resemble each other in virtue of nothing—an implication that would seem to be tantamount to maintaining that they do *not* resemble each other.

Since A's resemblance of B in respect to color cannot obtain independently of the colors of A and B, and thus cannot be basic in the way that the colors are, the nominalist can avoid acknowledging that there are universals only by arguing that A's color is *different from* B's color in that there is no single color quality manifested in both. Thus A's color is different from B's color and also from C's color and D's color, etc. Since no single color quality has an instance in each, a commitment to non-relational universals seems to be avoided. But this move by the nominalist is of no help at all in avoiding a commitment to *relational* universals. Since A resembles B in the way that it resembles C and in the way that B resembles C, etc., the resemblance relation has many instances: one in A's resemblance of B, another in A's resemblance of C, and a third in B's resemblance of C. Thus this relation is a universal—a relational universal.

The nominalist cannot avoid this conclusion by maintaining that there is no single relation that has an instance in each case of one blue ball resembling another. A nominalist may try to argue that each case of resemblance involves a relation different from the relation involved in any other case—that, for example, A bears relation R1 to B, A bears R2 to C, A bears R3 to D, B bears R4 to C, etc. But this will not help; for R1, R2, R3, and R4 must *resemble* each other, and so a higher-level resemblance relation would have an instance in each pair of these (first-level) relations. To maintain that each higher-level resemblance is different from every other merely repeats the problem on a still higher level, thereby creating an intolerable infinite regress.

Though we must realize that the realism-nominalism issue is a highly controversial and complicated one—one that we cannot explore extensively here—our reflections support the conclusion that reality includes objects other than the concrete particular things that typically concern us in our everyday affairs. More specifically, there apparently are several kinds of objects: concrete particulars, abstract particulars, and abstract non-particulars, i.e., universals. But some of the constituents of the world are not objects or reducible to objects. There are such non-objects as facts, states of affairs, events, states, and perhaps true and false propositions as well.[1] We need not try to formulate a complete list, however, as the ontologist may try to do in his search for the ultimate or fundamental categories into which everything real can be fit. Instead, at this point let us turn our attention to the natural world and the concrete particulars we find there.

SENSE QUALITIES AND SENSE EXPERIENCE

We are now taking for granted that in addition to you and your experience there are other people and things external to you. But what features do they have—what is true of them as they are in themselves? They must be something in themselves, apart from your experience of them, if they exist independently of you. And the question now is one of what this "something" is. Let us first focus on bodies—the physical objects around you, including your own body as well as those of other people—and then later attend to the minds or experiences of others.

You may have been assuming all along that these bodies or physical objects are, in themselves, just as you experience them to be. You experience a ripe tomato, for example, as red in color, as somewhat soft to the touch, and as having a characteristic taste and smell. And you may have simply taken for granted, as we commonly do, that the tomato has in itself these sense qualities, quite apart from your experience of it. But this assumption must be rejected, however natural it may seem to be. For it becomes clear, upon reflection, that your experience of it includes a very significant contribution on your part. Indeed, the dream hypothesis suggests that all the sense qualities you experience (viz., the color, the tactile impression of something soft, the taste quality, and the smell) are contributed by you. If you were merely dreaming that you are perceiving a ripe tomato, the sense qualities you experience would clearly be part of your contribution to the perceptual experience. But if you cannot eliminate the possibility that you are dreaming when you believe you are having a waking perception of a ripe tomato, then this conclusion about the sense qualities you experience again seems unavoidable. For if they were contributed by you in the one case but not in the other, this difference should show up in your perceptual experience in *some* way so as to enable you to tell conclusively that you are not dreaming when you are not.

Note that the dream hypothesis is a radical one which implies that the entire content of your perceptual experience is contributed by you (or, at any rate, has a source other than an external world of physical things).

Consequently, even though you are actually awake and surrounded by external objects, your apparent inability to rule out the possibility that you are dreaming indicates that these external objects enter into your perceptual experience only as cause of it and never as part of its content. For if they did appear in the content of your perceptual experience while you were awake, then (because they obviously do not do this in your dreams) there should be an observable difference between waking and dreaming—a difference that would enable you to eliminate conclusively the possibility that you are dreaming. Employing the distinction between direct and indirect knowledge, we might put the point as follows: Your apparent inability to eliminate the possibility that you are dreaming indicates that you have no direct perception or direct knowledge of any physical object, and so anything you do directly perceive must be distinguished from those objects themselves.

Though the dream hypothesis is apparently irrefutable, it may still seem preposterous and difficult to take seriously. So let us see what sober science implies about the relation between our perceptual experience and the physical objects that cause this experience to arise in us. More specifically, what does science imply about what is left of what we directly perceive after our contribution has been removed?

In the case of vision, it seems that we commonsensically suppose that our eyes are like windows through which we see physical things more or less as they are in themselves. We suppose that these things really do have in themselves the colors that are displayed in our sensory experience. But the scientific study of light and of our visual system not only fails to support this view but indicates that it must be rejected. There is no place for color as a feature of physical things as they are known to physics. Neither individual atoms nor the collections of them that form the physical objects around us have any color (not even the achromatic colors, black, white, and gray). Most of these objects reflect light, but that is a colorless electromagnetic wave. These waves have such properties as amplitude, frequency, and wavelength, but not color. If they are of an appropriate length they stimulate rod and cone cells in the retinas of your eyes. As a result of this stimulation, electrical impulses travel up your optic nerves to the occipital lobes of your brain and there generate an electrochemical disturbance involving hundreds of thousands of neurons. In conjunction with this disturbance you have an experience of seeing color. But the color arises at the end of the process of events leading from the external object to your brain disturbance and your visual experience. It is experience-dependent, forming part of the content of visual experience, and is not "out there" as an objective feature of external things.[2]

Though we may say that a ripe tomato reflects red light to our eyes, we should speak of "red-stimulating" light. For this way of speaking does not imply that the light itself is colored. Nor does it suggest that color is to be attributed to the reflective object. The object merely reflects certain light waves and absorbs others. But no color is involved in that activity. The difference between, say, red-stimulating and green-stimulating light waves is not a difference in color but in frequency and wavelength.

The conclusion, then, that color is contributed by the perceiver receives powerful support from science. But science also supports such a conclusion about the sense qualities we experience as a result of stimulation of the other senses (more specifically, tones, odors, tastes, and tactile impressions). With respect to hearing, what ordinarily stimulates the ear is a vibratory disturbance or "compression wave" in the air. This sonic wave consists of regions of compressed air separated by regions of expanded or rarefied air. When it is intercepted by the ear, the eardrum begins to vibrate in unison with the wave. This vibratory motion is transformed in the inner ear in such a way that electrical impulses begin to travel up the auditory nerves to the top inner fold of the temporal lobes of the brain. There an electrochemical disturbance occurs which, so far as we can tell, is very much like the one taking place in the occipital lobes due to stimulation by the optic nerves. This disturbance, however, is experienced as hearing pitches and tones. But again, as in the case of the color quality, the auditory sense qualities that we refer to as pitches or tones make their appearance only at the end of the series of events leading from the source of the air disturbance to the experience of hearing. They are, apparently, not to be found in the sonic waves or in either the vibrating activity of the eardrum or the electrochemical activity of the inner ear and the auditory nerve.

Though this account of the physics and physiology of hearing strongly supports the view that pitches and tones, like colors, are contributed by the perceiver, what is also worthy of notice is that although the experience of seeing color is radically unlike that of hearing tones, the brain disturbances which give rise to these very different experiences are remarkably similar. The kind of experience to which a brain disturbance gives rise seems to depend not upon the kind of disturbance it is but only upon where in the brain it occurs. Furthermore, the activity taking place in your auditory nerves when you are hearing is very similar to the activity occurring in your optic nerves when you are seeing. In other words, almost all of the physiological process which leads to the experience of seeing is remarkably similar to almost all of that which leads to the experience of hearing. Because of this we might have expected the content of the experiences to be very similar, but, of course, they are surely not.

To see how extraordinary this is we might consider a thought-experiment in which we imagine a case of someone (call her Susan) whose auditory and optic nerves are switched. Her optic and auditory nerves are severed; then the portions of her optic nerves attached to her eyes are spliced to the portions of her auditory nerves which lead to the temporal lobes of her brain, and the portions of her auditory nerves attached to the inner part of her ears are spliced to the portions of her optic nerves which lead to her optic lobes. What will Susan experience? Clearly, she will not see tones and hear colors.

Such a suggestion makes no sense. The fact that we cannot even imagine what it would be to see tones and hear colors is powerful support for our conviction that the experience of seeing color is radically different from that of hearing tones. Still, colors and tones will show up in Susan's experience. Since light waves falling upon her eyes will lead to a disturbance in the temporal lobes of her brain, they will result in her experiencing a pattern of tones; and since the stimulation of her ear by a sonic wave will lead to a disturbance in her occipital lobes, it will result in a display of color instead of tone. She would not hear anything in virtue of your speaking to her, but would have a visual experience instead; and when she focuses her eyes upon you, she has an auditory experience rather than a visual one. This would, of course, be quite peculiar and no doubt extremely confusing to Susan, at least at first; but it does seem to be an implication of the apparent fact that the mode of sensory experience depends upon the location of the relevant brain disturbance rather than upon the kind of disturbance it is. What is also important to note, however, is that this fact—that very similar physiological activities give rise to the radically different experiences of seeing and hearing—provides further support for the conclusion that there are no colors or tones in the world as it is independent of the perceiver.

The kinds of considerations which lead us to conclude that colors and tones are perceiver-contributed lead us to the same conclusion about odors and tastes. In the case of an odor, say the scent of the wild rose, the experience may arise in the following manner: As you bring the flower close to your nose to smell it, gaseous molecules emitted from it enter your nasal passageways. They stimulate receptor cells lining your nasal passageways, causing these cells to engage in chemical activity. As a result of this activity, electrical impulses travel up your olfactory nerves to the olfactory center of your brain and generate there an electrochemical disturbance. But this disturbance gives rise not to an experience of color or tone, but one of odor or scent—an odor you identify as the scent of the wild rose. And there is no reason to suppose that there is anything like the odor quality you experience in the rose as it is in itself, apart from its relation to you or any other perceiver.

The physiological account of how you are led to have an experience of tasting is very similar. You place a piece of peppermint candy in your mouth and experience a distinctive flavor that you identify as the taste of peppermint. How does this happen? The candy stimulates receptor cells in your palate, causing chemical activity in them which, in turn, results in electrical impulses traveling up your gustatory nerves to another region of your brain. An electrochemical disturbance then arises in that region, but, unlike those arising in other regions, this one is experienced as the distinctive taste of peppermint. Like the other sense qualities considered, there seems to be no room for the taste quality in the scientific account of the physiological process leading from your contact with the candy to your experience of tasting. It, too, apparently comes about only as the experience occurs and thus is perceiver-dependent. Perhaps some would try to maintain that it is merely your *awareness* of the taste of peppermint which arrives only at the end of the process, and that the taste quality itself is a property of the candy as it is independent of you or any other perceiver. But even if we have any idea of what it would be for a taste quality to reside in the candy itself, the fact that there is no place for such a quality in the candy as that substance is known to chemistry and physics seems fatal to any such view.

Of all the sense qualities, perhaps those experienced by way of the sense of touch (e.g., hard, smooth, and felt shape) are the most difficult to view as contributed by us. Suppose that you are seeing and touching a table before you. You may not have great difficulty believing that the color you see is not a property of the table as it is in itself. But it may seem preposterous to maintain that the table is not really hard, solid, and smooth. Yet this is precisely the conclusion indicated by the atomic theory of matter in conjunction with the scientific account of the physiological process leading from the stimulation you receive from the table to your experience of touching something hard and smooth.

According to atomic theory, both your finger and the table are composed of atoms. As the atoms composing your fingertip approach the atoms in the surface of the table, certain electromagnetic forces of repulsion become stronger; your fingertip and the table surface repel each other with a force which increases as the distance between them diminishes. When this distance becomes sufficiently small, the repulsive force becomes powerful enough to stimulate the touch receptor cells in your fingertips, causing chemical activity in them that results in electrical impulses traveling up nerves in your arm that lead to your brain. These impulses generate electrochemical activity in the neurons of still another region of your brain, and along with this activity, you experience a tactile sensation which is such that you are led to speak of feeling something hard and smooth. But again, the tactile qualities we denote with such words as *hard* and *smooth* are not in the table as it is known in atomic theory. According to that theory, what the table is in itself is a vast collection of atoms, each of which is thought to possess a structure that might be compared to the structure of our solar system. The atom's nucleus, which is composed primarily of protons and neutrons, is positioned like the sun, so to speak, while around it one or more electrons are orbiting at enormous velocities and at distances from it which are extremely great relative to the size of the sub-atomic particles themselves. Surely, there is no place in such a theory for the felt qualities of hard and smooth.

These considerations lead, in an apparently inescapable manner, to the conclusion that you must distinguish between what the world around you appears to you to be and what it is in itself, independent of its appearing to you. Colors, tones, odors, etc., are part of the world as it appears to you. There is no question about their reality since they must be real to be directly experienced. You couldn't have better grounds for acknowledging their existence. But since they are, apparently, contributed by you, they are not part of the world as it is independent of perception. And because they are not part of the world of things existing independently of our experience, we must wonder how we are to conceive of those things. If they have no color, odor, etc., then what features *do* they have? If what we directly observe is never these things themselves but only the effects they have on our sensory experience, what can we infer about their real underlying nature? There is, however, another question of equal importance: How does the world appear to others? An answer to this question will have important implications about the nature of reality. So let us attend to these questions.

THE EGOCENTRIC PREDICAMENT

Suppose that you and your friend are looking at a ripe tomato on the table. Both of you are seeing the very same tomato. You are seeing something having a certain color, shape, and size which you identify as a tomato; and the same is true of your friend. But if the color (or, more precisely, the colored expanse) which you see is contributed by you and not to be attributed to the tomato as it is in itself, two conclusions follow: (1) You are seeing the tomato only indirectly, that is, only in virtue of your direct experience of a colored expanse, and (2) the colored expanse (or instance of color) that your friend sees is not one and the same as the one you see. If the instance of color which you see is contributed by you, then the instance of color seen by your friend is contributed by her (for that color instance is surely not contributed by *you*), in which case these color instances cannot be one and the same. In other words, they are *numerically* different, or numerically *two* rather than one, although the two of them could be exactly alike.

The fact that the color instance you see is numerically different from the one seen by your friend seems undeniable when the situation is viewed in another way. Suppose that your friend is color blind, but is nevertheless able to employ the color vocabulary just as you do, calling ripe tomatoes and fire engines red, grass and emeralds green, etc. How do you find out about her color blindness? Certainly not by taking note of the color *you* see. Nor, of course, can you somehow make your way into her experience and literally see the instance of color that she sees. Such a suggestion doesn't even make sense. You find out by inference, for your knowledge of the color she sees is indirect. Unlike you, she cannot see, for example, the number five in an array of pale colored dots of various hues, and so you infer that she is color-blind, at least to some degree. But, clearly, you would not have to rely on this indirect way of knowing if the color instances you directly experience were one and the same as those directly experienced by others, for they would then be publicly displayed. But, of course, they are not. They are only privately observed. The instances of color that you experience cannot be experienced by another, just as no one else can feel your pains.

Now suppose that your friend is color normal, as you are. Perhaps she sees the very same shade of red that you do when the two of you are looking at the ripe tomato. At any rate, let us suppose that she does. We must still conclude, for the reasons already considered, that the instance of color which you see is numerically distinct from the color instance she sees, even though both are of the very same shade of color, that is, are identical with respect to color quality, or *qualitatively* identical. This is as close as you can possibly get to the sensory experience of another—you can have a sensory experience whose content is exactly similar or qualitatively identical to the content of that experience. But these contents, nevertheless, remain numerically distinct and only privately displayed.

Not only are we led to conclude that the instances of color that you see are seen only by you, but we must draw a similar conclusion about the other sense qualities as well. The instances of tones that you hear are heard only by you, even though someone else may hear an exactly similar tone. One might say that those instances are heard only in the privacy of your mind. And if every particular instance of every sense quality that you have ever experienced is, like your thoughts and your pains, experienced only by you, then, with respect to anything that you can experience directly, you are confined to the privacy of your own mind. You, along with everyone else, are in what has been called the egocentric predicament—you cannot have direct experiential knowledge of the experiences of others, nor can you have direct knowledge of the external world as it might exist in itself, apart from any experience of it. With respect to sensory experience, you cannot experience the contents of the sensory experience of any other sentient creature. Any knowledge that you can have of the world as it appears to any other creature must be indirect. And now we have reached by another route the conclusion implied by the fact that you cannot eliminate the possibility that you are dreaming. For direct knowledge of the experience of another, whatever that could be, would render the existence of that experience undeniable and would therefore show that the world cannot be merely a part of your dream.

Though it is possible for someone else to have a sensory experience exactly similar to one of your own, how do you know that this ever actually occurs? As we have noted, if you cannot eliminate the possibility that you are dreaming, you can have reasonable doubt that other human organisms are connected with any experiences at all. But here we should note that even when you assume that the dream hypothesis is false and that other human organisms exist independently of you, it remains a possibility that they are non-conscious, though complex, biological machines completely devoid of experience of any kind. They act as though they have thoughts and feelings, and also claim that they have; but they are really mindless automatons whose speech and other behavior is brought about by purely physical causes unaffected by any inner experience.

Your knowledge that this is false is indirect; it is based upon your knowledge of what is true in your own case. You have observed countless instances of connections between your experiences and your bodily states (e.g., stubbing your toe and feeling pain, opening your eyes and having visual experience), and this is your basis for believing that other human organisms are like your own in that they too are connected with experience. Of course, others would affirm that they have experience if you asked them, but their saying so is merely another behavior, rather than the experience (of understanding your question) which you believe underlies and accounts for what they say. So doubt that they have experience is not groundless; but even when it is put aside, you may still have reasonable doubt that their experience is similar to your own. You probably assume that when you and your friend are looking at a ripe tomato, you are both seeing a shade of *red*, even if the shade she sees is slightly different from the one you see. But could it be that she is seeing an entirely different color, say a shade that you would call green if you were seeing it, or perhaps even a color that you have never seen? Since this surely seems possible, we must ask how you know that it is not actually the case. She claims to see a shade of red, but that is because she has learned to apply the color terms just as you have: she calls ripe tomatoes, blood, and fire engines red, *whatever color she sees* when she looks at such things.

A better reason, you may say, for thinking that her experience is similar to yours is based upon the similarity of your eyes and nervous systems in conjunction with the fact that the two of you are receiving very similar stimuli from the object. We could observe that similar activities are occurring not only in the retinas of your eyes, but also in your optic nerves and in the occipital lobes of your brains. But, the skeptic would point out, we cannot observe the instances of color that the two of you are experiencing; and so for all we can tell from the outside, these colors could be very different. Even if brain science were advanced to the point where we could tell from the features of a certain disturbance in the occipital lobes of a person's brain that she would report seeing a shade of red, we would still have knowledge only of a correlation between brain states and *reports*, rather than between brain states and color experiences (except, of course, in one's own case, which is of no help at all in settling the question of what color *someone else* is seeing).

Again it appears that the skeptic's point must be acknowledged. You could be mistaken in believing that other human organisms are like your own in having experiences associated with them. And even if this belief is true, you could be mistaken in believing that the experiences of others are similar to your own. But his point is only that these beliefs *might* be false, not that they actually are. And though the burden of proof must be borne by the one who holds these beliefs, perhaps this burden may be borne by a "best-explanation" argument. The best explanation of the fact that other human organisms which have a physical structure very similar to yours also speak and act much as you do is that they possess an inner mental life similar to your own. At any rate, in view of the fact that you have no direct access to the experience of others, it is the best argument you have. So let us suppose that it is adequate. In that case, you know that there are material objects, that some of them are human organisms, that other human organisms have inner experiences just as you have, and that their experiences are similar to yours. One question remains, however. What are these objects in themselves, independently of their effect upon our sensory experience? In what does their reality consist?

MATERIAL OBJECTS

As we noted earlier, we have no direct knowledge of these objects. They cause us to have experiences of color, tone, taste, etc., though such qualities are apparently not properties of these objects, but instead are dependent on us (or, more generally, on *perceivers*) for their existence. So what *does* belong to these objects? To answer this question, we might think of how they are conceived in atomic theory and what our sense experience may reveal about them which is consistent with that theory.

According to atomic theory, ordinary material objects such as tables, stones, and trees are collections of atoms which in turn are composed of even smaller micro-entities. As we saw previously, there seems to be no place for such qualities as color, taste, and smell as properties of these collections. However, these objects clearly are located and extended in space, and consequently have such properties as shape and size. Atomic theory portrays them as having not only shape and size but also such properties as mass, radioactivity, being in relative motion or at rest, and electromagnetism. We are to think of them as located and extended in space even though they have no color and are not hard, smooth, or solid. Can we do this?

Our notion of spatiality arises primarily out of our senses of sight and touch—what we see and touch appears to be located and extended in space. But can we even *think* of a material object as spatial if it has no color and no tactile qualities? We wish to say of such an object that it has shape and size but no color. But can we think of these properties as pulled apart in this way? Perhaps not. Consider the fact that in visual perception they are necessarily tied together. You do not see anything that is not a colored expanse—that is, something with shape and size as well as color. Something must have color to be seen. Analogous remarks apply to the sense of touch. Thus it seems that we cannot even imagine seeing or touching a material thing if it has neither color nor tactile qualities. In other words, nothing comes to mind when we try to imagine directly perceiving such a thing if the only qualities it has that could be perceived are shape and size.

Note that the shape and size you perceive an object to have (i.e., the shape and size it *appears* to have) are perceiver-dependent, just as is the color it appears to have. For perceived shape and size vary with distance, perspective, light conditions, and other factors which affect perception, whereas, of course, the actual shape and size of the material thing do not. Besides, if the color an object appears to have is perceiver-dependent, then so is that which has the color; and that which has the color is also what has the shape and size.

But if perceived shape and size, along with all other perceptual content (as distinct from its cause), are perceiver-dependent, can we even *think* of an object as it is apart from any of this content? Yet this is apparently what we must do to think of *material* objects. And if this prevents us from even thinking of them as having shape and size, then it may well prevent us from thinking of them at all. If we are not entitled to conceive of them as spatial entities, then we may well be unable to think of them as entities to which we can ascribe the other properties which physics regards them as having. Even if a conception of them is not rendered impossible under these conditions, at best we may be able to have only a conception of an unknowable something or other that is able to affect our sense organs so as to give rise to our sensory experience.

However, our epistemic situation with respect to them is not as unfortunate as these concerns may lead us to believe. What we apparently cannot do is imagine directly *perceiving* them, but this doesn't prevent us from thinking about them at all or from making meaningful assertions about them. Though the shape and size that we directly perceive are perceiver-dependent and thus not identical to the actual (i.e., independently existing) shape and size of the material thing, this does not cast doubt upon the claim that some of the perceived shapes and sizes resemble, at least in a general way, the thing's actual shape and size. For example, when you are looking at a table under good light and you are near enough to it to move your hand along its surfaces, your reasons for believing that what you are perceiving resembles its actual shape and size seem as good as those you have for believing that there *are* things that exist independently of you. Even if there isn't *much* resemblance (given that the table edge as perceived is smooth and straight, whereas the actual edge is neither), any at all would be sufficient to justify the claim that we can at least *think* of these things as spatial entities, located and extended in space. And it seems clear that there must be *some* resemblance. For even if the perceived shape is very much unlike the actual (that is, material) shape, they are nevertheless alike in that both are *shapes*, and thus they still resemble each other to a degree to which no shape can resemble, say, a tone.

THE COMPOSITION OF THE NATURAL WORLD

We have now pushed our deliberations about the natural world far enough to provide a provisional list of the individuals and the very general kinds of things that constitute it. There is, of course, yourself and your world of experience—the world as it appears to you, composed of objects displaying color, emitting tone or scent, etc. Let us call these entities "appearance" objects or "phenomenal" objects, and the world they constitute your "phenomenal" world. You have direct knowledge of it and can have no reasonable doubt that it exists. In addition to this, there are other people and their phenomenal worlds. There are as many numerically different phenomenal worlds as there are persons. For to say that your phenomenal world is distinct from that of every other person is only to reaffirm the privacy of your sensory experience. There is, however, only one public world of material things—those things which, by affecting our bodies and sense organs, give rise to the various phenomenal worlds. Your knowledge of the material world and of phenomenal worlds other than your own is only indirect, but this fact does not prevent it from being genuine knowledge.

There is, however, another item that seems to require a place on our list; for without it, talk about your knowing anything, either directly or indirectly, seems senseless. In addition to the phenomenal objects of which you are directly aware and the material objects of which you have indirect awareness, there is your *awareness* or *consciousness* of them. Your consciousness of an object seems to be a reality distinct from that object. This may seem undeniable, especially if the object (e.g., a table) exists independently of your consciousness of it. Though few, if any at all, would deny that persons are conscious beings (or that many animals are as well), what the word *consciousness* denotes is much more controversial. What is also controversial is how these things fit together into a single world. Are persons, along with their conscious states and phenomenal worlds, just parts of the larger material world, or should they be seen as belonging to an entirely different category of reality? Is there only the material world manifesting itself in various forms, or are there non-material realities as well? These are the questions we will address in the next chapter (chapter 4).

QUESTIONS FOR FURTHER THOUGHT

1. If material things have no color, can we even imagine them as they are apart from our experience of them?

2. Can it be true that we (and other perceivers) contribute the color to a colorless world? If so, do we have any understanding of how we do this?

3. Consider the claim: Whatever is directly experienced is real. What does it mean? Is it true?

4. What is the egocentric predicament? Is it inescapable, as the text suggests? Does our being in this predicament support the view that we are not in direct contact with physical things?

5. What is a "phenomenal" object supposed to be? Are there any? Would there have to be if each of us is in an egocentric predicament?

6. Does the nerve-switching thought-experiment make sense? Note that what the ear is sensitive to (viz., sonic waves) is very unlike the electro-magnetic waves to which the eye is sensitive. Does this show that the experiment is ill-conceived?

7. When we think about nonexistent objects (e.g., a unicorn) we are not thinking about nothing. What then seems to be before our minds is not a concept but what the concept is a concept *of* (e.g., of a *unicorn*, not a con-cept of one). Does this fact imply that nonexistent objects have reality even though they do not exist? Can anything be real, or have any reality, if it does not exist?

8. Are there any universals? How might we determine that there are, or are not? Do we directly experience universals (e.g., shades of color) in sense perception? Or is it the case that what we directly experience in sense per-ception are *particular instances* of universals (if there are universals) rather than the *general* things that universals are alleged to be?

4

The MENTAL and the PHYSICAL

We live in an age of science. We habitually look to science to tell us what is in the natural world and to explain what happens there. But science finds only material things—material objects, events, and processes—and thereby leads us to believe that there is nothing else. The natural world that science discloses to us is a world of space, time, and matter in motion. And if these are the only ontological categories available, then even those things that do not appear to consist of matter (e.g., a pain, a mental image, or any conscious state) must nevertheless be seen as material phenomena of some kind. That they must be seen in this way gains further support from the fact that the natural world was entirely material before the advent of life. Consequently, someone who holds that mental phenomena are non-material is obliged to provide some account of how something non-material can arise out of an entirely material world. And that obligation may seem impossible to fulfill. Thus it is not surprising that a materialist view of the mental-physical relation is presently the dominant one.

MATERIALISM

Though there are many forms of materialism, all share the view that persons are entirely material beings. Perhaps the form that seems most plausible, at least initially, is central state materialism—a view which maintains that every mental state is identical to some state of the brain or central nervous system. Unlike other less plausible forms of materialism, it does not deny the very existence of mental states when understood as inner conscious episodes. Instead, it acknowledges their existence but maintains that as a matter of fact they turn out to be identical to physical states, namely, states of the brain.

Its appeal consists largely in the fact that, so far as we know, nothing ever happens in someone's mind or consciousness unless an event of a certain kind is occurring in that person's brain. You will not see a green afterimage in your visual field, or think about the next presidential election, or remember where you left your gloves, or decide to go fishing this afternoon unless, in the case of each experience, an activity of a certain kind is taking place in your brain. Nor will you feel a pain in your toe in the absence of the appropriate brain activity. An activity occurring in your toe is not sufficient by itself. The nerve impulses arising there must reach your brain and generate in it an appropriate disturbance. Without that disturbance you will feel no pain in your toe even if it is severely injured. On the other hand, if that disturbance *does* occur, then you *will* feel pain in your toe even if there is nothing wrong with it, or, indeed, even if it had been amputated some time ago. In other words, the occurrence of a brain disturbance of the appropriate kind is not only necessary but also sufficient (all that is needed) for you to have an experience of any kind. And so it may be tempting to conclude that an experience just *is* (identical to) a brain disturbance and that the mind is identical to the brain.

Yet upon further consideration this identity claim seems impossible to believe. At any rate, the difficulties standing in the way of accepting it are enormous. If an experience (E) really is one and the same thing as a brain process (B), then whatever is true of E is also true of B. Any (objective)[1] property of E must be a property of B, and vice versa; for if E and B are identical they are not two at all, but one and the same thing. And, of course, it is necessarily true that any single thing has all and only the properties that it has. But now suppose that upon closing your eyes after looking at a bright light you see a square, green afterimage and that a brain scientist is observing what is happening in your optic lobes at the time. He certainly does not observe anything green. Nor does he observe anything like the content of your other experiences. And he certainly doesn't observe your act of experiencing that content. Suppose, for example, that while you are smelling a wild rose and experiencing its distinctive scent, a brain scientist were observing the related activity occurring in your brain. He would not experience any scent. Even if he were foolish enough to try to observe what you are experiencing by smelling the relevant portion of your brain, there is surely no reason to believe that he would experience the scent of the wild rose. But even if he did, that would be *his* experience of this scent and not yours. We cannot even conceive of what it would be for him to observe your experience in the direct way that you do; and if he cannot observe it in that way, how can we conceive of him observing *it* at all? Your experience of the scent is a private phenomenon. The associated brain process, on the other hand, is a publicly accessible event, observable by anyone in the appropriate position and/or equipped with the appropriate instruments.

The materialist may acknowledge at this point that of course we cannot observe a person's experiences by looking at, or smelling, or, more generally, having a sensory experience of that person's brain. For that would result only in one's having a sensory experience of one's own. Rather, he may say, we must think of the brain as it is understood in physical theory and not as it appears in perception. But this suggestion fares no better. The brain consists primarily of neurons made up of molecules which, in turn, are composed of smaller physical entities. These neurons (or some subset of them) are engaged in a great deal of electrochemical activity whenever a conscious state is occurring. But when we think of the constituents of the neurons or of the electrochemical activity as these things are conceived in physical theory, we find no place at all for such sense qualities as aroma, tone, sweetness, or color.

The difficulties for the materialist do not end here, however. There are properties possessed by conscious states which, it would seem, cannot possibly be possessed by states of the brain, regardless of whether one thinks of the brain as it appears in perception or as it is conceived in physical theory. Note that you may have a desire *for* more education, a thought *of* or *about* the Pythagorean theorem, or a belief *that* the environment is becoming more polluted. Such conscious states are directed upon something. This directedness or "aboutness" has been termed "intentionality." But it seems nonsensical to suggest that a brain state can display such directedness or intentionality. It cannot be *of* or *about* something in this sense; it simply obtains. Furthermore, you can think of something, e.g., a unicorn, which does not even exist. But how can a state of the brain, or any other purely physical state, be *of* something, let alone of something that does not even exist? Also, your thoughts or beliefs may be either true or false. But the corresponding brain state cannot have such properties. It seems unintelligible to claim that the state of your brain associated with your present thought that, for example, the Pacific Ocean is larger than the Atlantic is either true or false. Since in this case your thought or belief is true, one would think that the associated brain state must have that property also. But it seems nonsensical to say that this brain state is true. It simply exists. It is true that it exists, but that is another matter. It is not itself true, as your belief is. Nor could it be. But if any doubt remains, consider someone's act of believing that the Atlantic Ocean is larger than the Pacific. It seems obvious that the associated brain state cannot be *false*. What would it be, we must ask, for a collection of brain neurons engaged in electrochemical activity to *be false*? The suggestion that it is seems nonsensical.

The materialist must argue that the apparent differences between an experience and the associated brain state or process are *only* apparent, that is, will turn out to be illusory when the mental-physical relationship is properly characterized. He must provide reason to believe that what we initially take the mental to be will either disappear altogether upon careful examination or will prove to be reducible to and thus nothing more than purely physical entities—physical substances, properties, states, and processes. The difficulties to be met in doing this, however, seem insuperable. Though the difficulties are many,[2] we might confine our attention to two major ones and consider them in some detail.

Two major difficulties for the materialist come into view when we see that within the realm of the mental, broadly construed, we can distinguish between the phenomenal and what we might call the "strictly" mental. In our deliberations about our sensory experience we were led to acknowledge the existence of phenomenal objects. What we should note now is that there seems to be no place for them in the material realm as that realm is understood in contemporary science. For we must remember that they are "appearance" objects, existing only when they are appearing to someone—a feature that no material object can have. Because of this, only two options are available to the materialist: argue either (1) that there simply is no phenomenal reality to create a problem for materialism or (2) that though the phenomenal must be acknowledged as real, there are no phenomenal *objects* (as contrasted with phenomenal *properties*). But the first option strikes one as a desperate maneuver that clashes head-on with our direct experience of colors, tones, and other sense qualities. It would imply that, for example, there is nothing that even *seems* to have color and thus would be very difficult to take seriously, let alone believe. The second option is more plausible in that it allows the materialist to maintain that there is a phenomenal reality in virtue of there being phenomenal *properties* possessed by physical particulars located in the brain. But it too is exposed to serious difficulties. First, the existence of phenomenal objects seems very difficult to deny. Afterimages and dream images, for example, seem to be much more plausibly understood as entities having properties (e.g., color and shape) then as consisting in nothing more than properties of something else. Secondly, even if we suppose that there are no phenomenal objects but only phenomenal properties of physical objects, we would still have to face the apparently insuperable difficulty of seeing how physical particulars could have *such* properties—properties whose reality depends upon their *appearing* to someone and thus unlike material objects do not exist independently of perceivers.

Though there is much more to be said on both sides of the issue as to how the phenomenal is to be understood, we can leave the issue at this point and attend to the problem that states or acts of consciousness (i.e., the strictly mental) presents for a materialist view of reality. Leaving aside the difficulty that the apparent non-spatiality of consciousness presents for materialism, let us focus on the directedness or intentionality of thought. Thinking is a conscious activity that seems to have an essential and intrinsic directedness. Its directedness is *essential* in that there can be no thought unless there is something it is a thought *of* or *about*. Its directedness or intentionality is *intrinsic* in that it has its intentionality in itself, not in virtue of standing in a relation to something else. Though there must be something it is about, i.e., its intentional object, its directedness upon its object is not separable from it and thus not some *other* item to which it could stand in some relation.

But can anything physical have intrinsic intentionality? If thinking is identical to certain brain states or processes, then they must be intrinsically intentional. But, as we have already noted, it seems nonsensical to suppose that states of the brain or any other physical states can be directed upon something, or, more precisely, possess in an essential way the intrinsic directedness of a thought. We should note that language and works of art display intentionality. The word *red* refers to (and is in this sense directed upon) a certain color, the sentence "The moon produces tides" is directed upon a certain state of affairs, and a painting or sculpture may be directed upon a certain scene or object that it represents. But these things have merely a *derivative* intentionality—an intentionality they acquire in virtue of expressing thought. Considered in terms of its physical properties alone, the spoken language is an ordered series of sounds, and the written language is a pattern of marks of certain shapes on paper or some other material. Of course, a language may take other forms with different physical properties; it may take the form of nonverbal gestures or the distribution of magnetic bits on a computer disk. But none of these physical items considered in themselves, independently of any interpretation we may impose on them, are directed upon anything. They simply occur or obtain. Nor do works of art, such as paintings, possess any directedness in themselves, independently of interpretation. A painting of a scene resembles the scene it is a painting of. But resemblance is not intentionality. To suppose otherwise is to suppose that, for example, two chairs that resemble each other in shape are directed upon each other in virtue of their resemblance—a supposition that seems nonsensical.

If even the physical items that may seem to possess intentionality have it only derivatively, then the conclusion that nothing physical can possess intrinsic intentionality appears unavoidable. What the materialist must do is show that the strictly mental doesn't have intrinsic intentionality either. She must show that contrary to appearances there really is no intentionality at all, or that the intentionality of the mental does exist but is reducible to non-intentional physical items. But the prospects for showing either look very dim.

A well-known attempt to show that intentionality is an illusion consists in arguing that apparently intentional items such as thoughts, beliefs, and language appear to possess intentionality only because they are *interpreted* as having it. Indeed, in this view there are no inner mental states such as thoughts and beliefs. Though we cannot avoid attributing thoughts and beliefs to ourselves and others, our doing so is the result of an interpretation we impose upon an entirely physical system that in itself possesses no intentionality. But the problem, which is apparently fatal to this view, is that the presence of an interpretation seems impossible to understand unless it has its source in intentional states of consciousness—conscious states directed upon what is being interpreted.[3] Of course, such states are precisely what in this view cannot be acknowledged to exist.

The other strategy consists in attempting to show that the intentionality connection between a thought and its intended object is reducible to, and thus ultimately nothing more than, some non-intentional relation between physical items. The difficulty, however, lies in seeing how any non-intentional relation can suffice. As we have noted, the resemblance relation will not do. A picture resembles what it is a picture of, but it cannot be *directed upon* what it is a picture of unless it is *taken by* a conscious subject to *represent* what it pictures. Furthermore, resemblance between the items connected is clearly not necessary for the intentionality connection to obtain. One's thinking about (say) a frog or a triangle certainly does not *resemble* what it is about.

Since thoughts and other mental states that possess intentionality are caused to occur, it may seem that the causal relation is the most plausible candidate for the non-intentional relation to which intentionality is supposed to be reducible. But what rules out the causal relation (along with other relations) is that it is a relation between existing events involving existing things. A thought, however, may be directed upon a nonexistent object or state of affairs, as when one thinks about a unicorn or plans for the future. Thoughts about the future are, of course, directed upon presently nonexistent states of affairs. Thus the intentionality connection is not reducible to the causal relation. For no causal relation can connect items that it connects, viz., existent thoughts and nonexistent objects or states of affairs. Nor can intentionality be a property of the brain, considered as an entirely material thing. For the workings of the brain, so considered, could consist in nothing more than causal interactions among physical substances acting in accordance with the laws of physics. In particular, it could not include nonexistent objects or anything connected to them.

We are now in a position to better assess the materialist claim that mental states are identical to brain states. If a mental state and the associated brain state are really one and the same state, then any objective property of the mental state must be a property of the brain state. Conversely, if the mental state possesses even one objective property not possessed by the associated brain state (or vice versa), then the mind-brain identity thesis must be rejected. What now seems clear is that the case for concluding that there is *at least one* objective property difference is very strong.

Functionalism

A recent attempt to salvage the materialist view proceeds by maintaining that mental states are functional states, that is, states whose mental natures are constituted by their causal relations. A mental state is essentially one with a particular kind of cause, say a sensory input, and which leads to a particular kind of effect, say, a behavioral output. The particular kind of cause or effect of a given mental state may be some other kind of mental state, and the totality of the causal relations into which that given mental state enters is called its "causal" or "functional" role. In other words, being a mental state of a certain kind (say, a pain) is having a certain kind of functional role. More specifically, what makes a certain kind of state a state of being in pain is that it is usually caused by some injury and usually results in such pain behavior as moaning, grimacing, and avoiding what brought about the injury.

The functionalist view of the mental does have some attractive features. In maintaining that what is essential to mind is what the mind *does*, i.e., its *function*, rather than the substance in which the function is carried out, the functionalist is able to avoid a difficulty that seems fatal to the mind-brain identity thesis—a difficulty not included in those we have already considered. The difficulty comes into view when we see that the identification of the mind with the brain entails that only creatures with brains can have minds. But this is a very implausible restriction. The brain and nervous system is an organic system in which the element carbon plays an essential role. Since computers, on the other hand, have a very different chemistry, one involving silicon chips bearing tiny electronic circuits instead of neurons engaging in electrochemical activity, this restriction would imply that even an advanced super-computer of the future could have no mentality. Nor could intelligent extraterrestrials whose chemistry is inorganic, that is, based, for example, on silicon in the way that ours is based on carbon. If there were such beings who appeared to have intellectual capabilities that match or exceed our own, we would surely want to allow the possibility that they have minds even though they lack carbon-based brains; and this is precisely what the functionalist is able to do.

Another reason why one might find functionalism attractive is the role it may be seen to play in providing a philosophical underpinning for modern computer and information-processing technologies. Modern computers have very impressive information-processing capabilities—capabilities enabling them to do what one would have thought only a mind can do. The fact that they appear mind-like in many respects, in conjunction with the support that modern brain science provides for viewing the brain as an information-processing machine, promotes the idea that the essence of mind is information processing. Functionalism embraces this idea in construing the mind as a biological information-processing machine. It would have us think of the mind as information-processing software capable of being run on many kinds of hardware, including our brains and nervous systems, which serve as its hardware in our own case. Thus it easily accommodates the intuition that intelligent extraterrestrials would have minds if they had silicon-based information-processing systems that function like our brains and nervous systems. In short, it may strike us as the most plausible science-based theory of mind available, given its intimate relation to the impressive advances in information-processing technology and its ability to avoid certain problems plaguing the mind-brain identity thesis in virtue of offering a more general conception of the nature of mind. At any rate, it seems to be currently the most widely held theory of mind, not only among psychologists and cognitive scientists but among contemporary philosophers of mind as well.

Despite these attractive features, however, it is difficult to see how this functionalist characterization of mental states can help the materialist at all with the problems we noted earlier. To begin with, reflections on our previous deliberations should lead us to conclude that any view in which the mental nature of mental states is constituted by their causal relations cannot accommodate the intentionality of the mental. Secondly, even if we assume that what makes a state a mental state is its causal relations, we will be unable to reach the conclusion that such states are material or physical states unless we add the premise that only physical items (physical objects, states, and events) can enter into causal relations (or, at any rate, into mind-body causal relations). And this premise certainly stands in need of defense. If, for example, your act of deciding to read this chapter is a non-physical event, then we certainly have evidence that some causes are non-physical. But suppose we allow this premise anyway. The materialist is still no better off. For if we assume that materialism is true, then even if we accept the functionalist thesis that what makes a state a mental state are its causal relations, every particular mental state will turn out to be a physical state (more specifically, a brain state); and thus we end up with a position exposed to all the difficulties we considered earlier.

Not only does the functionalist thesis fail to help the materialist, but that thesis itself must be rejected. For there is something which mental states are in themselves, apart from their causal relations to other things, that is, they have *intrinsic* characteristics; and this gets lost in the functionalist account. Consider again a case of someone's having a pain. If we agree with the functionalist that its mental nature consists in its causal relations (in, for example, an injury to her body, on the one hand, and to her pain-behavior, on the other), then we must also agree that it is something which need not have been *felt* at all. It seems easy to imagine a brain state of some human being or other animal that has precisely these causal relations to input and output even though no sensation of pain is experienced. In other words, the painfulness, i.e., the hurting, of a pain turns out to be an unessential feature, a feature it need not have had. But this seems clearly mistaken. Any adequate account of what pain *is* must acknowledge that hurting is essential to it. Without this inner felt quality there simply is no pain (though there may, of course, be tissue damage, bleeding, and avoidance behavior).

The problem that pain presents for the functionalist account is presented by other conscious states as well: In each case what is left out of such an account is the inner experienced character—what that state is for the person who experiences it. Thus it seems that we must reject the functionalist form of materialism along with the other forms. But this is to acknowledge that the world includes not only physical objects, states, and events, but a non-physical dimension as well. Our conscious states are apparently not physical states, or, at any rate, not *just* physical states, even though they occur only in conjunction with brain activity. How is this extraordinary fact to be understood?

PROPERTY DUALISM

One view of how this extraordinary fact is to be understood is the dual-aspect theory or property dualism. According to this theory, certain states or processes occurring in the brain have two aspects or properties, a physical aspect and a mental aspect. To illustrate, as you place a piece of peppermint candy in your mouth and experience its distinctive taste, the state or process occurring in the affected portion of your brain has the physical property of being an electrochemical disturbance but also the mental property of being a distinctive flavor. There is only a single event or process involved, but it has two quite different properties or aspects, much as a table top may have the property of being rectangular and the property of being smooth. The brain, then, is not a purely physical system: Some of the processes that take place in it have not only an external physical aspect that can be publicly observed, perhaps by surgically exposing someone's brain or monitoring its activity with instruments, but also an inner mental aspect that is observable only by the person whose brain it happens to be.

Property dualism is appealing in many respects. It does not deny the existence of the mental, as some forms of materialism do, nor does it maintain that the mental, when correctly understood, will be seen to be a material phenomenon. It acknowledges that the mental is a genuinely non-material reality, as our intuitions suggest. Still, it may seem very difficult to believe. Note, to begin with, how strange the brain turns out to be. Of course, the brain must be acknowledged to be a remarkable organ in any view, but it may seem so astounding as to be almost beyond belief if property dualism is true. Though the brain is a physical organ it also has a non-physical "insideness" to it: All the tones, scents, flavors, etc. that you experience, along with your experiencing or consciousness of them, are part of the "inside" of your brain. Of course, they are not inside your brain in the way that your brain neurons are, for they cannot be found by visual inspection of your brain or by any other publicly available access. As we noted, this insideness is non-physical and only privately accessible. Yet it is a property of a physical organ.

Can it be that brains are utterly unique among physical entities in their possession of this remarkable insideness? Can they be unique in their being part of the physical realm without being purely physical? It may seem difficult to believe that they are. For, at least as we ordinarily think of the brain, it is an extraordinary part of the body not because it is partly non-physical but because of its extreme physical complexity along with the fact that the processes which take place in it are intimately connected with our experiences. On the other hand, the view that the brain is partly non-physical, yet not unique in this respect, is even more difficult to believe. This view is called panpsychism, and it holds that all things in nature—even inanimate things such as stones—possess a non-physical insideness. You have direct access to the insideness of only one of these things, namely, your own brain; but all other things possess it as well, though probably in a less prominent manner or to a lesser extent than brains do.

A much more serious difficulty for the dual-aspect theory comes into view when we take a closer look at the properties that are supposed to fit together as dual properties of a single entity. We noted earlier that at least some mental states possess intentionality (i.e., they are directed upon something) and that physical objects, states, and processes seem incapable of possessing this. Yet according to the dual-aspect theory, a brain process may have *both* the physical property of being an electrochemical disturbance in a certain network of brain neurons *and* the mental property of (in the case of a thought) being about, say, the difference between an isosceles and a scalene triangle, or about the increasing size of the national debt. But if we cannot understand how a purely physical brain disturbance can be *about* anything, does it really help at all to suggest that there is something occurring in the brain which has the property of being a brain disturbance and is about something as well? Surely there is a problem with this suggestion—that properties such as these can be seen to fit together as properties of a single thing. One gets the impression that they were just slapped together for the sake of a theory.

We can have no doubt about the seriousness of this problem when we turn our attention to other mental states. Suppose that upon closing your eyes after looking at a bright light you see a green afterimage in your visual field. Though it is somewhat fuzzy at its edges, it is of a uniform shade of green throughout most of the space over which it extends. It is a homogeneously colored spatial expanse. But though the brain process with which it is associated also extends over a certain amount of space, this process is certainly not a *homogeneous* spatial expanse. Our brain science as well as our sensory observation of the brain leave no room for doubt about this. But clearly, no single thing can be *both* a homogeneous *and* an inhomogeneous spatial expanse. Since these are incompatible properties, they cannot be simultaneously possessed by a single entity.

There may well be other incompatible properties involved in this case. Note that your experience of the afterimage involves more than the occurrence of a certain event or the existence of a particular object, namely, the afterimage. It also appears to someone; there is your visual *consciousness* of it. Though the afterimage does not exist apart from your visual consciousness of it, it must nevertheless be distinguished from this consciousness that you have of it. For, of course, you can be visually conscious of other things as well. But now notice that although your afterimage appears in some part of your visual field, your *consciousness* of it does not appear to be there. Nor does it appear to be anywhere else. Though it is undeniably real, it is apparently a non-spatial reality; it has neither location nor extension in space. We cannot even conceive of finding it in some place. We know from our experience of our own conscious states that we do not encounter it in *that* way, that is, by observing it to be in some spatial location. But if consciousness is (or involves) a non-spatial reality, then it cannot be a property of anything which also has the property of being a brain disturbance; for nothing can have the property of being in space while having the property of being non-spatial as well.

MENTAL PARTICULARS

Though there are other serious difficulties with the dual-aspect theory, we are already in a position to see why someone who rejects materialism might well be led to embrace a more robust dualism—a dualism of things or particulars, as well as a dualism of aspects or properties. As we have seen, the property dualist acknowledges that there are mental properties which are genuinely non-physical but maintains that they are found only as properties of things, i.e., of particulars, which also have physical properties. One who defends a dualism of particulars, on the other hand (i.e., a "particular-dualist"), maintains not only that there are mental properties but that there are particulars which have *only* mental properties, viz., mental *particulars*.

Note that a dualism of particulars escapes the difficulty that seems fatal to property dualism. Properties that are incompatible and thus cannot belong to a single thing (as the property-dualist implies) are no longer problematic because they are possessed by different things. Since, for example, a green afterimage and the brain process associated with it are different things, the fact that the one is a homogeneous spatial expanse while the other is not does not present a problem. Of course, the fact that the mental enters the world only in association with brain activity may seem as remarkable as ever. We commonly assume (and have no evidence for thinking otherwise) that inanimate things and even such living things as plants have no mental states whatsoever. It seems likely that several lower forms of animal life are devoid of mentality as well. So mentality is apparently a rather rare phenomenon which, though genuinely non-physical (according to the dualist), occurs only in the presence of a fairly complex nervous system. This may seem inexplicable, especially if no appeal is made to a supernatural dimension as the source of the mental. For without such an appeal the mental must be seen as emerging out of an entirely physical natural world. Something utterly new and different comes into the world with its emergence.

But though we may marvel at the fact that the mental did emerge and thereby made our own existence possible, there may be no serious problem for the dualist lurking here. For although the truth of dualism implies the impossibility of a unified world-view in which everything can be seen as a material phenomenon of some kind, it does not imply that the mental is inexplicable. The dualist is at liberty to maintain that the mental is explained by a description of the conditions under which it occurs. When brain states of a certain kind (or set of kinds) occur, then mental states of a certain kind occur as well. A complete description of the conditions under which the various kinds of mental states or events come into the world may also turn out to be a complete explanation of their existence. It wouldn't be complete if there is a God who is responsible for the emergence of the mental (a matter we shall later consider), but it would be complete if the natural world is all there is.

MENTAL-PHYSICAL CAUSATION

Still, many may find such an explanation to be less than adequate. They may argue that it fails to provide us with any understanding of how, at least in naturalistic terms, a purely physical reality could have brought about something non-physical, that is, could have *caused* the mental to come to be. This points to a serious problem for the dualist—a problem that comes into full view when we focus on the causal relations between the mental and the physical. It is not merely a problem of how physical events can cause mental events[4] but also of how the mental can causally affect the physical. In other words, it is a problem of how the mental and the physical can causally interact. Once we acknowledge that there are mental particulars, it becomes very difficult to deny that they causally interact with physical things, more specifically, with brain events. But, so the argument goes, a non-physical mental reality is so utterly different from the physical that either (1) we cannot even conceive of causal transactions between them, or (2) even if we can conceive of this, our understanding of the physical realm shows that no such transactions occur. If a conscious state or event is a mental item with neither mass nor energy, and without either extension or location in space, how can it possibly move brain molecules or be affected by them? Furthermore, neurology and brain science not only make no mention of mental causes but apparently have no room for them. The brain as it is known to science is a physical system whose operations are physical processes which have physical causes—causes which, if known, would presumably provide a complete explanation of everything occurring in it. This difficulty seems to be the primary source of the widespread conviction among thoughtful people that a dualism of particulars must be rejected.

But where does this leave us? Our reflections about the nature of the mental have led us in a seemingly irresistible way to the conclusion that there are mental things and thus to a dualism of particulars. But then we encountered apparently compelling reasons for believing that this view cannot be true. We are now in a better position to appreciate the depth of the difficulties here and to understand why some philosophers have called the mental-physical relation "the world-knot." It may seem impossible to unravel. But let us take a stab at it anyway.

Perhaps we have misconceived the entire matter and so have made genuine understanding impossible without a fresh start with a radically different conceptual framework. But though we can speak of beginning with a new framework, such talk is empty if, as it seems, no one has any idea of what that might be. Given our present conceptual framework, our options are pretty well defined. Since, as we have seen, materialism is apparently unable to find any room for the mental as it is known to us in our experience of it, any hope for a resolution of the mind-body problem must lie with a dualist understanding of reality. And this brings us back to the problem with causation.

Explaining mental-physical causation is not as great a problem for the property dualist. He too has a problem with emergence if he is not a panpsychist. For if he is not, then he must hold that the purely physical leads to brain events or processes which have both mental and physical properties. But he does not have the burden of explaining how we might understand mind-brain interaction since he need not maintain that it occurs. Since he understands the mental to consist in mental properties possessed by things that also have physical properties, these things will have all the properties they need to interact with other physical things. Their mental properties need not have any causal efficacy, or at least none in relation to the physical.

But the particular-dualist does not get by as easily. Since he holds that there are mental particulars (e.g., your state of being conscious as you read this, or your act of deciding to turn the page), these particulars must causally affect the brain if the mind is to have any effect on the body. It is possible, however, to hold that these particulars do not affect the brain or any other physical thing. This position is called epiphenomenalism. In this view, mental particulars are caused to exist by brain activity, but they have no causal efficacy themselves (or, in some versions, none with respect to the physical realm). Their relation to the brain is like the relation a shadow bears to the object that casts it; the shadow owes its existence to an object that it is powerless to affect. The problem of how the mental may causally affect the physical does not arise, but the epiphenomenalist still has the equally difficult problem of explaining how the physical can causally affect the mental.

The main reason why epiphenomenalism is so difficult to believe (or, perhaps, even take seriously) is that it denies our commonsensical belief that our mental states have an effect on what we say and do. It implies that we could have gone about our business just as we presently do—building bridges, writing books, teaching classes, creating scientific theories about the world—even though entirely unconscious, without any mentality whatsoever. If it is true, then even our claims that we *have* mental states, or that they have a certain character, would be without basis; for these claims would be causally disconnected from our awareness of having such states. Such claims could be justified only if epiphenomenalism is false.

It is worth noting that property dualism does not escape this difficulty. As we have seen, the property dualist avoids the difficulty with causation if he maintains that the mental properties of a thing are not involved in any effect it may have on other things (or, at least, on the physical properties of other things). But then he ends up with a "property-epiphenomenalism" in which the mental has no more causal power than it has in the ordinary epiphenomenalist view. Thus we are led to the conclusion that the most plausible form of dualism is one which maintains that there are mental particulars having causal power to affect the physical realm. But then there is no escape from the problem of explaining how causal relations between the mental and the physical may be understood.

This surely seems to be a serious problem—a problem that may lead us to doubt that the mind-body problem can be resolved, or resolved in a dualist framework. But perhaps it can be. In any case, its resolution will certainly require a more careful look at what causation itself must involve. It is obvious that if causation must involve spatial contact or the transfer of mass-energy, there can be no mental-physical causation. If causation is this restrictive, then a mental particular which is non-spatial and without mass or energy will evidently be unable to enter into a causal relation with things having such features. These features may be involved in every case of *physical* causation, but they cannot be essential to the causal relation itself if mental-physical causation is to be possible. We certainly do not *know*, however, that they *are* essential. Indeed, we are apparently unable to provide a deep explanation of why any item, mental or physical, should have the causal powers and liabilities (potentialities to be affected) that we find it to have.

When we wonder how there can be mental-physical causation, we typically assume that physical-physical causation is unproblematic. But this is not so. We may suppose that one physical object is able to affect another (or, more generally, has the causal powers and liabilities that it has) in virtue of its mass-energy and volume or extension in space. But then we must wonder why volumes of mass-energy have the causal powers and liabilities, i.e., the causal properties, that they have. It will not do to say that ordinary physical objects have causal properties because their parts (e.g., the molecules or the atoms which compose them) have such properties, for the same question would arise with respect to their parts. Clearly, we should reject the view that the parts of a physical thing have causal properties by virtue of the causal properties of their parts, which, in turn, have their causal properties because of the causal properties of their parts, and so on without end. But to reject it is to acknowledge that there are physical items having certain causal powers and liabilities that admit of no further explanation. In other words, the fact that these items have such powers and liabilities is inexplicable; it seems to be a brute fact. As explanation comes to an end, we simply take note of what we find. But if this is true even of physical-physical causation, we should not be surprised to find that mental-physical causation is also inexplicable. In particular, our inability to explain how the mental and the physical are able to causally interact should not lead us to conclude that their interaction is impossible. Perhaps, in the end, all we can do is acknowledge that certain physical and mental items just do have the power to affect one another, without being able to explain why this should be.

We do not, then, know that spatial contact and the transfer of energy are essential to causation. But if they are not, then what is essential? Perhaps less than we would have thought. This is not, of course, a question that is easily answered. But suppose that the correct answer is "natural lawfulness" or "regularity in nature." Let us see what this comes to and how accepting it could point the way to a dualist resolution of the mind-body problem.

THE REGULARITY THEORY OF CAUSATION

Suppose that a brain process of a certain type, say B_1, occurring in someone's occipital lobes is always accompanied by a mental event of type M_1—an event which may be described as that person's seeing a round, green afterimage. The suggestion is that the brain process is the cause of the mental event not in virtue of any spatial contact or transfer of energy but because events of type B_1 are invariably accompanied, or closely followed, by an event of type M_1. There is an invariable, that is, regular, pairing or succession of events of these types ("events" that are understood to include not only happenings but states of a thing as well).

According to the regularity theory of causation, a causal sequence is an instance of a regularity in nature. A cause (C) of an event (E) is a member of a set of events or conditions (S), each of which is necessary for the occurrence of E and which are jointly sufficient (all that is needed) for E's occurrence. Which member, or members, of S we take to be the cause of E depends upon the context in conjunction with our beliefs and purposes. It may be the most conspicuous one, or the last one to be satisfied before the occurrence of E. Consequently, the event or condition we pick out of S and dub "the cause of E" is really only a causal factor which by itself is insufficient for the occurrence of E. For example, we may say that scratching the match caused it to light, but clearly the scratching of it is not by itself sufficient to light it. Oxygen must be present, there must be a combustible substance, that substance must be heated to a combustible temperature, the match cannot be wet, the surface on which it is struck must be of an appropriate kind, etc. When all of these conditions are satisfied, the match lights, i.e., the event E occurs. Together they are sufficient for the occurrence of E; and so it is the entire set of conditions or causal factors (what we have called S) which is the cause of E, even though we typically pick out one member of S and call it the cause.

Each member of S is, by itself, only a causal factor, and not the cause of E. Its presence is a necessary condition for the occurrence of E, even though not sufficient for E to occur. The presence of oxygen, for example, is a necessary condition for combustion to take place, though, of course, other necessary conditions (viz., the presence of a combustible substance and its attaining a combustible temperature) must be fulfilled as well. But to say that a causal factor C is *necessary* for the occurrence of E is to say only that an event like E (more precisely, an event of the type to which E belongs) never occurs without the occurrence of an event like C, and to say that S is *sufficient* for the occurrence of E is to say only that an event like E always occurs with the occurrence of a set of events or conditions like those in S. In other words, the relation between events like C and events like E is *lawful*; it is an instance of a regularity in nature which may be expressed as follows: If an event like C occurs along with the other events which together constitute a set like S, then an event like E occurs also; and an event like E never occurs in the absence of an event like C. C occurs either prior to or concurrently with E, but not after E. The causal relation is an invariable temporal relation, and the direction of causation (that is, what distinguishes cause from effect) is determined by the direction of time.

To provide a causal explanation of the event E is to show that E's occurrence is in accordance with a natural law or regularity, and to explain a regularity is to show that it is a consequence of a broader or more fundamental regularity. The regularity may be known by way of observation; or it may be postulated by theory, since a theory provides not only a characterization of the theoretical entities it postulates but a description of the lawful or regular ways in which they behave. In other words, explanation proceeds by way of appeal to lawfulness. For example, one may explain why the water pipe in the cellar burst last night by citing the fact that the cellar temperature at the time was well below freezing, along with the natural law, or regularity in nature, that water expands when it freezes. And one may explain why water expands when it freezes by citing a theory about the structure of the water molecule. One can, presumably, go on to explain why the water molecule has such a structure by appealing to more inclusive or more fundamental laws or theories that make reference to the properties of atoms and perhaps their subatomic constituents.

However, there is an end to this type of explanation, even if we can never reach it—an end which, in principle, is reached when one appeals to the most inclusive or fundamental regularities or laws of nature. Clearly, these regularities will not admit of explanation if explanation of a regularity requires appeal to a more inclusive or more fundamental regularity. On this level, explanation is replaced by description—a description of the most inclusive or fundamental regularities. We may still ask why nature displays *these* regularities and not others; but if we are looking for a *naturalistic* explanation (an explanation which makes no reference to anything beyond the natural world), then we are looking for something that does not exist. On this level, we can only take note of the way things are. After all, they had to be in some fashion if they are to be in the world at all. And that fundamental mode of existence can, at best, be merely observed and described.

DUALISM AND THE REGULARITY THEORY

Now let us see how this account of causation and explanation may be of help to the dualist in resolving the problem of causal interaction between the mental and the physical. A mental event, say, a pain (P) is the effect of a brain event (B_1) just in case the relation between events like P and events like B_1 is lawful in the sense we have specified. Similarly, your act of deciding (D) to turn this page is the cause of an event in your brain (B_2) if and only if the relation between events like D and events like B_2 is lawful. D and B_2, for example, need not be at all alike, nor does D need to have mass-energy or spatiality to affect B_2. Perhaps these lawful relations or regularities can be explained by revealing them to be consequences of a more inclusive or more fundamental regularity, but it is difficult to see what that could be. In any case, if there is such a regularity it would not provide an explanation of a different type, for it too would consist of a lawful relation between mental and physical things. Thus an account of how the mental and the physical causally interact would consist in a description of the lawful relations that hold between kinds of mental events and kinds of physical events.

We noted earlier that a dualist seems to have a plausible position in maintaining that the mental is explained by a description of the conditions under which it comes into the world, and we might now add that these conditions include its lawful relation to the physical. Though there is much more to be said about this matter (in particular, about whether the account we have examined can provide an adequate treatment of causal *direction*),[5] we have examined a dualist position in sufficient detail to at least indicate the direction it would take. Perhaps there is more to causality and causal explanation than what this dualist position can acknowledge. Yet it is difficult to see what this additional element could be. We commonsensically think of a cause as possessing a power to *produce* or *generate* its effect, and we may think that we directly observe this power in a volitional act such as a conscious decision to speak or to raise one's arm. But this power may seem to evaporate under our gaze as we subject the causal relation to a more careful examination: Perhaps all we directly observe are regularities, uniform successions of events. The impression of the presence of power may remain but now just dangles without any apparent basis in experience.

CAUSATION AS AN IRREDUCIBLE RELATION

However, the plausibleness of the dualist position does not depend upon the successful denial of the additional element. Suppose that the regularity theory of causation is false, in other words, that causation is not reducible to the regularities that constitute the laws of nature. Suppose that reduction runs the other way—that laws of nature are regularities in virtue of regularities in the causal powers and liabilities of objects (or subjects). These laws would then be what they are because of the causal features of the things entering into causal relations. Let us see what grounds there are for embracing such a view of causation—the view that the causal powers and liabilities of natural things are intrinsic and irreducible—and whether it is compatible with a dualist understanding of the mind-body relation.

If causation is not reducible to regularities in nature (or indeed to anything else); and if, as we noted earlier, neither spatial contact nor the transfer of energy between the causally related items is essential to causation, then what *is* essential? How should it be understood? Perhaps the answer to this question, or at least our best clue in our search for it, is to be found in our experience of (what we naturally take to be) the exercise of causal power in our mental and bodily lives. For it is in this experience of intentional action, as illustrated when you raise your arm by willing to do so, that our notion of causation arises. To understand our acts of willing is to have an understanding of ourselves exerting causal influence.

Perhaps our impression of exercising causal power, of *making* something happen, in exercising our will is an illusion, as the regularity theorist would have us believe. But we are now supposing that it is not, that in willing we have an immediate experience of causal power—an influence or power that is not reducible to a matter of an event of one type (e.g., your willing to raise your arm) merely followed by an event of another (e.g., your arm rising). We should note in passing that the view that there are real causal powers and liabilities, and that therefore causation is irreducible, has the great advantage of doing justice to our sense of the directionality of causation. Causation runs from cause to effect. This directionality is characterized by an asymmetrical dependence of one event upon another: Effects depend for their existence upon their causes, but the reverse is not true. The regularity theory implies, however, that this directionality is not intrinsic to the causal process. In that theory, the direction of the causal process is due to the direction of time, rather than to anything intrinsic to this process. For the regular successions of events to which causation is supposed to be reduced are intrinsically symmetrical: They could run the other way, as in fact they appear to do when a movie film or video is run backwards.

Clearly, then, the view that causation consists in the exercise of irreducible causal powers and liabilities has great appeal. Not only does it seem to be the view implicit in our commonsensical understanding of our acts of willing,[6] but it is in close accord with our intuitions about the directionality of causation. Moreover, it creates no special problem for the dualist. In response to the critic's concern about how one's non-physical act of willing can cause a brain event, the dualist is at liberty to say, "It just does." The fact that the mental and the physical do causally affect one another is a fact that we must acknowledge, however this fact is ultimately to be understood. Though at first glance this response seems to indicate a failure to appreciate the seriousness of the problem, further reflection reveals it to be quite appropriate.

In this view of causality, you exercise in your act of willing (say, to raise your arm) an irreducible causal power to bring about certain physical events in your body, and your body possesses a corresponding liability to be so affected. There need not be any spatial contact or transfer of energy involved; for, as we have noted, they need not be featured in every case of causation, even though all cases of physical-physical causation may involve them. There is, of course, the critic's objection that we cannot understand how something non-physical can possess the causal power to affect one's body, and vise versa. But this merely points to the ultimate mysteriousness of not only mental-physical causation but of all causation, given that causation is not reducible to anything else.[7] As we noted earlier, a similar problem arises in the case of physical-physical causation—we do not understand in an ultimate sense why physical things have the causal powers and liabilities to engage in the causal transactions that we witness.

We are not maintaining that the typical question we have in mind when we ask how one physical event causes another is unanswerable. For such questions are questions about what events intervene between cause and effect. Thus when we ask, for example, how the application of fertilizer makes the lawn grow better, the answer that we are looking for is one that provides a description of the process that begins with the application of the fertilizer and ends with the improved growth. It is a request for information about the intervening events. But this is not the kind of question we are asking when we ask how your willing to raise your arm causes a physical event in your body. For this seems to be a paradigm case of *direct* causation, i.e., causation in which no events intervene between cause and effect. Clearly, the mental must directly affect the physical at some point if it is to affect the physical at all, and the case of willing to move your body indicates that point as well as any case can. Once you have willed to move your body, there is nothing else you need to do (and, indeed, nothing else we can even imagine you doing) to initiate the physical process that constitutes the moving of your body.

Armed with the distinction between direct and indirect causation, the dualist is at liberty to contend that only in the case of direct causation do "how" questions become unanswerable and thus leave an impression of mystery that cannot be fully dispelled. When our search for explanation can no longer result in the discovery of intervening events but must confront an instance of irreducible and thus unanalyzable causal power, we seem to have reached the point where any further understanding can be attained only by acknowledging that this is the way things are and that further explanation is neither needed nor possible. No further explanation is possible by way of further analysis or more complete description of what is involved. Thus to demand that the dualist provide a "deeper" explanation of mental-physical causation is to unfairly demand of him that he meet a standard that cannot be met for any case of direct causation, even the supposedly unproblematic physical-physical type.

DUALISM AND THE WORLD-KNOT

It seems, then, that the dualist has a plausible account to offer of mental-physical causation, whether or not causality is reducible to natural law. But these accounts depend upon the plausibleness of denying that spatial contact and the transfer of energy are essential to all instances of causation—a denial that many find difficult to accept. Furthermore, there are other challenges to be met in showing that mind-body interaction is entirely compatible with what our most advanced brain science indicates about what is happening in our brains when we are conscious. A completed science of the brain must leave room for mental-physical causation if dualistic interactionism is to remain a tenable theory, and, of course, there can be no guarantee that it will.[8] Despite these challenges, a dualist understanding of the mind-body relation may still seem to be the most plausible one, partly because of the very great unattractiveness of the other views. It fares the best, not because it avoids serious problems, but because the competition is so weak.

In the end, however, we must acknowledge that the mind-body problem is a very complicated matter; and so it is difficult to attain much confidence that we have seen our way through the labyrinth, or, indeed, that we are even proceeding in the right direction. Thus it may seem that the world-knot is still rather secure and remains to challenge any attempt to attain a deep understanding of what we are.

QUESTIONS FOR FURTHER THOUGHT

1. Is it obvious that an activity taking place in your brain cannot be either true or false? If so, does this by itself show that your thoughts and beliefs cannot be (identical to) activities occurring in your brain?

2. Have you ever had a pain that you didn't feel? If you think you have, what would you say made that unfelt state a state of being in *pain*? Does the notion of an unfelt pain make sense? What might one say to someone who claims that it does?

3. Is it true that consciousness is not in space? Doesn't anything that exists have to be *somewhere*?

4. Is a green afterimage a non-physical thing? Does the notion of a *non-physical* thing make sense?

5. Could the mental, understood as a non-physical reality, have arisen out of an entirely physical natural world, as the text suggests? What would it be for this to happen? Do we know enough about our world to say with some assurance that it *couldn't* happen?

6. Do we know, or at least have good reason to believe, that there is more to causation than certain uniform successions of events? Can one event

cause another without producing it, as the text suggests, or even without a transfer of energy occurring?

7. Is direct physical-physical causation ultimately less mysterious than (direct) mental-physical causation? If it is, would that show that dualistic interactionism is an untenable view?

8. An eliminationist is a materialist who denies that there is any mental reality. Though the eliminationist acknowledges that we have a mentalistic language (containing such terms as "consciousness," "thought," and "pain"), she would deny that mental terms refer to mental things, or, indeed, to mental states, properties, or events. Do we *know* that the mental is real and, consequently, that the eliminationist is mistaken? If so, *how* do we know this?

5

SELF

Who are you? *What* are you? Can there be any real difficulty in answering such questions? Surely you know *what it is like* to be you, for that is who you have been all of your life. There is nothing that you know better than this, or so it would seem. But does pointing to this fact really answer these questions? Apparently not, for they are questions about who or what the word *you* refers to.

Perhaps your first response would be to give your name. But this is of no help. You certainly could have had a different name. And since a different name is something *you* could have had, your name certainly cannot be that to which *you* refers. It certainly cannot be at all constitutive of who or what you are. Nor would it suffice to cite your interests, your present job, your work history, your aspirations, or other such facts about you; for they too could have been different. Indeed, you may find it difficult to think of *any* truth about your life that could not have been different from what it actually is. You can, it seems, imagine being born at a different time and place to different parents, and having had a completely different childhood. You can imagine *yourself* in these circumstances, having experiences radically different from those you actually have. In other words, none of these differences prevents the life that you are imagining from being *your* life. And if there is a limit to the differences you can imagine, what that limit is, is not at all obvious. As you imagine more and more facts about your life as having been different— even to the point of your imagining having had a totally different set of experiences—there seems to be no point at which you discover that you are imagining the life of *someone else*. In every case, the person whose circumstances or experiences you are imagining is yourself. But anything about you that could have been different without thereby affecting your identity as a self cannot be constitutive of who or what you are. It cannot enter into that to which *you* refers (when it refers to the subject having the experience you are having).

This reflection may lead you to say that *you* refers to the self (or person)[1] who you are. For that could not have been different (i.e., some other self) if you are to be in the world at all. Though someone else could have been in your place, that is, in the world *instead* of you, *you* could not have been *someone else*. That much, at least, seems undeniable. But replacing *you* with *the self who you are* is only a verbal move. Since we have merely changed our terms, the question about what *the self who you are* refers to is still unanswered. This turns out to be one of the most difficult of philosophical questions. It is also one of the most important, not only because a deep understanding of ourselves is impossible without a satisfactory answer to it but because of the way this answer would bear upon such ethical issues as the morality of abortion and euthanasia, as well as upon the possibility of our surviving bodily death.

THE SELF AND THE BODY

It may seem at this point that there is a simple and very plausible answer to our question that we have not yet considered: *you* refers to your body. Of course, to speak of *your* body may suggest that it is something you *have*, rather than that which you *are*. But we need not be suggesting this, just as when we speak of *your* self we need not (and, indeed, should not) be suggesting that a self is something you *have*. So, with this in mind, let us consider the view that what you are is your body.

This view may seem, initially at least, to be the obviously correct one. You are a very complex physical organism—an organism whose complexity consists not only in its being composed of an enormous number of physical parts, e.g., cells, which are involved in complicated physical processes, but also in its possession of an inner mental life. If the conclusions we reached earlier are correct, then the mental must be acknowledged to be a non-physical reality; and so some reference to your mental states must be included in a description of what you are. But in this view the owner or possessor of these mental states or events is a physical organism. For they are *your* mental states, and a physical organism is what you *are*. And though this organism is so complicated that we may never be able to comprehend fully its composition or its workings, the self is not deeply mysterious in any further sense. We know what it is essentially, despite the fact that an enormous amount of detail remains to be uncovered.

The Possibility of a Body-Exchange

But as we look deeper into this view, it seems very difficult if not impossible to accept. To begin with, it appears that you could have been associated with a different organism. Earlier we spoke of facts about you that you can imagine as having been different from what they are. And now we note that you can imagine having had, or coming to have, a different body. Consider the following thought-experiment. You awaken one morning to find yourself in an unfamiliar bed in an unfamiliar room. You notice too that your body feels strange in a way difficult to describe. Let's just say it has a different feel to it—your bodily sensations are indescribably different from what you remember them to be. You have a sense that your body is larger and heavier than it was. You glance at your hands and they look strange. They are not *your* hands! Surprised and frightened, you get up. You seem taller, and your eyes seem out of focus. Although you do not wear glasses you see a pair on the dresser by the bed. You put them on and your vision is corrected. You now find a mirror in this strange place and are astonished when you see your image. You have never seen that face before! Now you hurry outside, hoping to encounter something familiar, but you are disappointed. You can't remember ever having been in this place.

After some investigation you discover that you are in Raleigh, North Carolina, and that the name of the person who lives in the house in which you awakened is Frank Reynolds. This explains why unfamiliar people whom you have met on the street have greeted you as "Frank." One of them who seems to regard you as an old friend begins to converse about some good times he apparently thinks the two of you have shared in the past. But you have no idea of what he is talking about; and so you quickly excuse yourself from this conversation, resolving to return to your home in Minneapolis as soon as possible. When you arrive there you are astonished to find in your home a person who could be your identical twin. You get the uncanny feeling that you are viewing yourself from the outside, as others do. This person has apparently just awakened and seems very confused. He doesn't know where he is or how he got here. But he claims to be Frank Reynolds and that he lives in Raleigh, North Carolina. With that information you grasp what has happened: The two of you have switched bodies.

This scenario seems easy enough to imagine, however astonishing and inexplicable its actual occurrence would be. You can imagine it happening to you. Though you can imagine having a different body, you can have no doubt about which person *you* are throughout this thought-experiment. Clearly, the suggestion that you could find yourself confused about who it is who has awakened in the bed (which turns out to be) in Raleigh is absurd. The experience of awakening is one you are directly aware of, and, of course, any experience of which you are directly aware must be one of your own. Since your identity is unambiguously tracked throughout the thought-experiment, only one conclusion is possible: You have survived a body-exchange. And if you can do *that*—if you can remain the self that you are even though your body is replaced—then you obviously cannot be identical with your body. In other words, if it is possible for *you* to survive a body-exchange but not possible for *your body* to survive a body-exchange, then you must be distinct from your body.

But have we really established that your surviving a body-exchange is possible? We apparently can imagine this scenario, but is it one in which our power of imagination reveals to us what is possible? This question does not admit of a simple answer. The kind of possibility that our power of imagination reveals to us in this case (if, indeed, it reveals anything at all about what is possible) is a very weak one.[2] Let us call it a *logical* or *conceptual* possibility and then distinguish it from what we often have in mind when we talk about a possibility. Sometimes we are speaking of what is within our power to do, or, in other words, of what is *technically* possible for us. A number of years ago heart transplants were technically impossible, but now they are possible in the technical sense. A complete brain transplant is still technically impossible. However, a brain transplant is possible in a broader sense: It is naturally possible. That is, the occurrence of such an event is consistent (so far as we know) with the natural laws of our world. These laws determine what is naturally possible or impossible. And so, if Einstein's special theory of relativity accurately describes the natural law of the physical universe, then it is naturally impossible (and thus forever technically impossible) for us to build a space ship that can travel faster than the velocity of light. However, we apparently have no problem conceiving of or thinking about such a space ship. Our concept of it is not inconsistent with the other concepts we must employ in thinking about it. In other words, its existence is conceptually possible, or possible in the weakest sense, even though it could not exist in the actual world.

Now let us apply these distinctions to the scenario we have imagined. Clearly, the fact that a body-exchange can be imagined does not show that such an exchange is technically possible, or even naturally possible. But this fact apparently *does* indicate (if it does not show) that a body-exchange is conceptually, or logically, possible, for what can be imagined is a guide (though not an infallible one) to what is possible, at least in this broad logical sense of possibility. All that is required for a state of affairs to be logically possible is that a description of it does not contain or imply a self-contradiction. It is logically impossible for there to be a round square. Here the implicit self-contradiction is apparent. Since a round figure cannot be a square, the reference is to a square that is not a square. Of course, we quickly see that though we can speak of a round square, we cannot imagine or conceive of a figure that is both round and square. A more complex example of implicit logical inconsistency or contradiction is a scenario in which you try to imagine yourself traveling into the past and killing your former self (i.e., yourself as you were at that earlier time). You may believe that this is logically possible until you realize that your killing this person would result in your nonexistence which, in turn, would entail that this person was *not* killed by you. But the body-exchange scenario seems quite different from these cases. Although a full description of this scenario would be complex enough to possibly conceal an inconsistency, it is difficult to see what such an inconsistency could be. Not only does the scenario seem easy to imagine initially, but no indication of any inconsistency appears even after carefully thinking it through. Thus it indicates (if it does not demonstrate) the logical possibility of a body-exchange. And so we can now state our earlier conclusion with more precision. If it is logically possible for you to survive a body-exchange but not logically possible for your body to survive a body-exchange (i.e., to remain your body when it is no longer your body), then you are not identical to your body and (logically) could exist in isolation from it.

The Brain-Transplant Scenario

The conclusion that you are not your body is also supported by thought-experiments that have the advantage of staying within the realm of the naturally possible. Suppose that you and your friend are badly injured in an automobile accident. Her brain is so badly damaged that she will remain permanently unconscious, although the rest of her body is uninjured. Your brain, on the other hand, is undamaged, but your body is so severely injured that you will die in a few days. Given these circumstances, a decision is made to surgically remove her brain from her skull and put yours in its place. The procedure of connecting your brain to her spinal cord, sensory nerves, etc. is enormously complicated, but the operation is successful. There is a survivor— one person is saved.

Of course, we can't actually perform such an operation, at least not yet. But there is every reason to believe that performing it would not violate any natural law. It is naturally possible though technically too difficult for us at the present time. We may wonder whether we should wish to do it even if we could, but our focus now is on the question of who the survivor would be. Since she has your brain and since brain activity is the immediate cause of experience, the experiences she has are your experiences; and therefore you are the person who survives. The experiences connected with your brain prior to the operation are your experiences. But there is no reason to believe that this relationship will change because your brain is connected to a different body. Hence, the survivor will have your experience, and that is something no one but you can have.

If, in spite of this consideration, we still had doubts about who the survivor is, we would very likely be able to find evidence to erase those doubts. We would very likely find that the experiences the survivor remembers having are (so far as we can tell) *your* past experiences. She knows everything about you that you knew, but nothing about your friend which you didn't know. Her interests and personality are like yours, and are certainly different from those of your friend. She refers to herself with your name and believes herself to be you. Given such evidence alone, we would be justified in concluding that the person who survives is you even though the body in which you survive is that of your friend.

We have answered the question as to who the survivor is, first by appealing to the fact that experience is connected with brain activity and secondly by examining the evidence that would be available from the outside. Both lines of evidence lead us to infer that you are the survivor. But *you* wouldn't have to *infer* this. For you would know this directly and conclusively. You have no difficulty imagining what it would be for you to awaken from the surgery, and as you do so you see that you could have no doubt about *who* has awakened. Perhaps others could have doubts about who has survived, but you could not.

The conclusion, then, seems clear: You would be the survivor. You go where your brain goes. But what should we infer from this—that you *are* your brain? The obvious inference to draw is that *you* cannot refer to your entire body, but we should also reject the inference that *you* refers to your brain. The importance of the role of your brain in this scenario is due entirely to its relation to your *mind*, i.e., to your experiences. The case for concluding that you are the survivor is a case for thinking that *your mind* has survived. Other people would draw this conclusion on the basis of the knowledge you have, the personality you display, what you remember, and who you claim to be. If these signs of the continued existence of your mind were not present, they would not infer that you have survived even if the brain transplant operation were successful in every other respect. And, of course, your knowledge that you are the survivor is not knowledge that your brain continues to function in another body. You may not even know that a surgery has taken place. Perhaps you were not informed, or have now forgotten, that it was to take place. But you know, in the most direct way possible, that you continue to exist, for you continue to have experiences—experiences which you know could not belong to anyone but you and which together with your other experiences constitute your mind. Thus it is only because your mind goes where your brain goes that you go there as well. And so now the correct conclusion seems to be that *you* refers to your mind. This conclusion, however, is tentative and one that we shall later examine more carefully.

The Persistence of the Self Through Time

Another set of considerations which seems to show that what *you* refers to cannot be either your body or your brain (or, perhaps, even your mind) arises from the way in which you have apparently remained one and the same self (or person) over time. You probably believe that you have remained the numerically same self for as long as you have lived. You would agree that you were born at a particular time and place, and that your presence in the world can be traced from that time to the present moment. You would surely reject as absurd the view that the infant born was someone else and that you later took that person's place in the world. Clearly, the relation you bear to that infant is not at all like the relation you bear to some *other* person. Although you have changed in many respects since the time when you were an infant, the person who has undergone these changes has certainly been *you* all along. More precisely, although you have changed qualitatively, you have nevertheless remained the numerically same person, that is, one and the same person. If this were not true, then we would have to conclude that you were never born and never were an infant—that these were events in the life of someone else. But of course they were not.

So the belief that you have remained one and the same self throughout your life seems unquestionable. But what is its basis or justification? Is there some fact about you—about the way you have endured through time—in virtue of which this belief is true? If there is such a fact, it must be crucially involved in an ultimate understanding of what you are. Let us see if we can uncover any such thing.

We might begin by considering the possibility that the fact in question is a fact about your body. If you are your body and you have remained the numerically same self over time, then your body must have remained the numerically same body. But the material or physical stuff that makes up your body now is numerically different from that which constituted your body when you were a child. We have good scientific evidence that the physical stuff or content which constitutes our bodies at any given time is gradually but continuously being replaced by different matter at a rate that results in complete replacement of all bodily material every six to ten years. In other words, there is no matter in your body now that was part of your body more than ten years ago. And so, if *you* refers to the matter that presently constitutes your body, then you are no more than ten years old.

You may have neurons that are more than ten years old. But such a fact does not conflict with the claim that none of the matter of your body has been part of it for more than ten years. For a neuron is a large complex cell that is comprised of a large number of smaller entities (atoms, for example), none of which were in it more than ten years ago. So we might say of each individual neuron what we might say of your body as a whole—that matter is continuously flowing through it, much as water may be continuously flowing through a swimming pool equipped with inlet and outlet pipes.

But though your body undergoes a complete replacement of its material content, we nevertheless speak of it as having remained one and the same body throughout your life. We say this not because we believe (falsely) that it has retained the numerically same material but because of the gradual manner in which its material has been replaced. More precisely, your body now (B_2) is one and the same as your body twelve years ago (B_1) if and only if B_2 has resulted from B_1 by a gradual process of material replacement of such a sort that it would be correct to say that B_1 and B_2 are one and the same. But what makes this correct to say is not some fact about B_1 and B_2 that would render incorrect our saying something else. There is no fact about these bodies that would falsify the claim that they are *different* bodies. Of course, it is a *fact* that B_2 has resulted from B_1 by a gradual process of material replacement. But it is also a fact that B_2 shares no material with B_1. Two people could agree about this—indeed, they could be in agreement about all the facts of the matter—and yet disagree about whether B_2 is one and the same body as B_1. But if they agree with respect to all the facts, their disagreement cannot be factual. Rather, it would be a disagreement about how the facts are to be described. And so, our claim that B_1 and B_2 are one and the same is the result of how we have *chosen to talk* about the facts—facts that could have been equally well described in a different way. In brief, since this claim is an expression of our linguistic conventions, your having retained one and the same body through time is a matter of convention, not of fact.

An analogy may help to make this point clear. Suppose that you bought a new automobile a long time ago and that you have been replacing its parts as they wear out. Some have lasted much longer than others, and so you have replaced them one, or only a few, at a time over the years. Yesterday you replaced the last original part. Do you still have the numerically same automobile as the one you purchased many years ago?

Note that this case is analogous to the case of your body persisting through time in that the entire material content of the original automobile has been more or less gradually replaced. Note too that though there is a strong case for answering our question in the affirmative, there is an equally strong case for answering it in the negative. When we reflect upon the fact that your present automobile (P) and the original (O) have no material in common, the negative answer seems to be the correct one. This is surely the answer we would have to give if P and O were both present before us at the same time. Yet this is something that could have happened. Suppose that as you replaced the parts of O you kept them instead of throwing them away, and that someone later reassembled them. Clearly, O would be the reassembled automobile, and under these conditions it certainly could not be numerically identical to P. On the other hand, it would be peculiar if the original parts of O were available for reassembly, and so let us suppose that they are not. Then when we consider the fact that P has resulted from O through a gradual replacement of O's parts, the affirmative answer may seem to be the correct one.

What is important to see, however, is that there is no fact about P and O which can provide grounds for preferring one answer over the other. Once we see how P has come about by way of the gradual replacement of the parts of O, we are in a position to know all of the facts relevant to the question of whether they are the same. And the point is that even if we were aware of them all we would not have thereby settled this question. It may seem that there must be some elusive "further fact" in virtue of which P and O are (or are not) one and the same. But there is not. Rather than appealing to some further fact, our claim (or denial) that they are one and the same reflects a decision about how the facts that we already know are to be described.

Whether or not P and O are one and the same is a matter of decision or lin-guistic convention rather than a matter of fact.

A defender of the view that what you are is your body may offer at this point the counterargument that your body has remained the numerically same body not because of the persistence of the numerically same material but because the organization of the material has persisted unchanged. Surely, he may argue, we must distinguish between the material constituting the body and the *form* that material takes, or the *way* in which the material is *organized* so as to function as a biological organism. Though many formal features of the body such as shape, size, and appearance do change a great deal over time, he may argue that on the micro-level a certain form or arrangement of material does persist. More specifically, he may argue that your genotype or genetic identity persists throughout the life of your body and that it is in virtue of this *fact*—the persistence of the genotype that came into existence when you were conceived—that you have remained the numerically same person over time.

But the problem with the view that your persistence through time consists in the persistence of your genotype is that your genotype is something general or abstract—something which, like a shade of color, may have several instances in the world—whereas you are a concrete particular, something there can be only *one* of. To illustrate, you might have had a genetically iden-tical twin (if you do not in fact have one). And if you had had such a twin, two instances of the very same genotype would have existed. One would have been yours and the other would have been that of your twin. Yet, of course, there would have been only *one* of you, for your twin is someone else. Thus we are led back to the view that if your persistence through time consists in the per-sistence of your body (as it must if you *are* your body), then the persistence of your body must consist in the persistence of something *particular* or *concrete*. In other words, we are back to the view we have already examined and found unacceptable, or at least difficult to accept. For if the persistence of your body must consist in the persistence of something concrete (as it must to constitute *your* persistence), then, as we have seen, this view implies that your persistence through time is a matter of convention rather than of fact.

We are now in a position to see why the view that you *are* your body is so dif-ficult to accept. If you are your body, then there is no fact which makes true your belief that you have remained the numerically same person throughout your life. Whether or not you have is not a matter of fact at all, but merely a matter of convention. This belief is grounded in nothing more than a con-vention—a decision as to how to talk about the facts rather than about what the facts are. The facts themselves provide no more support for *your* belief than they provide for the view that you have been in existence for less than ten years and that the child you think you once were was actually someone else. But this seems impossible to accept. Surely your belief that you have been in existence for more than ten years is grounded in a fact—indeed, in a fundamentally important fact—about what you are. But it cannot be if you are your body. Thus again we reach the conclusion that what *you* refers to cannot be your body.

THE SELF AND THE MIND

Let us now consider the view that *you* refers to your mind. But first we must make sure that we are sufficiently clear about what the mind is. Though the mind is composed primarily of experiences, it seems appropriate to consider dispositions to have experiences as part of the mind as well. More specifically, your mind is a unified set of experiences, along with dispositions to have experiences—experiences which, though strung out over time, are related in such a way as to form the unity of a single mind. These experiences are of various kinds—seeing, hearing, imagining, believing, feeling, thinking, wondering, etc. You are having experiences now as you read these sentences and think about them, but the great majority of your experiences either have already occurred or are yet to come. In addition to your experiences, which are all conscious states or events, your mind also includes non-conscious dispositions to have experiences. Beliefs, intentions, and desires, for example, are ordinarily held in a non-conscious dispositional manner. You may have held for some time the belief that St. Paul is the capital of Minnesota, but you do not consciously entertain that belief very frequently. When you are not consciously believing this, you nevertheless possess a disposition to consciously believe it. At those times you hold the belief in a dispositional manner, as part of the dispositional structure of your mind. Similarly, you may *intend* to finish college or *desire* to get all your debts paid off. You may hold such intentions and desires even when you are not conscious of them. These unconsciously held beliefs, intentions, and desires are dispositions to believe, intend, or desire consciously. They are part of the dispositional component of your mind.

The Unity of the Mind

As we noted earlier, your mind is not a group of scattered or unrelated mental elements. Rather, they are bound together to form a unity—the unity of a single mind. It is a unity that you experience. Let us call it the unity of consciousness. This unity is conspicuously displayed in your presently occurring conscious states. Suppose that as you are reading these sentences and thinking about what they state you hear the telephone ring. At that moment, perhaps because you are a bit startled, this book slips out of your hands into your lap. These experiences of seeing, thinking, hearing, and feeling the pressure of the book against you are virtually simultaneous. And though they are of very different types, they exhibit a unity which, though difficult to describe, is unmistakably present—a unity which may be best expressed by saying that each is experienced by *you*. But this unity of consciousness that is apparent in your present experience also extends across time to your experiences of the past. Your knowledge that it extends to the past is provided by memory. When you reflect upon what your memory reveals, you see that you remember past experiences as not only having displayed the unity you find in your present experiences, but as also displaying a unity *with* your present experiences in that all are undeniably experiences of *yours*. It is in virtue of this unity of consciousness present at every time at which you are conscious, and also extending across time, that your conscious states are states of a single mind, namely, your own.

Though the unity of the mind seems undeniable, at least in the case of a normal person, there is much disagreement as to how this unity is to be explained or understood. Three views seem to exhaust the possibilities. According to the first view, the unity is provided by the body. What unifies or brings together a number of experiences to form a single mind is the relation that each has to the one body. In the second view, the unity is provided by a subject of experience. Various individual experiences are unified into a single mind in virtue of the fact that all are states of that unitary subject. The third view, however, denies that there is any such subject. Here two versions may be distinguished: Either (a) the individual experience is subjectless or (b) though a subject is a component of every experience, that subject does not (or at least does not ordinarily) remain one and the same from experience to experience. In neither version is there any appeal made to a subject of experience in explaining the unity of the mind. Rather, this unity is due to certain relations which experiences that form a single mind bear to one another. Some of these experiences will be simultaneous or closely connected in time, some will resemble each other, some will be related as cause to effect, and some will be rememberings of others. Though there seems to be no satisfactory account of what these relations are, there is, in this view, nothing in addition to individual experiences and their relations to each other that could account for the unity of the mind. Let us call this the relational account of mental unity.

Now let us examine these views in more detail, especially with respect to what they imply about the issue of whether or how you have remained one and the same self for more than ten years. We have, in effect, already looked at reasons for believing that the first view must be rejected. The body-exchange scenario may be seen as a case in which mental unity is preserved through body-exchange. If it is logically possible for you to undergo a body-exchange and emerge with your memories, beliefs, intentions, etc. intact, then your mental unity cannot be dependent (in the logical sense) upon your having the particular body you do in fact have. But even if we ignore such considerations, we must agree that the body cannot confer upon the mind any deeper unity than it itself has. We have already noted that if you are your body, then your having remained one and the same self throughout your life is a matter of mere convention, rather than of fact. Consequently, if your mental unity is logically dependent upon your body, then your retention of one and the same mind throughout your life is also only a matter of convention. This view implies that there is no fact about you or your mind which would falsify the claim that the mind of the child you believe you once were is not *your* mind at all. And this implication must seem preposterous when you remind yourself that you have memories of your childhood.

Since you have such memories, it may seem that they, along with certain other relations that your experiences bear to one another, are what provide the unity of your mind. That is, it may seem that the third (the relational) view is the correct one. But a closer examination reveals great difficulties with it. If we appeal to it to justify the claim that what you are is your mind, then we must conclude that you are either a set of presently occurring experiences or a much larger set that includes past and future experiences as well. But each of these alternatives seems wildly implausible.

If *you* refers to your present experiences, then you are only a few seconds old. For your experiences change much more rapidly than the material composing your body. You have memories that extend far into the past. But, of course, your remembering of the past occurs in the present, for the past no longer exists. And your present experience of remembering soon gives way to other experiences such as thoughts about the future, auditory experiences, and bodily sensations. Even if we include your present non-conscious dispositions to have experiences, this view does not gain much appeal. For though these dispositions extend over a much greater period of time than experiences do, apparently they too undergo gradual change resulting in their eventual replacement, in which case the reasons for thinking that you cannot be your body also apply to your mind. More specifically, if you are your mind as it is presently (i.e., your present experiences and mental dispositions), and all of its constituents have been gradually replaced with the result that it presently contains no constituents that were in it more than ten years ago, then your belief that you have remained one and the same person for more than ten years is not driven by any fact about you, but by decision or linguistic convention.

Since this alternative is so implausible, we are naturally led to consider the other. But it turns out to be no better. If *you* refers to that much larger set of mental elements, which includes all your past, present, and future experiences as well as all your mental dispositions, then only a *part* of you is present now. You are not present in your entirety! But this seems implausible to the point of paradox. Your *life* is not present in its entirety, but *you* are. Or so we have been assuming. We may be able to give up this assumption if we do it for the sake of a view which is acceptable in every other respect. But, as we shall see, this view must be rejected on other grounds.

In this view what makes an experience part of your mind, and consequently one of *yours*, is its relations to other members of a very large, temporally extended set of mental elements—those experiences and dispositions that constitute your mind. But what relation or relations to other experiences could possibly make an experience one of yours? The memory relation seems to be the best candidate. One is inclined to assert that if *it* cannot do this, then *no* relation can. For memory provides us with an access to our past experiences which removes any doubt about whose experiences they were. You remember many of the experiences you had throughout the years, and you remember them, of course, as experiences that *you* have had. But though these experiences you remember were unquestionably experiences of yours, your remembering (or ability to remember) them is not what *makes* them yours. Rather, it is because they were your experiences in the first place that you can remember having them. What memory does is reveal, in a most compelling way, that they were yours when they occurred, for you remember them as experiences *you* had. But your *having* them is not some relation they bear to each other, and thus is something that can have no place in the relational view.

This point is of sufficient importance to merit further elaboration. The experience you are having as you read these words is certainly one of yours. Nothing could be clearer to you than this. But it is virtually as certain to you that a recent experience you are remembering—say, the experience of reading the previous sentence, which we shall call E_1—was also one of yours. Perhaps you could be mistaken about whether E_1 did occur (although this suggestion is very difficult to take seriously), but if it did occur you cannot be mistaken about whose it is. Let us say that E_2 is your experience of remembering E_1. Because of your having E_2 you can have no doubt that E_1 was an experience of yours. But your having E_2 *cannot* be what *makes* E_1 yours. For E_1 was yours when you had it, and E_2 merely reveals this to you. More important, E_1 was an experience of yours *because* it was *had by you*, and *not* because of any relation it may bear to E_2 or any other experience. Clearly, your having had E_1 cannot consist in any relation between experiences; it consists in your having been in a certain experiential state. This indicates that what you are is a subject of experience and that E_1 was an experience of yours in virtue of your having been its subject. What is also indicated is that E_1, E_2, and all of your other experiences are unified into a single mind in virtue of the fact that all are experiences of yours: They are your experiential states. But now we have arrived at the view that mental unity is provided by a subject of experience—a view we shall later look at in more detail.

We may already have more than sufficient grounds for rejecting the relational view. But the consideration of another thought-experiment should remove all doubt. Since this thought-experiment involves bisecting the brain, some discussion of brain anatomy and cerebral function is in order. The cerebrum is the part of the brain associated with conscious states. It consists of two hemispheres—the left and the right. A person may survive even if only one of them is functioning. This has been shown by actual cases of people who have lost the use of one hemisphere, due to a stroke or other brain damage. Because the full range of one's abilities to speak, remember, control one's body, etc. is usually not possessed by each hemisphere, such people will very likely suffer loss or diminishment of some of these abilities; and so some relearning will likely be necessary. However, it may well be that in the case of a few people, each hemisphere possesses the full range of their abilities. Let us suppose that you are one of these.

We have already noted that if your entire brain were successfully transplanted into someone else's body, you would be the survivor. And now we should note that you would be the survivor even if one of your cerebral hemispheres were destroyed, perhaps by some unfortunate mishap which occurred during the operation. Given our supposition that your hemispheres are equipotent, your experience in the new body would not be noticeably different from what it would have been if both hemispheres had been successfully transplanted.

The Divisibility of the Self

Now let us suppose that you are one of three identical triplets and that the three of you are involved in a serious accident. The brains of your two siblings are damaged beyond any possible recovery, but their bodies are otherwise uninjured. Your brain is uninjured, though you will soon die because of severe injury to your body. Given these circumstances, a decision is made to bisect your brain so that each half contains one of your cerebral hemispheres, and then to transplant one of your half-brains into each of the two uninjured bodies. Both transplant operations are successful—two offshoots are produced. But what happens to you?

Before we try to answer this question we should note that though these operations may strike us as bizarre and may always remain technically impossible for us to perform, they are surely conceivable. Not only are they logically possible but they may well be consistent with natural law (i.e., naturally possible as well). The duplication of capacity displayed by the cerebrum may be matched by a similar duplication of capacity in the lower brain. If so, then successful transplants of this sort are naturally possible. But even if they are not, such an impossibility would not affect the coherence of this thought-experiment. For its coherence rests upon the assumption that each cerebral hemisphere can, in the absence of the other, generate (or come to be associated with) a stream of consciousness—an assumption strongly supported by actual cases. We may, of course, wonder why anyone would want to perform these operations, but that is a matter irrelevant to our primary concern. For our primary concern is with the implications that these operations have for the relational view of the mind.

With respect to the question about what happens to you, there are only three possibilities: Either (1) you survive as both offshoots, or (2) you survive as one or the other of them, or (3) you do not survive at all. But (1) is wildly implausible if it implies that there can be *two* of you. Both intuition and common sense prompt us to declare that whatever you are, you are clearly something there can be only *one* of. Nor is (3) an acceptable alternative, not because there is any difficulty conceiving it, but because it lacks factual support. If you can survive the destruction of one of your cerebral hemispheres, then surely you can survive if this hemisphere is not destroyed but transplanted into another body. Thus there are no grounds for claiming that neither survivor would be you. In any case, this alternative would not be attractive to one who holds the relational view. For the experience of each offshoot would bear the appropriate relations to your experiences before the operation (e.g., each would seem to remember your preoperative experiences), and this fact would, in the relational view, imply that your mind includes the experiences of both offshoots. Rather than ceasing to exist, your mind has a branch in each of them.

We are thus led to the conclusion that (2) is by far the most plausible alternative: You survive as one of the offshoots.[3] You are not something that can divide, and so you cannot go where both halves of your brain go. Perhaps we cannot exclude the possibility that you do not survive at all; but if you *do*, then it is a fact that you are one of the offshoots and not the other.

This conclusion, however, is incompatible with the relational view. In this view, each offshoot is (for the reasons already mentioned) an equally good candidate for being you. If both can be you, then you have divided into two. And if it is impossible for both to be you, then neither can be. For there can be no grounds for picking one over the other. There can be no fact about one of them in virtue of which you are *that* one and not the other. Once we know how the offshoots came about and how their experiences are related to yours, we know all of the relevant facts. There is no further fact to distinguish them, but there would have to be if you were one of them and not the other.

The "Deep" Difference Between Selves

We now have before us a fundamental difference between the relational view and the view that you are a subject of experience. According to the latter view, there is a "deep" difference between you and every other person. This difference is sharp, radical, and absolute. There are no conditions under which it could even be blurred, let alone erased. It is completely unaffected by the close similarity of another person. Let us suppose that you have an identical twin who is as much like you as we can conceive anyone to be. The interests, personalities, characters, even the experiences of the two of you could not be more alike than they are. But, despite this great similarity, your twin is clearly someone else. You are one subject of experience and he, or she, is another. There is a deep difference between you and your twin which is as radical and as absolute as the difference between you and someone who is not like you at all. Similarly, in the case of the offshoots who are exactly alike, both physically and mentally, there is nevertheless a deep difference between them; and your being one of them and not the other would be a deep further fact. You are something extra, something in addition to an organism with a series of interrelated mental and physical states—states that could be matched by exactly similar ones of an exactly similar organism.

Because of this deep difference between you and anyone else, the question as to whether you are still in existence after the transplant operations must have a definite answer, either yes or no. We may be unable to discover what the correct answer is, but this does not affect the fact that there is a correct answer. For at no time can there be any ambiguity or indeterminateness about whether you exist at that time. This is an all or nothing matter: either you do or you do not. No one can be only partly you, nor can any experience be partly yours. Every experience whatsoever, whenever it occurs, is either yours or not yours. Thus if any experiences that occur after the transplant operations are had by you, then you have survived the operations. If all the experiences that occur then are had by others, then you have ceased to exist. Just as there can be no indeterminacy about whether an experience is one of yours, so there can be none about whether you continue to exist.

Now, a defender of the relational view must deny all of this, and the double half-brain transplant scenario is a picturesque way of drawing out the implications of his view. In this view, there is no deep difference between you and another. Consequently, the question as to whether you have survived the operations has become an empty one. When we ask, "Will you survive as both offshoots, as one or the other, or not survive at all?" we may believe that we are raising a question about which of several possible facts is the one that would actually obtain. But this belief is false; there is only one possibility, though there are different ways of describing it. Once we know that each offshoot has half your brain, along with experience which is appropriately related to yours (i.e., related to your preoperative experiences in the way in which the latter are interrelated), we know everything there is to know about the outcome. There is no deep further fact that must be known to know what happens to you. Though we can describe the outcome in various ways—that, for example, you have survived as both offshoots, or that neither is identical to you—we can reject these descriptions while agreeing about the outcome itself.

Indeterminacy and the Self

If the relational view is true, then, the question of whether you still exist after the operations has no definite answer. We could choose to say that you do, but your continuing to exist would be a matter of linguistic convention rather than of fact. Or we could choose to say that you do not, and have an equally good case for saying this. But irrespective of how we choose to describe the outcome, your existence does not consist in a deep further fact that would make true (or false) what we say about whether you still exist. Whether or not you do is indeterminate—a matter to be settled by convention rather than by discovery of fact.

It may already seem clear that we must reject any view in which there may be genuine indeterminacy about whether you exist. But let us temporarily put aside further consideration of this issue and focus instead on the implication that you cannot be just one of the offshoots. What we should note is how counter-intuitive this implication is. You can imagine waking up in one of the offshoots, and you can also imagine waking up in the other. But what you cannot imagine is splitting so as to become two. Perhaps you can imagine finding yourself in both bodies. That is, you may be able to imagine finding that you can see through the eyes of both, hear through both pairs of ears, and experience sensations in both bodies, etc. But this would not be a case of your division; for you would still be the subject of all these experiences. You have not imagined the division of that subject which you seem to be. And the fact that you cannot imagine *your* division supports the intuition that what you really are is a subject of experience—a psychological atom that cannot split into two.

Not only does the relational view imply that you may be divided, but also that you may be blended or merged with another. In other words, your undergoing both *fission and fusion* is possible in this view. The possibility of fusion is particularly important because of its implication for the indeterminacy issue. More specifically, the possibility of your fusing with another implies, in a clear and compelling way, that there could be someone who is neither you nor someone else; it would be indeterminate as to whether that person is identical to you. So let us look at a thought-experiment in which you apparently fuse with another.

The Possibility of Fusing with Another

Again suppose that you have an identical twin who is exactly similar to you, even with respect to your mental states and to the fine neural detail of your brains. Suppose also that the two of you are in the clutches of a mad scientist who is about to perform a series of brain operations upon you. He removes cells from your brain, a few at a time, and replaces them with the corresponding cells from the brain of your twin. He distributes his operations over your brain in such a way that the cells in every part of it (e.g., the cerebrum, the cerebellum, the medulla etc.) are being replaced at the same rate. There are, of course, a great number of such operations to be performed, but he performs them rapidly. When he is halfway through the series, half of your brain cells have been replaced with the brain cells of your twin and the other half are yours. At this point in the operations, who would his patient be?

You are clearly the person present at the beginning of the series, and your twin is the person present at the end. For the person at the end has the entire brain of your twin, and, as we have seen, a person goes where his (entire) brain goes. Consequently, something of great importance has happened during this process: You have (either abruptly or gradually) ceased to exist and have been replaced by your twin. But *in what manner*—abruptly or gradually— did you cease to exist? Our answer to this question will determine what we should say about who is present halfway through the operations. It may also lead us to a conclusion about what persons are.

If you are a subject of experience, then, as we have noted, you are something in addition to a body, a brain, and a series of interrelated mental and physical states. What you are essentially is a being who *has* experience, and your existence consists in a deep further fact. If there should occur an experience that is had by you, then you must exist at that time to have it. Just as no experience can be only partly yours, so no person can be only partly you. There can be no indeterminacy about these matters. Any experience is either yours or not yours; every person is either you or someone else. Consequently, the person present halfway through the operations cannot be partly you and partly someone else. Rather, that person is either you or your twin. This we know even if we are unable to find out which one of you is present then. Furthermore, your ceasing to exist occurs abruptly—as abruptly as the cessation of your last experience, and the arrival of your twin in what was your body is as abrupt as the arrival of his, or her, first experience in that body.

In the relational view, on the other hand, the brain fusion brought about halfway through the operations has resulted in your fusion with your twin. The person present then is only partly you, that is, neither you nor someone else. For in this view there is no indivisible subject who is either present or not. There is nothing in addition to a body, a brain, and a series of interrelated mental and physical states, and thus nothing indivisible here which you could possibly be. This series of states is, like the brain, a complex comprised of many parts that may be gradually replaced by similar ones. Consequently, your replacement by your twin is gradual. Thus there will be times during the replacement process when it is indeterminate as to whether the person present is identical to you.

THE SELF AS THE SUBJECT OF CONSCIOUSNESS

Perhaps this is the correct answer. At any rate, many contemporary philosophers of mind would accept it. But there are two compelling reasons for believing that it must be rejected. First, your fusion with another, like your fission into two, is unimaginable. It may seem that you can imagine your fusion by imaginatively getting outside yourself and viewing the product of fusion from a third-person standpoint. But this is not to imagine what it would be for you to *experience* fusion and thus not to imagine what it would be for *you* to be fused. Your imaginative effort must leave *you* out, for the person imagined is only partly you and the experience you attempt to imagine is only partly yours. Since the person imagined is *not* identical to you and the experience *not yours*, you cannot imaginatively enter into the situation as the person having the experience. It is as opaque to your power of imagination as your trying to imagine yourself having an experience that you imagine someone not identical to you as having. And if our power of imagination is in this case a trustworthy guide to what is possible, the conclusion is clear: Your fusion is impossible and the relational view must be rejected.

The second reason for rejecting the possibility of fusion may be even more persuasive. If your fusion with another is possible, then there could be a person who is neither you nor someone else. It would be indeterminate as to whether you are that person. But it seems that determinacy is an *essential* property of personhood. As we saw, you cannot imagine or conceive of what it would be for someone to be partly you, or for an experience to be partly yours. This is not a logically possible state for a person to be in. Thus if you are such that someone could be only partly you, then you are not a person. But you are a person if you are anything at all. Thus it follows from the possibility of fusion that you do not exist!

Perhaps the self we have been looking for does not exist. We have been looking for that apparently indivisible subject of consciousness, which is the *center* of conscious states or experiences, which is what *has* the experiences or *undergoes* the experiencing, and which, unlike the body, is directly known only from the first-person viewpoint one has on it. But perhaps what we have been looking for is only an illusion—an illusion generated by our language. So let us state our (tentative) conclusion as follows: Either you are a subject of experience, or you are not anything at all. Either *you* refers to a subject of consciousness, or it refers to nothing. If both these alternatives seem totally unsatisfactory to you, as they do to many, you may well end up concluding that what you essentially are is even more mysterious than our speculations have indicated and that finding our way to an understanding of the ultimate truth about ourselves is one of the most formidable intellectual challenges we face.

QUESTIONS FOR FURTHER THOUGHT

1. Can you imagine having a different body? If you can, does this show, or at least support the view, that you are not (identical to) the body you have? What can our power of imagination reveal to us about what we are?

2. Are you something that cannot be divided, as the text suggests? If you can, would this imply that there can be *two* of you? If you cannot, what would this fact imply about what you are?

3. Is there really a "deep" difference between you and every other person? What is this deep difference supposed to be? Can it be described?

4. Is determinacy an *essential* feature of personhood? Can you imagine someone being only *partly* you?

5. Can it be true that the self is an illusion? How should we understand the claim that it is—that you, for example, are *not* a self?

6. Is it true that you have remained one and the same person over time in just the way and extent to which your body has remained one and the same body over the same period of time? If it is not true, would this fact imply that you are something other than your body and logically separable from it?

7. If you are your body, then your body (or, more likely, some part of it) must be what undergoes, or is the subject of, the experiences you have. Can we identify any part of the body that is, or might be, undergoing the experience you are having now? Is it even meaningful to speak of some part or some process (say of your brain) that is now undergoing your experience? Would a negative answer to these questions imply that what undergoes your experience, i.e., yourself, cannot be your body?

6

GOD

When we wonder about why we exist, or why the world is the way it is, or why there is a world at all, we may find ourselves led to a religious explanation—the world owes its being to God. This view has held enormous appeal for great numbers of people throughout the ages. Perhaps the primary motivation for embracing a religious interpretation of reality arises out of our human condition. We are alone among creatures in possessing a full and terrible realization of our own inevitable and complete physical destruction. And it may seem that the only basis for our hope that we shall not be reduced to nothingness—extinguished from the universe forevermore—lies with the possibility that there is a God possessing the power and the will either to keep us in existence after bodily death or to bring us back into existence at a later time. But though it may be comforting to believe that God exists, this hardly provides support for the *truth* of that belief. So let us see what support we can find.

Before we examine our basis for believing that God exists, we should focus more carefully on what we should conceive God to be. Clearly, the question as to what the word *God* means (or, after reflection, should come to mean) must be answered at least to some extent if the assertion that God exists, or does not exist, is to be meaningful. Consider the suggestion that God is ultimate reality—that reality which underlies everything else in such a way that without it the natural world would not exist. Though we may agree that this suggestion expresses a truth about our concept of God, it leaves too much out to be acceptable. For if we agree that our concept of God is nothing more than our concept of that which is ultimately real, then we have trivialized the question about whether God exists. The question has become uninteresting and unimportant. If anything is real, then something is ultimately real; and so God's existence would be implied by the reality of anything whatsoever. Certainly our concept of God should be sufficiently rich and precise to enable us to distinguish theism from atheism.

GOD AS A PERSONAL BEING

It appears that what we must acknowledge to be part of an adequate concept of God is the notion of a personal being: *God* is the proper name of a personal being. Personhood seems to be an essential part of the concept, at least as it is understood in the theistic religions of the West. God is conceived as a being who is aware of the world, who intended that it should exist, who has complete knowledge of its composition and complete understanding of its laws, who cares about how we treat one another, who desires what is best for us, and who is grieved by our suffering. But caring, grieving, and understanding are states of a personal being—a being who has high-level mental states. Of course, this is not to suggest that God is a *human* being, or that His mind is limited in the ways characteristic of persons.[1] Rather, the concept before us is that of a conscious being who experiences the kinds of high-level mental states that persons experience. The concept is compatible with the possibility that the mind of God transcends our own in ways we cannot comprehend, but it must remain grounded in our experience of what it is to have a mind and to be a person. Without this experiential base we could have no concept of what it could be for God to be a personal being or to have the mental states we, implicitly or explicitly, attribute to Him.

In the light of our earlier deliberations about the nature of the self, we might say that the concept of a personal God is the concept of a supernatural subject of experience—a subject of conscious states. We may wish to add that we are talking about the *greatest conceivable* subject of consciousness, that is, a being who knows all truths, who can do anything that can be done, and who is perfect in goodness. But we need not add this, or, at any rate, not *all* of this, for the concept is intact without it. With this concept of God, the question as to whether God exists is, as it should be, an interesting and important one.

ARGUMENTS FOR GOD'S EXISTENCE

The central question now is one of whether we have any good reasons to believe that there is such a being. The reasons commonly offered fall roughly into two groups: (1) those which purportedly enable us to infer God's existence from the fact that there is a world or from the fact that the world has a certain character, and (2) those based upon the contention that God has revealed His existence, along with information about His character and wishes, to particular people or groups of people at particular places and times. Let us begin with those in the first group—those which do not depend upon the claim that some particular revelation has taken place.

The World's Existence Is Due to God

It has often been argued that we are entitled to infer God's existence from the undeniable fact that there is a world. The term *world* refers, of course, not only to the earth and our solar system, but to the entire natural order which includes everything known to physics and astronomy. Sometimes the argument appeals to the principle that everything has to have a cause, or causes. Consider the fact that you were caused to be. Your coming to exist was clearly not uncaused, nor could you have been the cause. For nothing can cause itself to be. Thus your existence must have been caused by something distinct from you. And the same seems to be true of all the objects around you. Indeed, all the items that constitute the world at any given time were caused to be. Thus it may seem that the entire world itself must have been caused to be. And since the world could not have been the cause of itself, there must be, or have been, a world-cause for there to be a world at all. But the only plausible candidate for the world-cause is God.

Though this argument may appear to have some force, it doesn't stand up under examination. It reaches the conclusion that there must be a world-cause by appealing to the principle that anything which exists must have been caused to exist. But this principle would also apply to God: there must have been a cause of God if God exists. To avoid this implication a defender of the argument may grant an exception to the principle and claim that God is the one being who doesn't require a cause. For God would have existed eternally if at all; and if God was always in existence, then there never was a time when He came into being. Consequently, no cause was required to bring about His existence. Thus God's existence would be uncaused. Obviously, if God never came into existence because of having existed eternally, then there could have been no event of His coming into existence which would require a cause.

Though this seems to be a good reason for not applying the causal principle to God, the problem which arises now is that the very same remarks can be made of the world. If there can be some one thing that doesn't need a cause, why can't that be the world *instead* of God? Even if no item in the world is eternal, the world itself could be, just as the human race could be eternal even though no individual human being lives for more than a few decades. Though the eternality of the world would imply that no cause was needed to bring it into existence (since there would have been no event of its coming into existence), this would not imply that any items *in* the world are uncaused. For in the case of every such non-eternal item, there would be others preceding it which could have brought it into existence. This remains true no matter how far back in time we go to select the item for consideration, for the series of items is infinitely long. Since the eternality of the world implies that the series has no beginning and thus no first member, *every* non-eternal item in the series would be preceded by others.

Now, if the world could be something that was not caused to come into existence, then we have obviously lost any grounds we may have thought we had for inferring that God must exist as the cause of the world. We would have such grounds if we knew that the world had a beginning, for then we could infer that it either "popped" into existence uncaused out of nothing or it was caused to come into existence by something else. And the latter alternative surely seems much more plausible. We could know that the world had a beginning if we could show that its having always existed is inconceivable. But we apparently cannot show this. Indeed, there seems to be no great difficulty in conceiving of the world as eternal. If, as it seems, we can conceive of time as extending infinitely far into the past, then why can't we conceive of the world as doing so as well?[2] There may be no more difficulty in conceiving of the world in existence at all times in the past than there is in conceiving of past times when it didn't exist. Thus any plausible attempt to infer God's existence from the fact that there is a world cannot depend uncritically upon the assumption that the world had a beginning.

So let us assume that the world is eternal, whether or not it actually is, and then proceed to inquire about whether we would have any grounds for inferring God's existence from the fact that a world exists. We are now wondering whether God is needed for there to be a world even though, on our present assumption, He is not needed to cause the world to begin existing. Perhaps the existence of even an eternal world could not be adequately explained without an appeal to God's existence. Let us look at an argument that may appear to establish this conclusion.[3]

The argument depends upon a very general principle called the principle of sufficient reason. It states that there is a sufficient reason or explanation, known or unknown, for every being and every positive fact that there is. This is a principle that we seem to accept without question, though it is probably held only implicitly by most of us. To see how plausible it may seem to you to be, suppose that while walking along a forest path you come upon a pink transparent cube about four-feet high. You would surely wonder how it got there and probably how it came about in the first place. You would reject without hesitation the suggestion that there simply is no explanation, whether known or unknown, of either its existence or the fact that it is now lying in this forest path. Nor would you take seriously the claim that its existence depends upon nothing beyond itself—that it somehow contains within itself the reason for its own existence. Perhaps we cannot find out how the cube came to be in the world or to be in the forest path now, but this would not shake our conviction that there must be some reason for or explanation of its existence and present location.[4]

Suppose, on the other hand, that you did *not* come upon such a cube during your forest walk. It would not occur to you to wonder why you didn't. This (negative) fact would not require explanation. Nor is an explanation required for the sheer nonexistence of some object, as contrasted with some object's ceasing to exist. If someone were to ask why you didn't come upon a light blue transparent cube, it would be entirely appropriate to reply with the question of why anyone would suppose that you should have. Its nonexistence just doesn't require any explanation. Though such an object is unusual and thus not something you would expect to encounter on a forest walk, this is not why its nonexistence requires no explanation. It merely illustrates the general principle that the simple nonexistence of something, unlike something's ceasing to exist, is not a matter that needs to be explained. On the other hand, the *existence* of an object, whether it be a strange blue cube or a common stone, always stands in need of explanation. And it seems very plausible to maintain that there must *be* an explanation, even if we cannot know what it is. But to maintain this is to embrace the principle of sufficient reason.

Since this principle states that there is an explanation of the existence of every being whatsoever, it implies that only two kinds of beings are possible: (1) those whose existence is explained by appeal to some other being or beings and (2) those whose existence is self-explanatory. Let us call a being of the first kind a *dependent* being, and one of the second kind a *self-existent* being. But there can be no being of a third kind—a being whose existence has no explanation.

Though two kinds of beings are possible, perhaps all actual beings are dependent. If every actual being could be a dependent being, we would be unable to infer the existence of a self-existent being from the fact that there is a world. Thus we would be unable to infer God's existence since our concept of God is, in part, a concept of a self-existent being. So let us consider the claim that every actual being could be a dependent being if the world is eternal.

The various things we encounter in the world—e.g., trees, animals, human beings, stones—are all dependent beings. Their existence can be explained by appeal to the causal activity of prior dependent beings, whose existence can, in turn, be explained by appeal to still earlier dependent beings, on and on without end. Since the series of dependent beings that constitute the world has no beginning if the world is infinitely old, the existence of each member of the series can be explained by appeal to the causal activity of an earlier member. This will be true no matter how far back in time we go to select the member for consideration, for there will always be an earlier member whose causal activity could explain its existence. In other words, there is *no first* member, that is, no member whose existence could not be explained by appeal to an earlier one.

At this point it may seem that we have no basis for inferring the existence of a self-existent being if the world has always been in existence. For the world may consist of an infinitely long causal series of dependent beings, each of which could have its existence explained by reference to a preceding being. Still, there would be something left unexplained—something that comes into view when we ask why the world should exist at all. Though every member of the series of dependent beings has an explanation, the series itself does not.

More precisely, the positive fact that there are and always have been dependent beings is not explained. This is a fact that obviously cannot be explained
by pointing out that this series has always been in existence. For that would be
an attempt to explain *why* there have always been dependent beings by simply
asserting *that* such beings have always existed. Since this fact cannot be
explained by appeal to the infinitely long series of dependent beings, it clearly
cannot be explained at all on the supposition that this series is all there is.

It now seems clear that if this fact is to admit of any explanation, the explanation must make reference to the existence of a self-existent being—a being
whose existence depends upon nothing but itself. Since such a being would
contain within itself the reason for its existence, it apparently could not fail to
exist if it exists at all. It would be a "necessary being" in that its nonexistence
would be impossible. By contrast, the nonexistence of any dependent being *is*
possible. In the case of the dependent beings with which we are most familiar—viz., the trees, chairs, roads, lakes, and buildings around us—their nonexistence is not only possible, but there actually was a time when they didn't
exist, and there actually will be a time when they will again fail to exist. And
this contingency (or possibility of nonexistence) seems to be a characteristic
of every being in the natural world, even those that are extremely old. The
reasons for inferring the existence of a necessary being again come into view
when we reflect upon this fact. Though planets, stars, and perhaps individual
atoms are extremely old, we are not at all tempted to suppose that they exist
by virtue of their own nature—that they owe their existence to nothing but
themselves. Even when we consider the suggestion that they may have always
been in existence, we surely do not regard their nonexistence as impossible.
On the contrary, it is easy to imagine them ceasing to exist, or not having ever
existed in the first place. Not only does this claim seem true of every entity in
the natural world but it also seems true of the natural world itself. We have no
difficulty understanding the suggestion that the entire natural world might
never have existed at all. Clearly, its nonexistence is possible; its existence is
not self-explanatory, and so, as we noted earlier, if the fact that there is a natural world is to admit of explanation, an appeal to the existence of a necessary being seems unavoidable.

Some philosophers have contended that the notion of a necessary being
makes no sense. The notion of necessity, they may say, applies to propositions
or statements but not to beings. For example, the statement "All white horses
are horses" is not only true but *necessarily* true. It doesn't just happen to be
true; it couldn't fail to be true. The notion of necessity is clearly applicable
here. But it also seems applicable to beings. The notion of a being that exists
by virtue of its own nature independently of anything else—a being that could
not fail to exist—seems quite comprehensible. After all, we have no difficulty
with the notion of a being that does *not* exist by virtue of its own nature and
whose nonexistence is possible, that is, a being such as you or I. And we must
wonder how we could have *that* notion if we were not implicitly contrasting it

with what it is *not*—namely, the notion of a being whose nonexistence is *not* possible. You could not have a concept of a dog, for example, without having a concept of what it is for something to fail to be a dog. And the same consideration apparently applies to the concept of a dependent being, i.e., our having it depends upon our having a concept of a being that fails to be dependent. Furthermore, we seem to make sense when we speak of an "impossible being" such as a round square—a being whose very nature guarantees its nonexistence. But if we have a notion of a being whose existence is impossible, then it seems undeniable that we also have the contrasting notion of a being whose nonexistence is impossible. If the one makes sense, then so does the other.

We have now reached the conclusion that there must be a self-existent being if the principle of sufficient reason (PSR) is true, and that this being cannot plausibly be regarded as either an entity in the natural world or as the natural world itself. But do we have adequate grounds for accepting this principle? More specifically, are we entitled to believe that there is an explanation or sufficient reason for every positive fact that there is? It may seem that we are, but consider a critic who disagrees, maintaining that the fact that there is (and perhaps always has been) a world is a *brute* fact—a positive fact for which there is no explanation. There is no reason why there should be a world; there simply *is* one. Its existence depends neither upon itself nor on something else, but on nothing whatsoever.

This challenge to the PSR is a formidable one—one that may be impossible to meet. For, as we have seen, there apparently are brute facts; and, if there are, the part of the PSR that denies this is false. But what is of most interest to us here is not so much the question of whether there are *any* brute facts but whether the fact that there is a natural world is such a fact. Taking it to be a brute fact seems especially difficult, even on the assumption that the natural world has always existed. We note that the nonexistence of the entire natural world was possible, and also that if this possibility had been actualized, i.e., if there had been nothing at all, then there would have been a state of nothingness—a state of affairs which strikes us as a paradigm case of a state that would *not* require explanation. On the other hand, the fact that there is (and perhaps always has been) a natural world appears to cry out for explanation, at least when contrasted with a state of nothingness. Thus we see why the question, Why is there something rather than nothing? impresses us as being not only an appropriate question but one of fundamental importance. Indeed, some philosophers have considered it to be the *ultimate* question.[5] But, of course, it doesn't have that status if we must accept the claim that the existence of the natural world is a brute fact. What is also clear, however, is how implausible that claim may seem to be.

We may have the impression, perhaps even the conviction, that the fact that there is a natural world stands in need of explanation. But how, the critic will ask, do we know that we can rely on this impression? What apparently gives rise to it is the underlying assumption that there is a *causal* explanation of this fact—an assumption that can be defended. Since the nonexistence of the natural world was possible, that is, since its existence is a contingent fact, it would seem that there probably is a causal explanation of its existence. For we have good inductive evidence that no contingent fact or event depends on nothing whatsoever. Both our ordinary experience and the findings of science testify to this. We find causal dependence even when we cannot explain why a cause has one effect rather than another. Of course, our inductive evidence is far from conclusive. There may be exceptions to the causal principle. And we obviously cannot verify that it holds in this case. Still, in the absence of evidence that the fact in question is an exception to the causal principle, we would seem to be justified in believing that it probably has a cause. Furthermore, its cause could not be contingent. If the fact that there are and perhaps always have been contingent beings stands in need of causal explanation, that explanation cannot be grounded in another *contingent* being.

Have we met the critic's challenge, even though we have not vindicated the PSR? Well, it seems that we have reached at least a stand-off with him and that we have rational grounds for inferring the existence of a self-existent being, for we can have such grounds even if the truth should be that no such being exists. But do we also have a rational basis for believing that this being is none other than God? Though we do think of God as a self-existent being, the fact that a being is self-existent may not be sufficient grounds for concluding that that being must be God. As we noted earlier, the question as to whether God exists becomes interesting and important only if God is conceived as having certain personal attributes. But it is far from clear that any self-existent being would have such attributes, even though this being is not part of the natural world. Our grounds for inferring the probable existence of a self-existent being have their source in the fact that there is a natural world, but we must now take into account the character of that world, i.e., the kind of world it is, if we are to find good reason to believe that this being has personal attributes.

The Argument from Design

Suppose that the world, or at least a certain portion of it, displays evidence of having been designed to bring about an end or fulfill a purpose that a being with personal attributes might be expected to have. Clearly, such evidence would support the claim that God exists as the self-existent being. Many people have been impressed with the great amount of order and regularity in the world, and have argued that the best explanation of their presence is that they are the result of intelligent design. Some have argued that the natural world, or at least some part of it, resembles a machine consisting of a large number of interrelated parts that work together to attain a goal or fulfill a purpose. But if there is some purpose that is being fulfilled by the existence of the natural world and the manner in which it is developing, then there must be a purpose-giver who, it would seem, must be a personal being. How are we to understand the notion of a world-purpose without thinking of it as the purpose or intention of a conscious, personal being? That we must think of it in this way seems uncontroversial. Rather, the issue is one of whether the natural world displays evidence that there is some purpose to it.

It would display such evidence if it did indeed resemble a complex machine. A complex machine is a teleological, or goal-directed, system—a system of parts that are fashioned and arranged in such a way as to fulfill some purpose. A wind-up clock is a good example of a human-made teleological system. It contains springs, gears, shafts, and other parts that are fashioned in such a way and adjusted to each other so as to serve a purpose, namely, to indicate the time of day. If it somehow fell into the hands of intelligent extraterrestrial beings who knew nothing about us, they would probably conclude that it must have been designed by intelligent beings—that it didn't just come about on its own as a result of the blind interplay of unconscious forces which could have had no prevision of the outcome. For it has the mark of intelligent design upon it.

But there are natural things that also seem to bear this mark. The human eye, for example, is a complex organ composed of many types of specialized cells that work together in harmony—in precisely the manner needed to make vision possible. It appears to be a teleological system. More impressive yet is the entire human organism. It consists of billions of cells appearing in various specialized forms in the various organs, but all functioning together to produce an elaborately organized creature finely tuned to its environment. Not only does every living organism appear to be a teleological system, but the natural world itself, or at least our little corner of it, also appears to be such a system. That is, it seems to be a system for producing teleological systems—living organisms that live together in that intricate pattern of relationships we sometimes refer to as the balance of nature.

What takes place in nature is indeed remarkable. The variety, the complexity, the interrelatedness, and the exquisite adaptation to environment that characterize the life forms we witness in nature may strike us as awesome. In any case, they set the background for our central question: Is the natural world the way it is because (1) it was designed by a conscious, personal being of great intelligence, that is, designed to fulfill a purpose which that being had; or (2) is it entirely without purpose (distinct, of course, from the various purposes we have), brought about by the blind interplay of unconscious forces incapable of intending or appreciating the outcome?

The second hypothesis may seem at first to be unworthy of serious consideration. The likelihood that life forms should have come about in the absence of intelligent design has been compared to the likelihood of a copy of Webster's dictionary coming about as the result of a monkey jumping around (for a lengthy time, of course) on the keys of a typewriter. Our intuitions tell us that even billions of years would not be enough to yield such a remarkable outcome. And so the hypothesis of intelligent design has seemed to many to be the only plausible one. But the other hypothesis has come to seem much more plausible with the availability of Darwin's theory of evolution, for this theory explains the *appearance* of design without conceding that there is any *actual* design. Our knowledge of natural law, as revealed through our study of chemistry and physics, enables us to understand how the most primitive life forms could have been generated out of inanimate matter simply by its being subjected to certain conditions—conditions thought to have obtained on earth during an early stage of its history. And evolutionary theory provides an account of how these primitive life forms could have evolved into the complex living things in existence now.

No conscious intelligence is needed to guide the evolutionary process, for that function is performed by natural selection: Those creatures most fit to survive tend to be the ones which are successful in the struggle for survival, and in surviving long enough to reproduce they are able to pass on to their offspring the traits that enabled them to be successful. There are genetically based differences among the offspring, making some more fit to survive than others; and, as in the case of the parents, the more fit tend to be the ones favored in the natural selection process. Different species come into being as a result of the fact that there are different ways of making a living, so to speak. But again, those most fit to make the sort of living in question tend to be the ones whose genes are passed on as a result of that mindless, non-purposive process of natural selection. In this way, the different species become ever more adapted to, and adept at filling, the various environmental niches that are available.

But though we apparently have no good reason to believe that any design or purpose lies behind the process by which living things on earth arose from non-living material and then evolved into the extremely complex organisms we now observe, it may nevertheless be true that the best explanation of why matter possesses the capacity to generate life under suitable conditions is that it has this capacity as a result of design. The generation and evolution of life forms proceeds in accordance with certain special natural laws; namely, the laws by which inorganic elements and molecules combine to form organic molecules, the laws by which organic molecules combine to form the simplest living things, and the laws by which these things evolve into more complex life forms. Given these laws, we have an account of how living things could have come about, but the laws themselves apparently stand in need of explanation. And it may be that the best explanation of *them* is that they are the result of intelligent design.

These laws arise out of the fundamental properties of matter. Physicists speak of four fundamental forces (the strong nuclear force, the weak nuclear force, electromagnetism, and gravity) and of a few different kinds of fundamental particles, e.g., electrons and protons. Each particle of a specific kind has a few defining properties (e.g., mass and charge) which characterize particles of that kind wherever they are found. On this fundamental level, there is a great deal of order. The laws by which these particles interact hold invariantly over enormous spaces and time.

Now we must ask whether or how this orderliness can be explained. It cannot be explained scientifically, for all scientific explanations are ultimately based on it. Since to refer to this orderliness is to refer to the most general natural laws, and since a scientific explanation of natural law is always in terms of a more general law, there can be no scientific explanation of this level of orderliness. All that science can do at this level is describe what it finds. So either explanation comes to an end at this most general level of orderliness, or we explain this orderliness as resulting from the purposes of a designer of great intelligence and power.

We might be inclined to accept the claim that explanation just *does* end here, especially if we believe it must end at some point in any case. But there is a further reason for thinking that it doesn't end here—that this order stands in need of explanation. For it seems that if precisely this sort of orderliness had not existed, life would have been impossible. We are told that if the four fundamental forces were not balanced as they in fact are, if they had differed even slightly from their actual values, or if some of the fundamental particles had had slightly different properties, then not even atoms would have been possible, let alone organic molecules and living organisms.[6] If, for example, gravity had been stronger by even an extremely minute amount–namely, by one part in 10^{40}–the universe would have collapsed in upon itself long ago, rendering impossible the genesis of any life. Similarly, if the strength of the initial explosion which gave rise to the universe in its present form had varied from its actual value by as little as one part in 10^{60}, the universe as we now know it would not exist. And if the electromagnetic and strong nuclear forces had been only moderately different, the formation of carbon, which is necessary for life as we know it, would have been impossible. Thus it seems that the universe is balanced on a "razor's edge." In the light of this, we must ask about the likelihood of matter having precisely these properties if it was not designed to have them by an intelligent being who intended to bring life about by means of it. Though we may be unable to quantify that likelihood, we may be left with the impression that it is extremely small and, consequently, that the hypothesis of intelligent design is the only plausible one.

We might say that the universe is fine-tuned to the needs of life. Even tiny changes in the fundamental properties of matter would have made life as we know it impossible. And the apparent unlikelihood that fine-tuning should exist seems very significant, not only because its unlikelihood seems to weigh against its being due to mere chance instead of design, but because it is a feature that is displayed throughout the known universe rather than a rare and local phenomenon, as the occurrence of life on earth may be. The possibility that life is an extremely rare phenomenon that occupies only tiny regions of space for relatively short periods of time may encourage the criticism that if one is going to suppose that there is any designer at all, one should conclude that there are several, each corresponding to parts of the universe that differ greatly from one another. But a fundamental feature that reigns throughout the universe certainly defuses that criticism.

Still, the evidence that fine-tuning provides for the existence of God is not compelling. Though fine-tuning may well be a highly improbable event, perhaps we should not find its improbability very significant, especially when we take the anthropic principle into account. This principle states that any universe containing observers must be observer-permitting. Though its truth is self-evident, it is not trivial, for it can be used to argue that the fine-tuning of the universe provides little or no support for the design hypothesis. Perhaps the universe was not fine-tuned to our needs throughout the great bulk of its history and, consequently, such that no observers were possible then. Perhaps it is true that during the enormously (if not infinitely) long history of the universe, all (or at any rate the great proportion) of the values that the fundamental forces and particles could possibly have had have already been actualized, and that the presently existing values, though necessary for life, represent nothing more than one possible fall of the cosmic dice. In other words, it may be that fine-tuning is a highly unusual state of the universe—a kind of cosmic accident—but nevertheless an accident that had to occur for us to be able to make any observations or do any speculating about this matter. What is certain, however, is that whenever and wherever observers *do* exist, the universe *must* be fine-tuned at those times and places. But the fact that fine-tuning is a necessary condition for our existence offers no explanation of why fine-tuning should exist. In particular, it apparently provides no evidence that fine-tuning exists for our sake. So instead of being amazed that the universe is fine-tuned despite the objective unlikelihood that it should be, we might instead see the fine-tuning of the universe simply as a necessary condition of our being able to observe it and thus as a condition whose objective unlikelihood is irrelevant to our assessment of its significance. But it was largely the impression that fine-tuning was not likely to occur by chance which led us to suppose that its existence provides substantial support for the design hypothesis.

So far our reflections on the anthropic principle indicate that the evidence for the design hypothesis is weaker than our initial awareness of the presence of fine-tuning prompted us to suppose. But we have been assuming the plausibility of a theory that is surely an extravagant one, for it is the theory that, in effect, an infinite (or, at least, enormously large) number of universes have preceded this one—universes in which the fundamental physical elements and forces were markedly different from those that presently exist. Against the backdrop provided by such a theory, the balancing of our universe on a razor's edge appears as nothing more than one unlikely position among an enormous number of possible though equally unlikely ones. But we have no evidence for the truth of this theory. Furthermore, its extravagance alone weighs against our accepting it. The simplest theory that accommodates all of the known facts is the one that we should prefer; and this seems to be the theory that there is only the one universe—the one we know. Of course, we may uncover other facts that will lead us to change our minds, but this hardly affects what it is rational for us to believe now.

These considerations imply that if the razor's edge position of the universe, as we now know it, is to be viewed as a mere chance occurrence, then it should be understood to be the result of a single roll of the cosmic dice. But then its occurrence would seem extremely improbable—so improbable that the design hypothesis seems preferable.

We must acknowledge that if the universe is a unique entity, then it is very difficult if not impossible to quantify this improbability with any precision, and that, consequently, we may be overestimating it. But despite this possibility, the specter of a universe balanced on a razor's edge may continue to strike us as extraordinary and to diminish our confidence in even the most plausible naturalistic accounts of things.

So what should we conclude from all this? Perhaps the evidence for the design hypothesis is too weak to render it quite probable (or even more probable than not) that there is a personal God. Still, this evidence seems to make the personal God hypothesis more probable than it otherwise would have been. What we might consider now is whether there is any good evidence on the other side of the issue—evidence that there is no personal God. An open-minded, impartial approach requires that we look at evidence that may weigh heavily on the other side, even if we would like to believe that there isn't any.

AN ARGUMENT FOR THE NONEXISTENCE OF GOD

We have been looking for evidence supporting the claim that there is a personal God, though we realize that even if the evidence is scant or nonexistent this claim could still be true. Rational belief in the existence of such a being would not be clearly ruled out. It would be ruled out, however, if there were conclusive, or even very strong, evidence that there is no such being. Some have argued that the existence of evil provides evidence of this sort and indeed have dubbed the resulting argument "the proof of the nonexistence of God"! Let us see if they are correct.

The argument may be stated in the following way.

P1: If God exists (i.e., if *God* denotes an existing personal being), then there is a being who is omniscient (all-knowing), omnipotent (all-powerful), and perfect in moral goodness.

P2: An omniscient being would be aware of the presence of any evil.

P3: An omnipotent being would be able to eliminate all evil.

P4: A being perfect in moral goodness would want to eliminate all evil.

P5: But evil does exist.

C: Therefore, there is no such being: God does not exist.

This argument is clearly a valid one; that is, the conclusion is correctly drawn from the premises. Thus, if all the premises are true, the conclusion must be true as well. So we must look very carefully at the premises.

The first premise gives expression to our concept of a divine personal being—the concept of God that is central to the theistic religions of the West. God is conceived to be a perfect being—perfect in knowledge, power, and moral goodness. Of course, one might deny that God has all these attributes, or even any of them. But this reply has much going against it. Denying that God is omniscient is not an effective reply; for even if God fails to know everything that can be known, He must surely be aware of the evil in the world if He is aware of the world at all. And if He is aware of the evil but so morally deficient as to be insensitive to it, then He is not worthy of worship. So the moral perfection of God seems unchallengeable. It is much more plausible to deny that God is omnipotent; for if He is not, He may lack the power to eliminate evil. But omnipotence, too, seems to be part of the traditional theistic conception of God, and is, in any case, an attribute of a personal being conceived to be perfect in all the respects that make such a being great. So it appears that we should accept the first premise.

We must also accept P2 and P3, for their truth follows from the definitions of omniscience and omnipotence. Thus their truth is undeniable. But P5 too must be accepted. Surely there is evil in the world; indeed, there is a great deal of it. Thus if there is a flaw in this argument, it must lie with P4.

P4 may also seem undeniable, at least at first glance. A morally perfect being could not help but be opposed to evil, and so would do everything in His power to eliminate it. But perhaps the evil that we observe could not have been eliminated because it is necessary—necessary in the sense that its elimination would have resulted in the elimination of a greater good. In other words, it may be that the evil in the world is necessarily tied to certain goods that outweigh the evil's negative value. If this is so, then although God could have eliminated it, His doing so would have resulted in a world with less overall value than this one. This would imply that He must have been willing to tolerate the presence of a considerable amount of evil in order to create the world with the most value, i.e., the best possible world. He doesn't like the evil but sees that it must be tolerated. Given such a relationship between good and evil, P4 would be false and the entire argument would be unsound.

But the plausibility of this attack upon the argument depends upon our grounds for believing that all the world's evil may be necessary in the specified sense. And so we must try to determine whether we have any such grounds. With this attack we have, in effect, shown that the original argument must be replaced with a modified version. P4 is to be replaced by P4b: "A being perfect in moral goodness would wish to eliminate all *unnecessary* evil," and P5 by P5b: "*Unnecessary* evil does exist." Since P4b is a necessary truth and thus undeniable, our focus must shift to P5b. Can we find good grounds for believing that it is false—that there is no unnecessary evil?

At least some of the world's evil certainly appears to be necessary. Evil that results from our free actions appears to be evil that God would have to permit in any world containing free agents. Thus it is evil that He would regard as necessary for the existence of free agents, that is, of *persons*. If our moral choices are to be free, then we must be free to choose evil as well as good. Of course, it is logically possible that we should always freely choose what is good, even though we don't; and so it may seem that God could have created us such that this is what we always do. But the truth is that He could not have done so. Though God could have created beings who would always choose what is morally good, He could not have done so without having been the cause of their choosing the good. Consequently, their choices would not be self-initiated (or self-caused), and so these beings would not be capable of *freely* choosing the good. They would not be *persons*. In other words, if God is to create *free* beings, then His task is to create beings whose choices He cannot control. And if they sometimes, or frequently, choose what is morally evil, there will be evil in the world that He must permit.

Theism and the Problem of Suffering

Clearly, much of the world's evil is of this sort. Human beings are the source of an unspeakable amount of suffering endured by people and other sentient creatures. We might think of the Holocaust, the ravage and plunder of war, the torture of political dissidents and others unfortunate enough to be in the clutches of sadists, the burning of religious heretics at the stake, the suffering of innocent victims of terrorist activity, and the mass starvation of innocent people whose food supply has been cut off by ruthless tyrants. But in addition to these flagrant displays of moral evil, there are innumerable occasions when we succeed in hurting each other in relatively minor ways. Sometimes we are insensitive, or even rude. Sometimes we lack compassion or generosity or a full appreciation of the desperate plights of others, so that we do nothing when we could be of help. And when we take all of these occasions into account, we cannot fail to be impressed with how widespread and, in many instances, how outrageous is the evil resulting from our free choices.

But though the evil that is brought about by our decisions (and which, therefore, must be tolerated by a deity willing to put up with *us*) is abundant and deplorable, it does not amount to all of the world's evil. That it does not becomes clear when we see that there are two kinds of evil: moral and natural. Moral evil results from wickedness. It consists in the pain and suffering that we bring about in virtue of our being morally responsible agents. But there is also natural evil—pain and suffering for which we are not responsible. Because it is not due to us and thus not the result of our free will, God's reason for allowing it would have to be different from that which would explain why He tolerates moral evil. Its existence constitutes a further, and daunting, challenge to anyone who maintains that there is no unnecessary evil in the world.

It is obvious that there is an enormous amount of pain and suffering for which we are not responsible, either directly or indirectly. Earthquakes, volcanoes, hurricanes, fires, droughts, floods, and disease are the cause of great suffering not only of humans but of other animals as well. The plight of wild animals seems especially troublesome, not only because of the manner in which they must struggle to survive and because their suffering is hardly ever relieved by our intervention, but because their suffering is entirely undeserved. One might argue (though very implausibly) that because of our inherent wickedness we deserve everything we get. But such an argument is extremely implausible when applied to animals. For they are not morally responsible beings.

Though it is obvious that such suffering exists, what may not be obvious is that we should regard it as a form of *evil*. Not to do so is to implicitly assume that all evil must be moral evil or wickedness. But we see that this assumption must be rejected when we come to realize that what makes wickedness something bad or evil is (at least in part) its connection to pain and suffering. Clearly, what makes it wrong to betray your friend, to be rude and uncaring, or to forget about those who are depending on you must include the fact that people are *hurt* by these actions. Surely the primary reason why the torturing of a human being or other sentient creature is so awful is that it brings about great pain and suffering. What these reflections indicate is that suffering is intrinsically bad or undesirable, if anything is. Of course, it is sometimes if not always causally connected to certain goods, and these goods may be so valuable that they outweigh the negative value of the suffering. Suffering may sometimes *lead* to goods, as when an unbearable pain in your side leads you to discover that your appendix is about to burst. Also, suffering may lead to knowledge that is probably not obtainable in any other way. On the other hand, suffering may *result* from goods. Our free will, for example, is a good that may be used to make bad choices and thereby result in the suffering of animals as well as people. But we should not allow these truths to obscure the fact that the suffering itself, considered independently of what it leads to or results from, is intrinsically bad if anything is. This is further evidenced by the fact that no sentient creature enjoys suffering or seeks it for itself.

If the production of suffering is what makes an action or event evil, then there can be no question about the existence of *natural* evil. Consequently, the following question becomes unavoidable: Can we see how the world's natural evil might be regarded as necessary, that is, needed for the existence of a greater good? This problem may well constitute the greatest challenge to belief in God's existence. But perhaps it can be met. It certainly seems that a deity who wanted to bring about free agents who can be held morally responsible for their actions would also want to create the sort of world in which those beings could undergo moral development. This would require a world whose natural laws display enough uniformity or regularity to enable those beings to predict the moral consequences of their actions, despite the fact that the uniformity needed would sometimes lead to the suffering of innocent creatures. A knife, for example, must continue to cut whether it is wielded with intent or by accident, and whether the material cut is bread or the flesh of a person. And the law of gravity cannot be suspended for a child who falls out of a tree. Nor can the laws of chemistry and physiology be suspended for a creature that eats some toxic substance. Clearly, much suffering would be a result of the uniformity requirement. But a great deal of suffering would be required anyway, for the world in question must contain enough adversity to ensure that such moral virtues as generosity, courage, forbearance, fortitude, and compassion can be exercised. Obviously, they could not be exercised in a paradise free of suffering. There must be real needs and deprivations, real dangers, and events that are sufficiently awful to bring about genuine heartache and despair if these virtues are to arise in the first place and then be developed through further exercise.

Some have argued, however, that virtuous actions are valuable only because they reduce or eliminate suffering. They have value insofar as they promote happiness and minimize suffering; but they have no value in themselves, i.e., no *intrinsic* value. Without the existence of suffering, there would be no need or justification for their existence. Consequently, one cannot explain the existence of suffering arising from natural causes by arguing that it is needed for their development. If the virtues are good only because they reduce suffering, then it cannot be true that this suffering is good, i.e., leads to good, because it makes possible the development of the virtues. If each is needed only for the sake of the other, then why should we suppose that *either* is needed?

Though this argument has force, it does not seem compelling. It assumes that happiness, or at least the absence of suffering, is the only intrinsic good; and that the virtues have only instrumental value, that is, value only insofar as they lead to what is intrinsically good. But this assumption is based on a value judgment that a rational being need not make. A deity who set out to create free agents capable of acting in a morally responsible manner may well regard the virtues as having *intrinsic* worth. And if He did, He would see natural evil as necessary.

Perhaps we have come upon a route that will lead to an understanding of how all of the world's evil may be necessary. Formidable problems remain, however. One concerns the magnitude of natural evil: how abundant it is and how ruthlessly destructive it can be. Though some natural evil is necessary for the existence of virtue, it may seem impossible to understand how all of it can be. Some instances of natural evil (e.g., some cases of terminal cancer) are so horrible that they exceed the limits of human endurance, and others, even if endurable, end up breaking one's spirit instead of encouraging any character development. Some plunge the victim into the depths of despair, crushed by the circumstances of his life, perhaps cursing any god there may be, and unable to go on in any constructive way. Examples abound of human suffering on a gigantic scale, as when epidemics strike or famines occur. Perhaps such conditions, though unspeakably awful, nevertheless provide some opportunity for the generation of value in allowing some of the afflicted to respond with great courage and forbearance in a heroic effort to overcome the forces that will inexorably and tragically defeat them. But the positive value of whatever good may come to those who suffer in such frightful circumstances seems not to even approach, let alone exceed, the negative value of the suffering and the mass destruction of human life. Perhaps even worse, however, are those cases of debilitating brain disease, such as Alzheimer's, that demean as they destroy, that rob us of our dignity and of our very humanity as they relentlessly lead us to our destruction. To sensitive souls, it may seem perverse to suggest that the staggering amount of negative value presented by such a level of human misery may be necessary for and outweighed by the good arising from the development of virtue.

The second problem is the problem of animal suffering—a problem importantly different from, and perhaps even more intractable than, the problem of human suffering. Since animals are not free agents and cannot develop virtue, it may seem impossible to understand how God could regard all of their suffering as necessary. The enormous *amount* of animal suffering becomes apparent to us when we reflect upon how animals typically live and die in nature: how they engage in a perpetual and intense struggle for survival, how species prey upon species, prompting the slogan that nature is "red in tooth and claw," and how disease, starvation, brutality, and bloodshed seem so commonplace in nature that we run the risk of becoming desensitized to it. The great *intensity* that animal suffering can reach becomes apparent to us as we consider the horrible circumstances under which some animals die—an impala being eaten alive by a pride of lions who have not yet succeeded in killing it, a lamb, alive and helplessly suffering, as its flesh is being devoured by maggots, and a deer fawn, severely burned in a forest fire, suffering terribly for several days before death finally arrives.

Clearly, the problem that animal suffering presents may well be the most difficult of all for those who wish to embrace a theistic view of the world. Though a theist can argue that some of the suffering of animals is the result of our free choices (and possible those of Satan and other fallen angels, if such beings are assumed to exist), the remainder of it (which is very considerable) must, apparently, be due to their existing in a world designed for our character development, thereby making them subject to its natural law just as we are. One might say that they suffer for our sake.

We are now in a position to see how much the virtue development explanation must be stretched to cover, if it is the only explanation available. There is an enormous amount of suffering that would have to be deemed sacrificial in the sense that any virtue development resulting from it would have to occur in creatures other than those who experienced the suffering. Not only do the animals, which never had a capacity to develop virtue, suffer for the sake of our virtue development, but so do those unfortunate people who have suffered unto death and have thereby lost the capacity to develop virtue, at least in this life. As we have noted, many suffer without the eventual reward of having their virtue enhanced, often because death intervenes; and so any benefit that might ensue from their suffering must be registered in the accounts of others—others whose compassion, generosity, and sensitivity to the hardships of others is increased by the awareness of those who suffer without any atonement or benefit to themselves. One has to wonder how such a state of affairs could possibly be seen as necessary for the production of a greater good, even if it were seen from a "God's-eye view" in which everything is taken into account.

We can now fully appreciate the magnitude of the problem that natural evil presents for a theistic view of the world. No problem presents a greater challenge to theism. What the theist must do is provide reason to believe that *all* of the world's natural evil might be necessary for the production of good that outweighs the enormous negative value of the evil and thus could be viewed by God as permissible. If this can be done at all, it is surely a formidable task. Let us see what might be said in defense of theism.

There appear to be two distinguishable though closely related explanations of why the world's natural evil may seem to us to be impossible to reconcile with the existence of God. First, we begin by assuming that God could have, and would have wished to, create the best of all possible worlds. We then note that a slightly better world is so easy to conceive, and thus so easy to regard as possible. Thus we are led to the conclusion that our imperfect world is not a world that God, if He existed, would have created. Secondly, given the enormity of the world's natural evil, we may find ourselves unable to conceive of what good resulting from it might outweigh its negative value. What we may find upon reflection, however, is that neither of these considerations is as persuasive as we may have thought it to be initially.

The first consideration or reason for rejecting theism seems to attain compelling force when we focus on some particular case of extreme natural evil such as that of the suffering fawn and imagine the alternative ways in which the world would have contained a little less natural evil if the fate of the fawn had been different. The forest fire might have missed the spot where it was lying, it might have escaped the fire by running to a different area, or it might have perished quickly in the fire instead of suffering intensely for several days. Though some other changes would have had to occur had any one of these alternatives been actualized, it seems impossible to believe that any such changes would have resulted in a world with a less-favorable balance of good to evil than the actual one.

The "Best" Possible World

But the problem with this line of thinking is the assumption that there is a *best* of all possible worlds. For this is an assumption that a theist may plausibly deny. A theist may plausibly maintain, as Thomas Aquinas did, that any world created by God would imitate or reflect His divine perfection. But since God's perfection is an infinite good, it can be imitated in an infinite number of ways. It is inexhaustible and thus unattainable in any finite created order. This implies that whatever world God decides to create and however much it may imitate the divine perfection, there will always be an infinite gap in which other even better worlds could occur.

This reply by the theist is important not only because it allows the theist to avoid the onerous task of arguing that, contrary to appearances and rational reflection, our world is the best possible world, but because it defuses the criticism that God should have (and thus, if He existed, *would* have) created a better world, e.g., a world in which the fawn avoided suffering, or at least suffered less. God cannot be legitimately criticized for not having created a better world, simply because the very same criticism would apply with the same force even if He had done so. A criticism is legitimate only if the one criticized could have acted in such a way that the criticism would not apply. However, if there is no best possible world, but only an infinite number of possible worlds, each of which can be located on a continuum from better to worse, then God could not have acted in a way that would enable Him to avoid such a criticism. Hence, the criticism itself is misguided and so cannot be used to argue that God should have created a better world than this one. Nor can the fact that the world could have been better be used to infer the nonexistence of God.

The Moral Depth of the World

The second reason why the world's natural evil may seem to be incompatible with the existence of God is that it is so abundant and in some cases so horrible that we cannot see what good resulting from it could be great enough to outweigh it, or even match it. But again the theist has a plausible reply in questioning the motivating assumption—in this case, the assumption that if there were such a great good we would (or probably would) know what it is. Since we don't know what it is, or even what it might be in addition to the (apparently insufficient) good consisting in the development of virtue, we are inclined to infer that it probably doesn't exist and that, consequently, God probably doesn't exist either. The theist, however, may advise us to resist this inclination, arguing that we have good grounds for believing that God's reasons for permitting evil would not be fully known to us.

A theist may begin by pointing out that any good great enough to outweigh the world's natural evil would very likely be extremely complex, perhaps knowable only by God, whose cognitive powers are immeasurably greater than our own. The theist may claim that the world may have a much greater moral depth than what is presupposed in most thought about the problem of natural evil and that, accordingly, the total good being developed in the world process may be much broader and more complex that we have been implicitly assuming. Perhaps we grasp some part of the total complex good (Gt) when we grasp the connection between natural evil and virtue development, but our grasp of their connection may not be clear enough, or otherwise secure enough, to give us much confidence that we have properly assessed their relative values. If Gt is very complex, it has many constituents, each of which cannot be fully understood independently of its place in the whole. Thus if we do not have a grasp of the whole (of Gt), we cannot accurately assess the value of even that part of it that we are able to grasp.

Nor would we be justified in assuming that in cases of horrendous natural evil, there *must be*, if theism is true, certain specific goods resulting from the evil and outweighing its negative value, whether or not we can *know* what those goods are. For this would be to assume, without justification, that the value of Gt's constituents may be properly assessed in isolation from one another. Such an assumption would be false, however, if, as may well be the case, Gt's value transcends the values of its constituents when each is considered independently of the others, much as the aesthetic value of a beautiful painting transcends the aesthetic values of its parts (however they may be determined). In other words, additional value obtains in virtue of the way the parts fit together to form the whole. Thus it may be a mistake to look for some specific good resulting from and outweighing some instance of horrendous natural evil, not only because there may be no such good but because the fact (if it is a fact) that no such good exists is not what ultimately matters in the determination of the theological significance of natural evil. What ultimately matters is the positive value of Gt since it includes all goods, known and unknown, that weigh against the natural evil of the world. And given the complexity of Gt and its epistemic inaccessibility to us, we cannot rule out the possibility expressed in the following conjunction: The positive value of Gt outweighs the total negative value of the world's natural evil *and* all of that evil is necessary for Gt to exist. Of course, these considerations do not rule out the possibility of a better world—a world in which the balance of good and evil is more favorable than that of the actual world. But, as we have noted, such a possibility loses its theological significance if there is no best possible world.

That the world does have great moral depth, much of which lies below that surface layer visible to us, may seem to be sheer conjecture. But there are considerations that provide some basis for it, even if they fail to constitute good grounds for believing it. Perhaps the world in its entirety includes many dimensions in addition to the one in which we exist and that Gt is dependent in part upon what happens in some of them. If, for example, there is an afterlife that is the source of part of the good constituting Gt, then the truth about the overall balance between good and evil is not something that we could determine without taking that afterlife into account, even if we had complete knowledge of the natural realm.

The existence of such an afterlife would render the problem of natural evil much more tractable. It would open up the possibility that those who suffer and die before realizing any significant benefits resulting from their suffering in this life eventually realize such benefits, among others, in the afterlife. Also, even if the natural evil of our world should equal or outweigh the good brought about in our world as a result of the evil, the consequences for theism would not be especially problematic. For a theist could remind us that Gt is the only good that ultimately matters in these considerations and go on to argue that it outweighs the natural evil of our world (along with any other relevant natural evil that may exist) in virtue of the fact that its magnitude is a function of the good developing in the afterworld as well as in this one.

The view that the world may have great moral depth is supported not only by what we have just considered, namely, the possibility that the world contains other dimensions whose moral relations to our own realm render much more complex the relations between its good and evil, but also by the likelihood that our knowledge of those relations is very imperfect even if they are not rendered more complex by what may be true of other possible realms. This second possibility is suggested by what we have discovered about the depth of the physical world. About four hundred years ago, Francis Bacon, among others, held the optimistic view that the ultimate constituents of physical reality along with the causal relations they bear to one another lie close to the cognitive surface, so to speak, readily apprehendable by us. Indeed, Bacon believed at the time that these matters would be pretty well pinned down in another twenty years or so if scientists followed the methods that he had articulated. But he could not have been further from the truth as we understand it today. We can no longer think of the vast variety of physical things that we encounter in sense perception as different combinations of a few different kinds of atoms whose behavior is governed by the laws of classical mechanics. Now we must contemplate a hoard of such microentities as mesons, leptons, quarks, and strings, whose behavior is so exceedingly strange that it can be described, to the extent that it can be, only by the virtually incredible laws of quantum mechanics.

Physical reality, then, appears to be astonishingly deep and bewildering in its complexity. One must wonder if our cognitive powers are too feeble for us to fully comprehend it. In any case, we certainly regard it as having a depth that Bacon did not suspect. What is of central importance to our present concern, however, is the theist's suggestion that the world may have a similar *moral* depth. The suggestion is not that good and evil may have a deep underlying nature that would open up the possibility that we may be completely mistaken about what constitutes good and evil. As we shall later see, we can hardly be entirely mistaken about what good and evil fundamentally *are*. Besides, if we were, we would have no reason to believe that there is any problem of natural evil or that there is any real distinction between good and evil to be drawn. Rather, the suggestion is that, in addition to the possibility of there being deep moral good, what may be cognitively deep are the interconnections between good and evil, and the ultimate balance into which they enter.

We are now in a position to draw some conclusions about the problem that natural evil presents for the theist. Formidable as this problem undeniably is, the theist does appear to have a plausible response to it in the two-pronged argument that we have now examined: namely, that (1) if there is no best possible world, God had no obligation to create a better world, and (2) there is no reason to believe that God's reasons for permitting natural evil would be fully known to us, given the moral depth that the world would likely have if it were designed by God. Furthermore, the theist might add, since God's existence is incompatible with the existence of unnecessary evil, the various arguments for God's existence are arguments for believing that no evil is unnecessary. Consequently, the problem that natural evil presents to the theist cannot be fully assessed independently of the other considerations that bear upon the truth of theism.[7]

In conclusion, then, the arguments available to the theist, though lacking compelling force, have enough force to prevent us from knowing that some evil is unnecessary. Hence they prevent us from knowing that P5b (unnecessary evil does exist) is true and, consequently, that the so-called proof of the nonexistence of God proves anything. This putative proof would prove that there is no God if P5b were true and its truth were known to us. But for all we know, it could be false. The truth could be that God does exist and sees from His "God's-eye view" that all of the world's evil is necessary. Nothing that we have looked at rules out that possibility.

THE SIGNIFICANCE OF THE HOLY BOOKS

Our deliberations so far lack the conclusiveness for which we may have hoped, especially in a matter as important to our ultimate concerns as this one is. But we have not yet taken into account what may seem to be the most convincing line of evidence—the evidence that God has revealed His existence to us, not only on momentous occasions in the past, but also more recently and less dramatically in the everyday lives of ordinary people. Let us first consider those revelation accounts that lie at the source of the great world religions, particularly those of the West—Judaism, Christianity, and Islam. Don't the holy books of these religions provide compelling evidence that a personal God has revealed Himself to us? Though it is tempting to think so, more cautious reflection should lead us to wonder whether any of these accounts that purport to be revelations are indeed revelations from God. The fact that a holy book contains many claims that state or imply that it is the word of God does not imply that any of these claims are true. We are not calling the word of God into question; rather, we are wondering if what purports to be the word of God is indeed what it claims to be. If we already knew that an account was in fact the word of God, then we should, of course, believe that what it states is true. But without already knowing this we are certainly not entitled to infer that the account is the word of God merely because that is what it *claims* to be. We need independent evidence that this claim is true—evidence independent of the claim itself.

The miracle stories contained in the holy books may constitute such evidence, but only if we have reason to believe that any of these stories are true. If a miracle story were true, its truth might be compelling evidence that God has revealed Himself to us. But the same doubts about whether we should believe any of the revelation accounts also apply to the miracle stories. How do we know that any of *them* are true? But even if some particular miracle story is true, it may not report the occurrence of a genuine miracle, that is, a genuine violation of the laws of nature. Consider, for example, stories about apparently miraculous healing. Perhaps some of these stories are true; but even if they are, we don't know that what they report are miracles because we don't know enough about the laws of nature. In particular, we don't know enough about the extent to which the mind can affect the body or about the power of the body to heal itself.

There is, however, a further problem with the holy books—if they prove anything at all about God, they prove too much; for they contradict each other. They disagree about God's character, God's intentions and actions, and even about God's existence. For example, Theravada Buddhism claims that there is no God. Of course, even if they were in agreement in what they say about God, this would not prove anything, but at least we wouldn't have to choose among them. As things stand, however, we do have to choose, for they cannot all be true in the respects in which they conflict. We acknowledge that one of several conflicting accounts could be true, and that, perhaps, one of these is in fact true. But how do we tell which one that is? We certainly cannot tell by surveying the religious beliefs that people hold. Typically, people believe the religion that they have been taught to believe as children. Though this explains, in the case of many people, why they believe what they believe, it certainly does not by itself constitute any grounds for these beliefs. But, of course, the *grounds* for a belief, as opposed to how someone may have been caused to hold it, are what we must examine as we attempt to answer the question of whether the belief is true. And our concern for truth should lead us to view the holy books with that open-minded, impartial, and even critical attitude we should employ in scrutinizing any other book that purports to be giving us the truth about something. But, as we have seen, when we do that our grounds for believing any of them may appear to be disappointingly weak.

RELIGIOUS EXPERIENCE AND ITS SIGNIFICANCE

Still, our evidence that God has revealed Himself to us is not confined to the testimony of the holy books. Numerous individuals throughout history report having had direct personal experience of God. They have claimed to have come to know God through a direct experiential encounter. Some of these religious experiences are mystical in character. A mystical experience of the deep, introversive kind is characterized by a complete, undivided unity. It seems to the person having the experience that all differences that separate one thing from another have disappeared. Even that fundamental distinction between the self having the experience and the world (or that part of it) that is being experienced seems to disappear as self and world blend into an undivided unity in which there is no duality or division. Since this is not an unconscious state, consciousness must still be present; but it no longer displays intentionality—it is no longer *of* anything, not even of the unity. For if it were, there would still be a duality consisting of the consciousness, on the one hand, and what it is a consciousness *of*, on the other.

Those who have had such an experience are convinced beyond any doubt that it is of the highest importance, not only because of their conviction that it has brought them into epistemic contact with ultimate reality but because of its emotional quality—it is pure beatitude, ultimate bliss, "the peace that passes all understanding."[8] Unfortunately, it is also said to be ineffable or beyond all description—a fact that makes its significance very difficult to assess. Though a great many mystics regard their experience as having profound religious significance, often thinking of it as a God-encounter, their doing so is almost certainly a result of their imposing an interpretation upon it rather than the result of an effort to simply describe something inherent in the experience itself. For we should note to begin with that there is nothing inherently religious about an undivided unity. Secondly, some mystics do not attribute any religious significance to their experience. The great mystic Plotinus did not. Nor are Buddhist and other non-theistic mystics inclined to do so. And thirdly, the mystics who do see their experience in a religious light tend to speak of it in terms that express the concepts and doctrines of the particular religions that they embrace. So although we should have no doubt about the reality of mystical experiences, it seems clear that whatever religious significance they have is a result of an interpretation imposed upon them—an interpretation that could be mistaken. Thus we are led to ask whether the religious interpretation constitutes the best explanation of these experiences.

The naturalistic explanation of them is certainly not implausible despite the extraordinary impression they make on the people who have them and despite the fact that those people almost always think of them in a non-naturalistic way. They are undoubtedly connected with changes in the electrochemistry of the brain. They are usually preceded by one or more of such unusual practices as prolonged fasting, self-flagellation, sensory deprivation, extensive meditation, and getting in and out of a series of unusual body positions. Those in whom they occur spontaneously tend to display physical and/or mental abnormalities. Some powerful hallucinogens, e.g., psilocybin, have been shown to produce experiences that, judging by the descriptions their subjects gave of them, were indistinguishable from mystical experiences had by some of the great mystics of the past. So perhaps they are nothing more than peculiar hallucinations—totally subjective creations that provide no evidence of any objective encounter. But even if they do provide exposure to a dimension of reality with which we otherwise have no contact, it is far from obvious that the best explanation of them is a religious interpretation that would have us believe that a personal God has been encountered. So the grounds they provide for the belief in a personal God seem weak at best.

Non-mystical religious experiences may seem more likely to provide substantial support for this belief. Unlike the full-blown mystical experience, these are not extremely rare, nor are they so commonly associated with the extraordinary. They range all the way from an undefined and unspecifiable (though unmistakable) sense of divine presence to the dramatic and moving sensory experience of the sort had by St. Paul on the Damascus Road. With them, the religious interpretation arises quite naturally out of the experience, as the experience often takes the form of an apparent communication with another, or at least a sensing of the presence of another—more specifically, an *other* who is taken to be divine. But the conclusion that one has been in the presence of God is nevertheless based upon an interpretation that goes beyond the experience itself. And so again we must ask if the religious interpretation is the best explanation of such experience.

Unfortunately, there is good reason to believe that it is not, for again the alternative naturalistic explanation seems quite plausible. The need (or at least the strong desire) to believe that God exists is apparently very widespread, at least in the West. This belief is central to the great Western religions and is impressed upon children by their parents and the Church at a time when children lack the critical/analytical resources needed to evaluate it adequately. What is impressed upon us at an early age often has a long-lasting if not permanent effect upon us. The inclination to look at it critically may be accompanied by feelings of guilt and wrongdoing. Besides, as children become adults who attain a more vivid, reflective awareness of our human condition, they may find themselves recoiling from the relative bleakness of a world without God and thus more inclined to suppress any doubts they may have had about what they were taught as children. This tenaciously held belief in a personal God who brought us into existence and now oversees our lives is an overarching belief that guides the believer's interpretation of his experience. He sees God behind the world process, thinks about His presence, prays to Him, spends time in worship of Him, and often interprets significant events beyond his control as expressions of His will. Given this focus, it is not surprising that many people report having had religious experience. What we bring to our experiences—in particular, the psychological baggage—has a significant effect on the experiences themselves, and it may be that one who interprets his religious experience as a God-encounter may be fairly compared to the person who comes upon his own footprints but mistakenly assumes that they were made by someone else.

Perhaps this naturalistic explanation, or one along these lines, is more plausible than the religious interpretation. But even if they are equally plausible, the naturalistic explanation has the advantage in that it is the simpler hypothesis: It assumes the existence of a smaller number of entities. Besides, the entities involved are independently known to exist. There is no question about the existence of the natural world, and this explanation makes no appeal to anything beyond that world. It stays within the realm of what we believe people are capable of doing. We know that people are capable of hallucinating, of misinterpreting their experience, and of persistently deluding themselves, especially if the delusion is a comforting one that reduces fear and feelings of helplessness as well as satisfying deep-seated hopes and desires. At the very least, this explanation must diminish our confidence in the religious interpretation.

THE ROLE OF FAITH

Our search for evidence sufficient to sustain rational belief in God may seem disappointing. We have been appealing to reason and looking for evidence to support such belief. But we have not yet taken into account the role of faith. Perhaps belief in God should depend on faith rather than on reason and evidence. In any case, many would insist that faith is the foundation of religious belief. But we must ask how this can be so.

To believe on faith is to believe without adequate evidence, and to hold that belief *must* be based on faith is to concede, at least implicitly, that there is no such evidence. But without evidence we have no evidential basis for deciding what the object of our faith should be, i.e., *what* we should believe on faith. Among other problems, we would have no evidential basis for selecting one holy book over another as the genuine source of revelation from God. Worse yet, what do we say to someone who claims to believe *on faith* that God does *not* exist? Without an anchor in any evidence, this "faith" is just as legitimate as the purely faith-based belief that God exists. If faith is not guided by evidence but still not entirely arbitrary or unguided either, then what *does* guide it? Do we decide *what* to accept on faith simply on the basis of our hopes and desires?

Well, that is apparently what we will do if we take this route at all. But can we really take it after seeing its implication that the objective truth is irrelevant? If, in the absence of evidence to provide a rational basis for determining what is objectively true, we choose to believe *on faith* anyway, we thereby show that we are willing to regard what is true as irrelevant to our concerns. Perhaps this route should strike us as a display of desperation—a failure of nerve. In any case, we seem forced to the conclusion that such disregard for the truth is beneath what we should expect of ourselves; for it appears to be a shirking of the intellectual responsibility we have as beings able to conceive of objective truth and reality.

Faith, then, does not constitute an alternative route to rational belief in the existence of God. Perhaps there are no routes at all to such belief. However, our deliberations have not led us to the conclusion that God does *not* exist. The belief that God exists could be true even though the evidence for it is insufficient. And though the lack of evidence may render *belief* irrational (or at least rationally unjustifiable), *hope* is not similarly affected. It seems irrational to hope for what one knows is not even possible, but we are not so unfortunate as to be in that situation. If one is looking for certainty, then this conclusion will be disappointing, if not simply unacceptable. But perhaps the demand for certainty, though understandable, is itself quite inappropriate, given our limited powers in relation to the bewildering complexity of the world. Though certainty about God's existence may seem crucially important to us, an impartial objective assessment of our human condition indicates that we must learn to live without it. We are not entitled to assume that the world was made for us and thus not entitled to assume that it is a place in which our desires—our desire for certainty, for example—can be satisfied. Our challenge is to adapt ourselves emotionally to what our best evidence indicates the world to be, rather than to insist on viewing it through the lens of our desires.

INTIMATIONS OF A NON-NATURAL REALM

Before we bring our reflections on the subject of God to a close, we should note how some of our earlier conclusions about self-consciousness and the mental bear upon this subject. The undeniable presence of consciousness, mentality, and especially self-conscious subjects of experience in an otherwise entirely material natural world might strike us as so astonishing as to prompt us to believe that they must have a supernatural or transcendental ground. It is tempting to believe that matter (at least as presently understood in physical theory) simply lacks the capacity to give rise to an immaterial reality. As we noted earlier, the mental and the physical certainly appear to be radically different types of reality, and this may lead us to think that the emergence of the mental from the physical is extremely unlikely, if not downright impossible. But the unlikelihood of emergence is equivalent to the likelihood that the mental is more securely grounded in reality than what a purely naturalistic view of the world could acknowledge, that is, grounded in a non-natural order or dimension of reality beyond the natural world. And any evidence that there is a nonnatural or supernatural order is certainly congenial to the view that God exists.

That there may, after all, be something non-natural about us, and thus something about us that points to a supernatural or transcendental ground, comes most clearly into view when we focus upon ourselves as self-conscious subjects of experience. Consider the fact that you might have had an identical twin who is exactly similar to you, both mentally and physically. Now consider the fact that you might have been one of three identical triplets, or one of five identical quintuplets. All of this seems easy to do. Finally, let us think of an entire world containing millions or even billions of people each one of whom is exactly similar to you. We need not worry about how all these people came to be. Perhaps your genotype was replicated in some type of cloning process. The point is that there is nothing incoherent or unintelligible about the conception of such a world. It is a world that is surely conceivable, however bizarre it may seem to be.

Now consider a different possibility—that the person who would have been your identical twin (if you had had one) is in the world *instead* of you. Your place in the world might have been occupied by some other person who is exactly similar to you in every way. And then consider the possibility that any one of those billions of people exactly similar to you might have been in your place. When you do this, you may find it astounding that you are in the world at all. The likelihood that some one or other of these countless billions of people should have been in your place seems so great that *your* actually being in this place instead of any of them may seem to be nothing short of miraculous.

We are now in a position to see what a peculiar relation a subject of experience bears to the natural world. As science gains more and more knowledge of the natural world, it may at some point be able to tell us virtually everything we might want to know about human beings—everything about our minds and our bodies, as well as our relations to other things. But though science may someday be able to explain how a person with all of your mental and physical characteristics came to be, as well as virtually everything else about this person, it would never be able to show that this person is *you*—the subject of *your* experience. For all science could tell, this person could be any one of the countless numbers of people exactly similar to you who could have been in your place. It could never tell that you are the person under scientific study; for you, considered as the subject of your experience, are something that lies beyond the items available to it. Though all of your physical and mental characteristics—indeed everything true of you that would have been true of someone exactly similar to you who might have been in your place—may be inextricably bound up with other items in the natural world, you yourself are apparently not. For they might have been in the world without you, bound up with, e.g., causally related to, other items in the natural world just as they are now. Since all your characteristics might have been the characteristics of someone just like you existing in your place, what you essentially are must be distinct from all these characteristics. And since the entire natural world could have been just as it is now if such a person had been in your place, you appear to be curiously disconnected from that world, and perhaps not even a proper part of it. If this is a truth about you, then there is a truth that seems very hard to fit into a naturalistic view. It is more congenial to the view that there is a non-natural order—an order of the sort we have in mind when we think about God.

It appears, then, that we have come upon three indicators of the presence of a realm beyond the natural world, a realm in which this world may be grounded: (1) the difficulty in seeing how mentality in general and a subject of experience in particular could have arisen or emerged out of an entirely material world; (2) the apparently great unlikelihood, even given all of the natural facts just as they were prior to your existence, that you should have come to exist at all; and (3) your apparent disconnection from everything else in the natural order. Perhaps at last we have found a weak though respectable basis for belief in God. But even if these considerations fail to provide a rational basis for belief, they have, at the very least, sufficient power to liberate hope.

QUESTIONS FOR FURTHER THOUGHT

1. When we think of God as a personal being, should we be thinking of a supernatural subject of experience? Do we have a concept of such a subject?

2. Is the principle of sufficient reason a plausible principle? Is there any way to show that it is true, or that it is false?

3. Should the fact that the universe is fine-tuned to the needs of life be interpreted as evidence that the universe was designed for us and other life forms? If so, does this fact provide enough evidence to justify the belief that there is a universe-designer?

4. Is there any unnecessary evil? Can we be certain that there is, or is not? Is the possibility that the world has great moral depth a sufficient basis for doubting that there is any unnecessary evil?

5. Do the holy books, or some particular one of them, provide stronger evidence for God's existence than the text suggests? How might we show that they do?

6. Is there something "non-natural" about us? Or do we fit into the natural world as well as everything else known to us?

7. Does the suffering of animals constitute a greater challenge to theism than human suffering? Is it plausible to suppose that animals, especially those with much simpler nervous systems, suffer much less, or less intensely, than humans do?

8. The text suggests that the problem of natural evil may well constitute the greatest challenge to a theistic interpretation of the world. Is this cor-

rect, or does it seem to you that the problem is overstated? Is there some other problem for theism that is as great or greater than this one?

9. Is it plausible to deny that there is a *best* possible world? Though it seems easy to conceive of a morally better world, can we also conceive of a morally best or morally perfect world? Is it more difficult to conceive of a morally perfect world than a morally perfect God?

10. Should we be persuaded by the argument (presented in the text) that begins with the premise that there is no best possible world and ends with the conclusion that God had no moral obligation to create a better world than this one?

11. Is it plausible to suppose that if God did exist the world might be so morally deep that knowledge of the ultimate balance between the good and evil in it would be impossible for us? Would the plausibleness of this supposition defuse the argument from evil for the nonexistence of God?

7

FREE WILL

In our reflections about God we have been assuming that we are capable of making free choices and that, as a consequence, we can justifiably be held morally responsible for our actions. In particular, we can be held accountable for the moral evil in the world. This is certainly not an unusual assumption to make. The assumption that we are free beings (in virtue of our having free will) is central to our conception of ourselves and plays a crucially important role in our dealings with one another. We hold each other morally and legally responsible—we praise and we blame, we reward and we punish. And when we hold people responsible for their actions, we assume, whether implicitly or explicitly, that they could have chosen to act other than as they did. Unfortunately, there are seemingly compelling reasons for believing that this assumption is mistaken—that free will is a mere illusion and that, accordingly, we must completely rethink our present understanding of ourselves as morally responsible beings.

THE DETERMINIST THESIS

These reasons are based on the evidence that the world is deterministic, that everything that happens in it happens in accordance with causal laws. If the thesis of causal determinism is true, then every event, whether mental or physical, is caused to occur exactly as it does and, given its cause or causes, could not have been different from what it is. In other words, there are antecedent causal conditions, known or unknown, which determine the entire state of the world at any given time. Given these antecedent conditions, nothing could have differed even in the slightest from what it actually turned out to be. And these antecedent conditions were determined to be exactly what they were by conditions obtaining prior to them which, in turn, were precisely determined by earlier conditions, and so forth indefinitely (or perhaps infinitely) far into the past. If the world is eternal, then these chains of causally determined events had no beginning.

The past was caused to be what it is and is now causally fixed. But so is the future. Even though it has not yet occurred, what it will be is already causally fixed; for it is already predetermined by the causal conditions obtaining now. Since whatever occurs is just the outcome of what happened previously, every event is causally fixed. The time at which it occurs makes no difference.

If the world is deterministic, then whatever happens was bound to happen and thus was unavoidable. For nothing happens unless it is caused to happen, and, as we have seen, the cause (C) of an event (E) is the necessary and sufficient condition of E's occurrence. Since C is necessary for E, E *cannot* occur without C; and since C is sufficient for E, E *must* occur if C does. Clearly, if E's occurrence (and thus the occurrence of *every* event) is necessitated or rendered inevitable, the implications for our belief in free will look grim indeed.

With this in mind let us consider a case in which your freedom to choose seems undeniable. At this moment it surely seems to you that you can either close this book and, for example, watch a TV program or continue on reading. Suppose you choose to do the latter. Even though you did not choose to close the book, it probably seems as evident to you as anything can be that you *could have* done so. Clearly, this action was within your power, and any theory that implies otherwise must be false. Or so it seems to us, at any rate.

But the determinist thesis *does* imply otherwise; it implies that continuing to read was the only course of action open to you. For this was the course of action that was the inevitable result of the conditions obtaining just prior to it—conditions sufficient for bringing it about. In other words, it was the course of action for which there was a cause. On the other hand, there was no cause for any action contrary to this one, such as your closing the book. That action could not have occurred because there was no cause to bring it about. Though we can easily conceive of either of these actions occurring, only the one that is caused can actually occur. Indeed, it is necessitated by the antecedent conditions, whereas the one that lacks a cause could not have occurred. Thus regardless of how convinced we may be that alternative courses of action were open to you, we must come to acknowledge that, given the antecedent conditions exactly as they were prior to your action, only one course of action was possible for you, namely, the one you actually took.

A determinist could apply this argument to every case in which you believe that different alternative courses of action are open to you. The case we have just considered has no moral significance. But many cases have; sometimes your decision concerns how other people should be treated. A stranger needs assistance. Should you help? You found a lost billfold containing owner identification and a substantial sum of money. Are you obliged to return it? Your terminally ill friend who wants to die in order to end his/her suffering and helplessness requests your assistance. What should you do? These are obviously morally significant cases. But a determinist would argue that in these cases too, like every other, only one course of action is open to you—the one necessitated by the antecedent conditions. Given precisely those conditions, there was nothing else you could have done.

Suppose, for example, that you decide to keep the lost billfold. The determinist thesis would imply that given the antecedent conditions you could not have done anything else. But if no other course of action were possible, so that you could not help but keep it, then holding you morally responsible for keeping it seems totally unjustifiable. For we do not, or at any rate *should* not, hold people morally responsible for doing that which they cannot help doing. And what the determinist thesis implies is true of you in this case also extends to every other case of someone appearing to deliberate about what to do. This thesis has universal application; and so it implies that in every case of someone appearing to choose among alternatives, the antecedent conditions permit only one course of action—namely, the one that they predetermine. Thus the person taking that predetermined course of action could not help but take it; his taking it was inevitable and, consequently, unavoidable. Therefore, no one can justifiably be held responsible for anything!

At this point it may seem that the determinist thesis is utterly at odds with our understanding of ourselves and thus *must* be rejected. Any view which implies that our deliberations are totally illusory, that there are no alternative courses of action open to us, that we could not have avoided taking the course of action we actually did take, and that no one is responsible for anything he does seems so counter-intuitive as to be impossible to accept. But the reasons for believing that it is true seem equally powerful. As we have seen, it is nothing more than a thesis of universal causation—the thesis that every event is caused. Considered as such it seems to be implicitly accepted by both science and common sense. We encounter a horrible disease, AIDS, for example. How it comes about is at first a mystery to us. But we subject it to scientific study and eventually learn a good deal about the antecedent conditions that lead to it. Knowledge of these causal factors is extremely important—well worth the enormous amount of time and effort expended—because we can remove the disease itself if we can remove its cause. But underlying all of this activity is the assumption that this disease, like everything else, is caused, that it didn't just pop into existence out of nothing, and that removing its cause removes any possibility of its getting into the world. At the outset we were unaware of how it was caused and, one might say, even lacked knowledge *that* it was caused. Presumably, it could have been causally disconnected to everything else. Although that is a logical possibility, it is surely not one that we take seriously. We assume that such disconnection is not possible in the actual world. It is, we might say, contrary to the natural law of this world or *causally* impossible. But to say this is to embrace the determinist thesis.

Consider another example: the weather. Though the weather has been notoriously difficult to predict with great accuracy, we are getting much better at predicting it. However, we are still utterly unable to predict with considerable accuracy the weather conditions that will prevail at some specific location (say, where you are now) at some distant future time (say, three years from this moment). In accounting for this inability we would not even consider the suggestion that some weather conditions are uncaused. Every weather condition, we would insist, is just the outcome of the antecedent conditions—conditions that predetermine or causally necessitate its occurrence. Our ineptitude at predicting on this level is sufficiently explained by the fact that these conditions are too numerous and complicated for us to attain the detailed grasp of them needed for such highly sophisticated predictions. It certainly doesn't call into question our assumption of universal causation.

Though science and common sense apparently accept (at least implicitly) the thesis of universal causation, they could be mistaken in doing so. But we have reasons for accepting it that are independent of whatever support they provide. For it does seem very hard to believe that something that begins to exist at some time, i.e., is not eternal, should have come into existence without being caused to exist. To assert that it came into existence out of nothing is hardly to provide a sufficient explanation of its existence. And to claim that its coming into existence simply doesn't stand in need of any explanation seems wildly implausible.

INDETERMINISM

So the reasons for accepting the determinist thesis seem very powerful, if not compelling. But suppose that (perhaps out of desperation) we reject this thesis anyway, on the grounds that it is incompatible with our belief in free will and moral responsibility. Though we still believe that the vast majority of events are causally determined, we now maintain that this thesis is not true with respect to certain events involving persons—more specifically, those events that consist in persons deliberating and choosing. A person is able to choose one of several alternatives, each of which is a genuine possibility because none of them is causally determined by antecedent conditions. In this view the alternative that is actually taken *just happens* to be taken. Taking it was an uncaused event. Other alternatives were genuine possibilities because any one of them could have been the one that just happened to be chosen or taken. Each was genuinely possible because none was causally determined to occur. In other words, sheer indeterminism reigns in the realm of deliberation and choosing,

An indeterminist may go on to argue that the notion of an event that "just happens" seems to have application on the quantum level. Quantum physics provides evidence that at least some events involving certain micro-entities (more specifically, those entities to which the laws of quantum mechanics apply) are uncaused. They just happen, so far as we can tell. Of course, it may be that a deeper understanding of nature will yield an interpretation in which there is no indeterminism even on the quantum level. But at the present time, this seems unlikely. So if the present indeterminist interpretation can be sustained, we may simply have to learn to accommodate the notion of an uncaused event. In any case, this interpretation does appear to confer some respectability on the notion.

But an appeal to sheer indeterminism will certainly not yield a resolution of the free-will problem. Even if there are quantum-level events that are uncaused, indeterminism is very likely confined to that level. The behavior of all larger physical entities, even if they are no larger than atoms, is causally determined. And though there are quantum-level events occurring in our brains, it seems highly unlikely that any indeterminism on that level could be invoked to support the claim that our choices are uncaused. But the central reason why an appeal to indeterminism cannot be of any help in solving the free-will problem is that if our choices were uncaused, they could not have been caused by *us*, in which case we should not be held responsible for them or anything resulting from them. Clearly, if some activity involving your body was not caused by you, then it was not something *you* willed. It was not *your* doing, and we could have no grounds for holding you responsible for it. The fact that your body was involved makes no difference. It would be like a case in which you accidentally slip on the ice and knock someone else down. Though you may have chosen to walk on the ice and, perhaps, to walk somewhat carelessly, the slipping itself was not willed by you; and you are not morally responsible for it.

We are now in a position to appreciate the depth of the free-will problem and the formidable challenge it poses to us as we attempt to arrive at an adequate understanding of ourselves. For it now appears that free will and moral responsibility are illusions whether our choices are caused or not caused. If the determinist thesis is true, then free will is an illusion and no one is morally responsible for anything. If, on the other hand, this thesis is not true when extended to our deliberation and choosing (and thus not true at all), then our "decisions" are not caused by us, and so again we are not morally responsible for them or for anything else. Not only would there be no free will, there would be nothing that counts as *our* willing. For the activity in question is not caused by *us*. But obviously the determinist thesis is either true or not true. These are the only alternatives. Thus free will and moral responsibility turn out to be illusions in either case, i.e., in *every possible* case. Yet, we would insist, they cannot be illusions if we are *persons*. For they seem to be essentially involved in what a person *is*.

SOFT DETERMINISM

This is indeed an unfortunate situation. Our understanding of the world process clashes head-on with our understanding of ourselves. When faced with such a situation we would be well advised to take another look at the route by which we arrived at this impasse and to wonder if we have not misconceived something important. At any rate, this is what a "soft" determinist may suggest we do. A soft determinist is a determinist who believes that determinism is compatible with free will. Unlike the "hard" determinist who holds that the determinist thesis is true and that the free-will thesis is false, he believes that *both* theses are *true*. And he would also suggest that we reexamine what we seem to have in mind when we conceive of someone who is acting freely.

Not surprisingly, the soft determinist has some definite opinions about what an adequate conception of free will would be, i.e., about what it is for someone to have free will. He would argue that you act freely when you act in accordance with your choices and desires—when you do what you want or choose to do. Your action is neither impeded nor compelled. Nothing is preventing you from doing what you want to do, nor are you being forced to do otherwise. He would also point out that though your volitions and desires are the effects of antecedent conditions, your actions may nevertheless be unimpeded and uncompelled, that is, *free*. And if they are free you are morally responsible for them. Thus the reality of free will and moral responsibility are entirely consistent with the truth of the determinist thesis.

This may strike us as a very appealing view, especially since it seems to allow us to eat our cake and have it too. The absurdity of indeterminism is avoided, yet free will and responsibility are saved. It certainly merits a closer look. In this view, a free act is causally determined like every other event. It is free in virtue of *how* it is caused. An act of yours is free if it is caused by something within you, namely, your own choices, volitions, and desires. But your act will be the result of your own inner states, and thus free, only if nothing external to you is preventing you from acting in accordance with them or compelling you to do something other than what they would have led you to do. It is true that, given the antecedent conditions just as they were prior to your action, only one course of action was open to you—the one you actually took. And this fact may lead us to doubt that you were acting freely, since no alternative courses of action were possible for you, that is, since the future was not open or unfixed with respect to what action you would take. For the implication is clear: There is nothing else you could have done. But the soft determinist has several arguments that he could offer in an attempt to eliminate such doubt.

The causal determination of an event *does* exclude the possibility of any other event taking its place. This much must be acknowledged; after all, we are talking about causal *determination*. But, the soft determinist may counter, if the absence of causal determination is the absence of causation, then we must acknowledge that our actions are causally determined. For they are surely not uncaused. In other words, the view that our actions are causally determined is apparently the only alternative to the absurd view that sheer indeterminism reigns with respect to them. Furthermore, he may add, alternative courses of action are impossible only in a relatively weak sense of "impossible"—they are *causally* impossible. Though the causal determination of an action does rule out alternative actions, other courses of action are conceivable; they are *logically* possible. Indeed, some alternative course of action would have been the one taken if the antecedent conditions had been different. Perhaps it is only because alternatives are conceivable that we regard them as causally possible as well.

However, the soft determinist provides what is probably the most cogent defense of his view when he reminds us that causation is not compulsion—that, for example, when we say of someone that his action was caused we certainly do not, or *should* not, mean that it was coerced or compelled. If we discover that your behavior was caused by your own volitions and desires, then we would say that it was *not* compelled. For what is implied is that there were no external forces compelling you to act as you did. And we should conclude that you acted freely, for what conflicts with free will is compulsion, not causation. Causal determination is incompatible with indeterminism, but not with free will. On the other hand, an act of free will cannot be a compelled act, but it is surely one that is caused to occur. Thus free will is compatible with universal causation.

The tacit assumption that causes compel their effects may arise from confusing two very different kinds of laws. We can predict and explain human behavior by appeal to causal laws, for example, the laws of psychology. The fact that we are getting progressively better at doing this certainly supports the claim that human behavior too, like that of inanimate bodies, is causally determined. But a focus on causal laws also helps to dispel the myth that causes are compelling. Some laws do compel, namely, the laws of government. These laws are prescriptive; they prescribe a certain behavior. People are forced, under threat of punishment, to comply with them. But causal laws, i.e., laws of nature, are not like this. The laws of psychology, for example, do not prescribe how people are to conduct themselves. Rather, they describe how people do in fact behave under a certain set of conditions. Since they are descriptive rather than prescriptive, the notion of compulsion doesn't apply to them. When we say that a person's will obeys psychological laws, we do not mean that his volitions and desires are compelled by these laws to be whatever they are. Rather, we are merely describing what desires he in fact has or what he actually wills to do under a given set of conditions.

Does the soft determinist have the solution to the puzzle about free will? Many have thought so, and we can now see why. To answer this question, we must focus more carefully on what it is for an action to be free. Consider your present act of reading this page. It is a free act of yours, but what makes it such an act? The correct answer seems to be that it satisfies two conditions: (1) it was initiated by you—you were the cause of it, and (2) you could have done something else. The satisfaction of these two conditions certainly appears to be both necessary and sufficient for your action to be free. Let us examine them more carefully to see if the soft determinist view allows them to be satisfied.

With respect to the first condition, if an act of yours is to be free, then it must be caused by *you*. Now, according to soft determinism this act like every other was caused. But could *you* have been the cause? It appears that you could not. Rather, the cause was some inner state or event, e.g., a certain desire along with the belief that this desire could be satisfied by a certain course of action. But this inner subjective state is not *identical* to you. As we have seen, the soft determinist correctly denies that your behavior is free when it is caused by external circumstances. It is free only when it is the effect of your own subjective states, that is, items *not* identical to you. Thus, unless you are the cause of these states, the behavior that results from them is not even *your* action, let alone your *free* action. But you apparently cannot be the cause of them; for they are the effects of prior mental and/or physical states, which in turn are the effects of earlier states or conditions, etc. In other words, they are part of a causally determined chain of events that extends infinitely far into the past.

The problem arising here for the soft determinist is that his view contains no room for the notion of an *agent*, that is, of a *being who acts*, as opposed to a passive being who is merely acted upon—a being whose behavior can be nothing more than the effect of antecedent conditions. But we think of ourselves as agents—as self-determining beings who are not merely acted upon but who have causal powers that can be exercised in alternative ways. What seems to be implied in this notion of ourselves as agents is that we can *initiate* causal chains. We do not think of ourselves as passively swept along in causal chains of events that are infinitely long and that therefore causally determine our actions before we came into existence. As agents we initiate causal chains with our free acts.

But it appears that if soft determinism is true, the only behavior possible for us is what is causally determined by that which acts upon us. Thus self-determined action is ruled out. This problem remains even when our behavior is the causal consequence of our own mental and/or brain states, and thus of something that is part of us. Even such behavior is not *self*-determined, for we are distinct from these states. They too merely act upon us as they were acted upon by prior states and conditions, which were acted upon by prior conditions, and so on without end. One gets a mental image of an infinitely long line of dominoes. Before us one domino is falling and knocks the one in front of it down, which in falling knocks the one in front of it down, and so on endlessly. In the forward direction the dominoes are still standing; in the rearward direction they have all fallen. Each domino is acted upon by the one behind it. The fall of each is both an effect of being acted upon and a cause that acts upon another, but there is no room for any agency in this. An agent would be analogous to something that causes the fall of the first domino in a series. It initiates a causal chain. Its activity is not causally necessitated by its being acted upon by something else.

If these difficulties fail to convince us that soft determinism is not the answer, a look at the second requirement for a free act should remove all doubt. If you cannot act freely unless alternative courses of action are open to you, then the conclusion is clear: You cannot act freely if soft determinism is true. The soft determinist will likely concede this without hesitation. In any case, it is implied by his position. He may try to ease us into this conclusion by pointing out that what is causally necessary need not be logically necessary and that you could have acted other than you in fact did if the antecedent conditions had been different. But this is a feeble reply that we should dismiss without further consideration once we see that the antecedent conditions *could not* have been different. For they were causally determined to be what they were by prior conditions, which in turn were causally determined by earlier conditions, and so on endlessly. Thus the antecedent conditions could not have been different and so you could not have acted other than as you did. The fact that we can conceive of you acting in some other way makes no difference. Since no other action was causally possible for you—since nothing else was actually within your power to perform—you are not (and thus should not be held) morally responsible for what you did.

It is also of no help for the soft determinist to point out that causal laws fail to compel in the way prescriptive or civil laws do if the causal laws permit only one course of action, namely, the causally determined one. Since that is precisely what they permit, no one can help but do that which he does. He could not have acted otherwise because no other action was causally possible. The soft determinist argues that you act freely when you act in accordance with your own inclinations, desires, volitions, etc., that is, in accordance with your own given nature, free from external compulsion. But now we must ask why it should make any difference whether it is because of external compulsion or because of your own given nature that you cannot help but do that which you do. For if you could not help but do it, then you should not be held morally responsible for doing it. The claim that you ought to have done x implies that you *could* have done x. This implication must be acknowledged. But soft determinism implies that given the antecedent conditions, which could not have been different, no one could have acted other than he in fact did. Hence it implies that no one is morally responsible for anything.

It seems obvious that if no one is morally responsible for his actions, then *holding* anyone morally responsible would never be justifiable. Yet it is important for the soft determinist, like almost everyone else, to hold people morally responsible, for the social consequences of not doing so would be disastrous. A society could not exist if no one were held responsible for anything. But the soft determinist who agrees that we must hold people morally responsible must also concede that we can have no moral justification for doing so. For in his view they are not morally responsible. He might try to avoid this conclusion by claiming that we are justified in treating them *as if* they were morally responsible because of the benefits that such treatment provides. But this will not do. It cannot be morally permissible (or morally justifiable) for us to treat others as if they were morally responsible, for we would not be morally responsible either and thus could not act in a morally justified or unjustified way. Since the notions of moral responsibility and moral justification have no application in a soft determinist world, they cannot be implicitly appealed to in attempting to justify some mode of conduct. Yet a group of interacting individuals in which these notions do not apply could hardly be a society of *persons*, though it might be a colony of ants or a hive of bees.

Clearly then, soft determinism must be rejected if freedom and moral responsibility require that a person could have acted other than he did. The soft determinist must deny that this is a requirement, but his denial is extremely implausible. He would claim that you act freely, and so can be justifiably held responsible, when you do what you will or desire to do, unconstrained by external forces. The fact that you could not have done anything else under the prevailing conditions is not supposed to matter. But we see how unsatisfactory this is when we see that, in his view, your volitions and desires are beyond your control. For they are causally determined to be what they are by antecedent conditions, which in turn are causally determined by earlier conditions, and so on endlessly. Thus your volitions and desires at any given time are the inevitable outcome of conditions that were in existence before you were. If we are going to hold you morally responsible for the volitions and desires you presently have, then we might as well hold you responsible for having an inherited disease. For both are the inevitable outcomes of events that took place before you were born. But if you cannot be justifiably held responsible for your volitions, desires, etc., then you cannot be justifiably held responsible for the behavior that is causally determined by them. Thus we reach the conclusion that freedom and responsibility *do* require one to have had the power to act other than one did, and so soft determinism must be rejected.

Once again we appear to be faced with the paradox that free will and responsibility are illusions, whether determinism is true *or* false. The failure of soft determinism leaves only hard determinism—the view that determinism is true and freedom is an illusion. And if the falsity of hard determinism implies that simple indeterminism is true, then our choices and actions are not caused by us, and therefore are not really *ours* at all. Both views seem preposterous and completely at odds with our commonsensical conception of ourselves. At the same time, we seem to be locked into one or the other, since it must be the case that the determinist thesis is either true *or* false. It obviously cannot be both or neither.

THE AGENCY THEORY

Fortunately, however, there does seem to be a third view—a way of slipping between the Scylla of hard determinism and the Charybdis of simple indeterminism. Let us call it the agency theory. We have already looked at most of the elements that enter into it. Let us now bring them together to see if the view that emerges is both intelligible and faithful to our commonsensical intuitions.

We have already reached the conclusion that you are a subject of experience if you are anything at all. This fits well with the agency theory. For, as we have noted, if an act of yours is to be free, then *you* must be the cause of it, not merely some part of you or some event occurring within you. Furthermore, you must be a self-determining being, not something that is merely acted upon, that is, not something whose activity is causally determined by antecedent conditions. But if you are a physical organism, then what you are is a collection of things and events, e.g., organs, cells, and brain events. No agent can be found in such a collection. Each item in it is merely acted upon; its activity is causally determined by antecedent conditions in accordance with the physical laws that describe the behavior of all physical things and processes. But even if some member of this collection—say, the cause of your present behavior—did at least *look like* an agent, it would be something within you or part of you, and thus *not identical* to you. For in this view the immediate cause of your present behavior is a process occurring in your brain; and, of course, that is not what you *are*. These difficulties are not avoided in the view that what you are is your mind, understood as a collection of experiences (that is, what we earlier called the relational view of the mind). Although we saw good reason to believe that mental states and processes are non-physical, this feature doesn't enable us to see how an individual mental item could be self-determining. But even if some of them were, this fact would not support the claim that *you* are a self-determining being, for in this view you are a collection of such items and not identical to any one of them.

If, on the other hand, you are a subject of experience, then you are not a collection of items, but a unitary being. You would be such that *you yourself,* rather than some part of you or element within you, could be the cause of your own choices and actions. This is supported by our earlier conclusion that a subject of experience is indivisible, indeed is apparently without parts. If, as it seems, you are such an entity, then you cannot be split into two. Though you have a great variety of experiences (e.g., of seeing, thinking, imagining, remembering, etc.), they are all experiences of *yours.* You are the subject of them all. They are not parts of you but *states* of yours. And when you think of yourself as the *subject* of your experiences, then it seems undeniable that you are something that is not divisible into parts. The notion of an experience that is only partly yours or that is experienced by only a part of you is nonsense. Thus if you are a subject who acts at all, you act as a unitary being.

As we noted earlier, if some decision or act of yours is to be free, then *you* must be the cause of it. It must be self-determined. And we have just looked at an account in which this condition is satisfied. What remains to be shown is that the second condition—that you could have done something other than what you did—can be satisfied as well. This requires a breach of causal continuity. Although your free action was caused by you, you were not causally determined to act as you did. You could have done something else. Thus your deliberations about what you should do are not illusory; you really do have alternative courses of action open to you. Consider again a case in which you find a lost wallet containing a substantial amount of money. After deliberating about what to do, you decide to return it. You were the cause of that action, but nothing caused you to choose that alternative. Here is the breach of causal continuity—the break in the causal chain. With this action you initiate a causal chain. But you could have decided to keep the wallet, in which case you would have initiated a different causal chain. Thus some causal chains have beginnings; they are not infinitely, or at least not indefinitely, long as the determinist thesis implies.

Of course, you do not deliberate in a vacuum. You consider reasons for taking one course of action rather than another. At any rate, you take reasons into account if your decision is both free *and* rational. But these reasons do not causally determine what you decide. Rather, *you* do that. If they did it, then your decision would be neither self-determined nor the first member of a causal chain initiated by you. You may act on the basis of reasons, but you are not merely acted upon by them. You may take them into account as you deliberate about what to do; but when you make a free decision, only you can causally determine what that decision shall be.

This, then, is the agency theory. It lays out a route between the absurdity of simple indeterminism and the unacceptable implications of the determinist thesis that causal chains are infinitely long. The agent is the cause of its decisions (thereby preventing them from being uncaused) and initiates causal chains which begin with those decisions. This is a theory that may strike us as enormously appealing, for it offers an explanation of our unshakeable conviction that we are free beings, capable of acting other than as we do.

Consider once more the lost wallet case. You have a powerful desire to keep it, along with a keen sense of a moral duty to return it. Desire clashes with duty. Suppose that after considerable deliberation you choose to go with your desire. What is incontestably clear to you at this moment is (1) that it is *you* who chooses, that this choosing is genuinely *your* act rather than some accidental happening or the activity of something not identical to you, and (2) that even though you didn't you *could have* risen to the occasion and done what you were morally obliged to do. Someone looking in from the outside may believe that you were causally determined to go with your desire, that given such a desire along with the other antecedent conditions, there is nothing else you could have done. But *you* could not be convinced of this, and you have the unique perspective of the inner observer. What is happening here is introspectively available only to you. Indeed, you may retort that no *theory* that clashes head-on with what is introspectively evident to you has any credibility. Anything evident to you in this way, you may insist, must be regarded as a *datum* that any credible theory must somehow accommodate. Herein lies the enormous appeal of the agency theory, for it not only accommodates this datum but interprets it to be just what it appears to be.

The agency theory has its critics, however. Some would argue that it doesn't really avoid indeterminism after all. It may appear to do so, but in fact does not. A critic may argue that if in some set of circumstances you could have decided to do something other than what you actually did even though there would have been no change in any of the circumstances affecting you at the time—that is, no change either in any of the external circumstances or in any of your beliefs, desires, inclinations, emotions, thought processes, etc.—then what you do is causally detached from all these circumstances. In other words, if you could have engaged in some alternative course of action, then the alternative that actually occurs is random relative to the other alternatives supposedly available to you. But if your so-called free decision was a random event, then it was not within your control. Obviously, if this objection can be sustained, the agency theory collapses.

RATIONAL DETERMINATION

The problem is to provide a coherent account of how the course of action you decide to take was within your control even though none of the factors that influenced your decision—e.g., your consideration of reasons and your weighing of alternative courses of action, along with your current beliefs, desires, inclinations, and brain states—causally determined it and thereby prevented you from doing anything else. Perhaps what is needed here is a notion of rational (as opposed to causal) determination—a determination in accordance with the laws of rationality rather than causal laws. There is influence but without causal necessitation. The control you exercise is a "rational" control that exists in virtue of your awareness of various alternative courses of action open to you, in conjunction with reasons for and against taking each alternative. The influence that your mental states—in particular, your awareness of the alternatives and your deliberation about them—have on you prevents your decision from taking place in a vacuum and thereby prevents the action you bring about from being a purely random event. But this influence is weaker than causal determination; it does not amount to a causally sufficient condition for your choosing as you did. Your choosing some other alternative was causally possible. To repeat, what we have here is what we might call rational determination—an influence on the agent that is neither causal determination nor non-determination (i.e., indeterminism) and that leaves room for (causal) control by the agent. It is consistent with our concept of an agent as a self-moving being. The agent moves (i.e., causes) itself to act, not in a random manner, but in accordance with the laws of rationality.

The charge that the agency theory cannot avoid indeterminism now seems to be effectively met. The critic making the charge would have us believe that if in some set of circumstances you could have decided to do something other than what you actually did even though all the circumstances, both external and internal, remain exactly as they were in the actual situation, then your so-called free action would be causally severed from these circumstances and thus would be a chance or random occurrence. As a chance occurrence, it would not only be inexplicable but would be something for which you are not morally responsible. But the critic seems to be simply presuming that the absence of causal necessitation is also the absence of causal influence and that the only adequate explanation of a choice is of the type that explains why *only that choice* could have been made, given the set of relevant external and internal circumstances in existence at the moment of choosing. The agency theorist, however, is in a position to reply that explanations of the type demanded by the critic—explanations appealing to factors that necessitate an outcome and thus allow a fully informed observer to predict the outcome with certainty—*are* precluded by the agency theory, but that this fact does not render the theory implausible, much less incoherent. For the agency theorist offers a different type of explanation of the behaviors that are to count as our free actions.

In the agency theory (or at least the form of it that we are considering), a free action is the freely initiated behavior of an agent motivated by a consideration of certain reasons for so acting. The action is not a chance occurrence; it is controlled by the agent and the control is causal. Reasons influence the action, but do not cause it. By themselves they do not yield an explanation of the action. Reasons get linked up with action only by way of the agent's free exercise of his causal capacity. The explanatory scheme of the agency theory requires both the agent-causal initiation of an action and the presence of consciously considered reasons for acting.

Perhaps there are insuperable problems involved in any attempt to defend an agency theory within a materialist framework. We would have to wonder what physical particular or system of physical elements could possibly qualify as an agent. For there are good reasons to believe that nothing physical could qualify as a basic or irreducible subject of consciousness.[1] Yet an agent must be a subject of consciousness, whatever else is held to be true of it. Indeed, it seems appropriate to speak of a subject-*agent*. At any rate, such problems, along with those that may arise for the dual-aspect theorist,[2] do not arise for us, given the apparent strength of the case we have previously established for believing that the self exists as a subject of conscious states.

It seems, then, that armed with a coherent conception of an agent and the notion of rational determination, or influence by reasons, we have at least the rudiments of an understanding of how an agent's deciding to take a certain course of action rather than some alternative one is neither causally determined nor a random event. At any rate, let us suppose that we do. Then what problems, if any, might we have in accepting the agency theory? First, if our actions are not causally determined, then they would not be knowable in their entirety prior to their occurrence, i.e., they would not be completely predictable. Though this consequence accords well with our prescientific conviction that we could have acted other than we did, it imposes a limit on the reach of any science of human behavior. Such science could never be complete if completeness requires complete predictability—a consequence that may strike many as not only in conflict with science but impossible to accommodate within an entirely naturalistic understanding of the world. Secondly, if as agents we act upon our brains, then this apparently implies that no physical science of the brain can yield a total understanding of brain activity, even if that science is complete. Brains would be, in that respect, unique among physical items, and this may seem impossible to believe. Thirdly, the agency theory appeals to entities that may seem inexplicably strange. The subject of experience again appears to be a very remarkable being. Its apparent indivisibility is a feature we have already noted in our reflections about the self. This feature by itself may give us pause, for both minds (understood as collections of experiences) and bodies are composite things. But now we see that if the subject is an agent (and it seems to be the only thing that could be), it is a self-moving being—a being who *acts* instead of one who is merely acted upon. And this feature would render it absolutely unique in nature. Though some events on the quantum level may be uncaused, only an agent *causes itself* to act in one way rather than another, without being caused to do so. A subject of experience that is also a self-moving being is a peculiar entity indeed. And if that is what we are, then we may well be the most mysterious things we encounter in a deeply mysterious world.

QUESTIONS FOR FURTHER THOUGHT

1. Is it true that there really are no alternative courses of action open to you—that at this moment you cannot decide either to continue to read or to close this book and, say, watch television? Even if it is true, can you *believe* it?

2. Do you act freely simply when you do what you want to do, even if you could not have done anything else? Should we think of freedom as requiring anything more than this?

3. If you are an agent who initiates causal chains by acting on your brain, then some of your brain states will be caused in this way rather than by prior brain states. Does this imply that what goes on in your brain could never be entirely understood by any physical science of the brain, even if that science were complete? If so, does this render the agency theory unacceptable?

4. What does the agency theory imply about what you are? Does it imply that you are neither your body nor your mind?

5. Can you accept the agency theory and also be a materialist? Can we conceive of a material entity (perhaps the brain or some part of it) or some function of a system of material entities that might be identified as an agent? If it seems that we can, would we be able to specify, in a non-arbitrary manner, which material item the agent is supposed to be?

6. Can the notion of a self-moving being—a being that can act without being acted upon—survive careful scrutiny? Is an ultimate account of agent-causation likely to be more problematic than a comparable account of any other kind of causation?

8

VALUE and MORALITY

We have been, for the most part, trying to approach the world in a value-neutral way. We have attempted to provide a description of its most general or fundamental features, along with how we come to know about it and what must be true of us for our overall account to make most sense. But this approach is incomplete in that it ignores the fact that our experience of the world is *not* value-neutral. Many of the items in the world and much of what happens in it *matter* to us. We do not merely take note of what is happening; we also care about it and often hope for one outcome rather than another. We speak of the good and the bad, of the beautiful and the ugly, and of right and wrong. In so doing, we are making value judgments. But how is this activity to be understood? What is value, and how is it to be fit into our general understanding of the world? Is the value that we seem to find in things actually *in them*, independently of us? The shape and size of a gold bar are properties that it has independently of us. But would we wish to say the same of its preciousness, that is, of its *value*? Perhaps we are saying more about ourselves—our attitudes, feelings, desires, preferences, etc.—than about the things to which we attribute value.

Closely related to questions about the nature of value are questions about the foundation and justification of our value judgments. These questions are especially important when raised about moral value, about matters of right and wrong. What is the basis for our distinction between right and wrong? Are there principles or standards that may be used to determine the correctness of a moral judgment or to show that an action is immoral? If there are, are they such that an appeal to them should settle, or at least mitigate, such controversial issues as those concerning the morality of abortion, capital punishment, and euthanasia? Though it may seem clear that there are such principles, we are hardly entitled to assume that we know what they are until we inquire into their basis and see what it is that makes them worthy as guides to determining how we should conduct ourselves. The principles themselves may turn out to be abstract and general, but we must not lose sight of the fact that the study of morality is ultimately concerned with the concrete and practical task of influencing and guiding our action.

Whatever value turns out to be, it certainly pervades our lives. To confirm this we need do no more than listen to our speech. In a great deal of our speech we find ourselves saying of something or other that it is good or bad, or better or worse than something else. Many of these utterances are concerned with moral goodness, or with the morality of some action or practice, such as abortion. But others have nothing to do with morality. When we say of a painting or a musical composition that it is a good work of art, we certainly don't mean *morally* good. We are speaking of beauty—a variety of *aesthetic* value. We find it in nature, e.g., in a beautiful sunset, as well as in our own creations. This is the sort of value involved in matters of taste. We give expression to it when we say of something that it has a good taste or aroma, or, less frequently, that it has "a good feel to it," as we might say upon touching a silk shirt. But there are other goods that are neither moral nor aesthetic—health, for example. Though one's health is of great value, it is not valuable in either the moral or aesthetic sense, though, of course, it is the condition for participating in or enjoying these other goods. So there is a variety of different kinds of value. Yet they apparently have something in common in virtue of which they are values rather than something else. To find out what that something is, is to answer our question about the nature of value and to put ourselves in a position to see how value may be fit into our overall conception of reality.

THE SUBJECTIVITY OF VALUE

As we try to understand how value fits into our ontology or general theory of reality, questions about whether it has any reality independently of us become central. Our language suggests that it does. When we say of something that it is good (or that it is bad), our speech suggests that the object referred to (say, an apple) has the property of being good (that is, of having a good taste), and that it has this property independently of us, just as it independently has properties of shape and size. This suggestion of a property that is possessed independently of us seems somewhat stronger when we say of a painting or some scene in nature that it is beautiful. Clearly, what this *language* suggests, if not the speaker as well, is that the object has in itself the property of being beautiful.

But perhaps the suggestion that things have value (positive or negative) in themselves independently of us becomes most conspicuous in the case of those involving *moral* value. When we consider some heinous act—an act of torturing someone, for example—we may be inclined to declare that such an act is not only horribly wrong but *intrinsically* wrong, that is, wrong in itself, independent of the attitudes and feelings of all sentient beings. But this, apparently, would be a mistake. Value, whether positive or negative, has no reality apart from an evaluator. Important as the things we value are to us, the value we attribute to them is apparently not part of the fabric of the world as it is in itself, distinct from anyone's experience of it.

This conclusion that there can be no value in a world devoid of beings who have feelings, cares, and desires is powerfully supported by thought-experiments in which we imagine such a world. First let us consider a world just like the actual one except that it is totally devoid of life. There is nothing in it capable of having any experience. What comes to mind is an environment like that of the moon. There are material objects and material processes taking place, but it seems clear that nothing would be good or bad, right or wrong, or beautiful or ugly. The existence of value depends on the existence of experience.

But not just any sort of experience or consciousness will suffice. To see this, consider a world in which there are conscious rational beings that resemble machines in that they are completely devoid of what in us is the affective/volitional aspect of our nature. They have no feelings, no desires, no will to do anything. They are aware of themselves and perceive what is happening around them, and their capacity to acquire knowledge and reason from it is equal to our own. But they have no cares or concerns; nothing matters to them. If it begins to rain, they will not bother to take shelter, even if the rain damages them. They have no desire to do anything or to avoid anything. If they are on a collision course with something that could destroy them, they would be aware of the impending collision but would do nothing to avoid it. For it would not matter to them if they were severely damaged or even destroyed. If nothing matters to them, then even that wouldn't matter.

Obviously, such beings would strike us as extremely peculiar. But this reaction merely underlines how profoundly we are affected by the affective/volitional aspect of our nature. We may seem to have difficulty imagining a conscious rational being that perceives its environment without taking any interest in what is going on around it or even in what happens to itself. But if we do, we are probably thinking of it as a highly evolved animal, that is, as a conscious being adapted to living in a potentially dangerous environment. This is understandable, for all the perceivers known to us are animals. And it does seem very difficult to imagine a highly advanced animal that has no interests, desires, concerns, or purposes. On the other hand, if we think of these beings as essentially machines capable of perceiving their environment and drawing inferences from what they perceive, there is no longer any difficulty at all in conceiving of them as devoid of feeling and will. Now the only difficulty is in viewing a machine as a conscious perceiver. But any such difficulty is surely diminished by our experience with computers. There is hardly any more difficulty in seeing how consciousness could come to be associated with a non-protoplasmic system such as a computer than there is in seeing how it could have come to be associated with our brains.

Since nothing matters to these beings, nothing would seem good or bad to them. But theirs is the *only* standpoint; there is no other from which things might seem to be different. Thus nothing would *be* either good or bad. If they do not value anything, then there would be no value in their world. For it seems clear that nothing can be of value without being of value *to* someone.

So although the existence of a conscious being is necessary for the existence of value, this is not a sufficient condition. What else is needed is that this being should have feelings, concerns, desires, and purposes. There must be an affective/volitional aspect to its nature. With the existence of even one such being, value comes into the world. Now there is good and bad, but it exists only in relation to this being. What is good furthers its interests, satisfies its desires, fulfills its purposes. What is bad does just the opposite: It is what disappoints, negates, frustrates, prevents fulfillment. It is what injures or harms, broadly understood. In short, the good is what promotes this being's *enjoyment*; the bad is what leads to its *suffering*. There could be no other value standard in a world containing only a single sentient being. In particular, there is no basis for a further distinction between what is good for it and what is good as measured by some higher standard. For the distinction between good and bad arises in the first place only in relation to that solitary being's desires and purposes.

Though good and bad exist in a world of a solitary sentient being, no morality has yet entered the picture. There can be no moral obligation in such a world because there is no one to whom this being could have such an obligation. It cannot be morally obligated to itself, and there isn't anyone else. When it acts to further its own interests, it will bring about what is good in its world, but it is not morally obliged to act in that way. It may fail to act in its own best interest, perhaps out of ignorance, but it does not thereby engage in any moral wrongdoing. For it does not interfere with the interest of anyone else. Since there is no one else to be injured or to have interests that may conflict with its own, there can be no occasion for its actions to be either morally right or morally wrong. The notions of right and wrong pertain to conduct in relation to others.

The possibility of moral and immoral behavior arises, however, upon the arrival of a second sentient being. Since each will have its own desires, aims, and interests, the possibility of conflict arises. Each may desire something that cannot be possessed by both. Now it is possible for one to hinder or prevent the satisfaction of the desires or the fulfillment of the purposes of the other. On the other hand, there is also the opportunity for cooperation. By helping each other they may be able to render both of their lives more secure and more fulfilling than would have been possible via their individual efforts. In any case, morality enters the picture with the opportunity they now have to help or to harm, or to refrain from harming, each other.

Though we have arrived at an answer to our questions about the nature of value in general, we need to look more closely at moral value. For, as we noted earlier, moral value, as reflected in our moral judgments, is of special concern to us. Of course, our conclusions about value in general will likely have important implications for what we should say about moral value, and, consequently, about moral judgments and moral principles as well. So let us take stock of where we are.

We have argued that values are not intrinsic to the universe, that is, not part of it as it exists independently of us. Rather, they are contributed by us, as part of our response to what we encounter. They do not exist independently of our attitudes, feelings, and preferences. And so our talk about the value of things should not be understood to be descriptions of those things, as statements about their shape and size would be. Instead, they give expression to our feelings and attitudes concerning those things. We have, in effect, argued for a view that we might call "value subjectivism." Value is a contribution of the subject of experience and is not to be found in the object to which it is attributed—at least not as that object is in itself, independently of the subject of experience. Value objectivism, on the other hand, would have us believe that value statements *do* describe the objects to which they refer. They describe by making reference to its "value properties." A beautiful painting, for example, has the value property of being beautiful, just as it has the properties of shape and size. Of course, the value property is quite different from these other, value-neutral properties. Nevertheless, they are alike in that all are possessed by the object as it is in itself, independent of anyone's experience of it.

An important consequence of value objectivism is that value utterances are either true or false. A value statement is true if it attributes to an object a value property which that object actually has, and false if it does not. And so in the case of a value judgment (e.g., This painting is beautiful) and its negation (This painting is not beautiful), one must be true and the other false. They are just like factual claims in this respect. Also, *knowledge* of value is possible in a straightforward sense. For knowledge is knowledge of *truth*; and in the objectivist view, there is a truth to be known in matters of value.

In embracing value subjectivism we are, of course, committed to denying this consequence. Value judgments are neither true nor false, at least not in the sense suggested above; for they do not ascribe properties to things as they are independently of the feelings, preferences, and attitudes of the subject making the judgments. Perhaps our denial that our value judgments—e.g., that torture is morally wrong, that Jesus Christ was a good person, or that the Mona Lisa is a beautiful painting—are either true or false should make us feel uneasy. For this is to deny that the Mona Lisa, for example, actually has the property of being beautiful. However, we are *not* denying (indeed, we are affirming) that it actually has a set of properties that affect us in such a way that we speak of its beauty. Its having those properties *is* a matter of fact. It has them independently of us. It is also a matter of fact that something having those properties affects beings of our nature in a certain characteristic way. But what we might call the beauty itself, or the property of being beautiful, is not in the object itself. Indeed, we might wonder what one could mean in saying that it is, other than that the object has a capacity to elicit a certain sort of response in *us*. But that, of course, is the subjectivist view.

We should also add in defense of subjectivism that if questions about value were, as objectivism implies, like scientific questions and other questions about what the facts are, then we should have at the very least a conception of what evidence, if we had it, would answer them. Issues about what the facts are *do* get settled, often conclusively, as in the case of the issue of whether heavier objects fall faster than lighter ones (they don't); and even in the case of those that are very much unsettled, we generally have a good grasp of what evidence *would* settle them. But value issues seem radically different in this respect. Consider a matter of taste—more specifically, whether chocolate tastes better than peppermint. Perhaps we ordinarily refrain from debating such matters, but we wouldn't be too surprised if someone did. In any case, if we don't, that is not because we are in complete agreement but because we ordinarily have little or no motivation to try to get others to agree with our value judgments about taste. But suppose this did become an issue that we wished to settle. Could we do it? Having the chocolate lovers and the peppermint lovers describe to each other what it is about chocolate or peppermint that made them like it, assuming they were able to do this, would be of no avail. Nor would taking a poll. A poll may tell us that there are more chocolate lovers, but this information would do nothing to persuade the peppermint lovers that chocolate tastes better than peppermint. Our problem here is not so much that we have no idea of any possible evidence that would settle this issue. Instead, we apparently come to see that no evidence *could* settle it, as the subjectivist has insisted all along.

Since the subjectivist is apparently correct in contending that value exists only in the presence of an evaluator, we might expect what is valued, i.e., the object of value, to vary considerably from person to person. To a great extent, this is what we find, particularly in the realm of taste. There is widespread disagreement even in the realm of moral value, where disagreement may have very serious consequences. At the same time, there appears to be substantial agreement on a more fundamental level. While there may be a great deal of disagreement about whether chocolate tastes better than peppermint, there is, one would think, almost universal agreement that both taste better than crankcase oil. Similarly, we should expect to find near universal agreement that a wild rose smells better (has a more pleasing aroma) than a skunk or a partially decomposed animal carcass. And while we may never secure widespread agreement about the morality of abortion or capital punishment, there is such agreement that torturing someone and betraying one's friends are morally wrong.

The fact that there is widespread moral agreement on the most fundamental level turns out to be a godsend for us. One has to wonder if we could have survived, let alone prospered, as a species without it. For it motivates and guides our search for universal moral principles and makes possible the widespread conviction that we *should* treat each other in accordance with these principles, even when we don't. If we did not share a concern for our own well-being and to avoid pain and suffering as much as possible, along with the capacity to recognize that others are like us in these respects, we would lack the motivation to restrict our behavior to principles of action that further these concerns.

Though it is fortunate for us that there is substantial agreement on a fundamental level, such agreement may also seem to weigh against the subjectivist position we have taken. For we may be reminding ourselves of the fact that considerable agreement is what we should expect to find if value objectivism were true. If values are properties of the things we value, as being round is ordinarily a property of things we see as round, then of course there should be considerable agreement with respect to matters of value (even if, as an objectivist may claim, values are much more difficult than shapes to accurately detect), just as we have little disagreement about the shapes of things we perceive.

But there really is no problem lurking here for the subjectivist, nor is there any help for the objectivist. The extent to which we agree in our value judgments is fully explained by the fact that we share a common human nature, at least with respect to its physical basis. We have very similar nervous systems and sense organs, and the character of our experience is heavily if not totally dependent upon them. Thus it is not at all surprising that we agree in our value judgment that, for example, the scent of the wild rose is better than the odor of rotting flesh. We are merely expressing an experiential effect of a nervous system of the human kind.

It appears, then, that value subjectivism is the view that expresses the truth about values.[1] With this in mind, let us return to our focus on morality. The first point to note is that value subjectivism implies moral subjectivism. For moral judgments are value judgments, and value subjectivism is a general theory about the nature of all value. Thus we are committed to the view that our moral judgments about persons and their actions are not descriptions of them but expressions of our attitudes and feelings concerning them. Such judgments are not judgments about what the truth is; they are neither true nor false. This, however, does not diminish their significance. They are of fundamental importance; and, as we shall see, though they are rooted in feeling, knowledge of fact and the employment of reason are deeply involved in moral deliberation.

PREFERENCE AND THE MORAL POINT OF VIEW

We have already answered, at least implicitly, some very general questions about morality. Morally right action is action that brings about, or is intended to bring about, what is good for others as well as for oneself, more specifically, that which tends to maximize the production of good and minimize the production of harm or evil; and what is intrinsically good (i.e., good for its own sake) are feelings of enjoyment, satisfaction, contentment, well-being, etc. Accordingly, what is intrinsically bad are feelings of suffering, frustration, discontentment, and misery. Perhaps there are other intrinsic goods—knowledge and virtue, for example. But we need not try to formulate a complete list.

We have also arrived at a partial answer to the question as to what a moral judgment *is*. Like any other value judgment, it is an expression of attitude, preference, or feeling. But the preference is of a special type; it pertains to conduct—to how people treat one another. Furthermore, unlike an expression of an ordinary personal preference, which expresses one's personal interests, likes, or dislikes with no intent to persuade others to share them, a moral judgment expresses how one would like to see everyone treat one another. Since it has implications for the conduct and preferences of everyone else, it must be interpreted as an attempt to influence the attitudes and preferences of others.

Suppose, for example, that you believe capital punishment to be morally wrong under all circumstances. What are you doing when you give expression to this belief? According to our analysis, you are expressing your feeling of disapproval of this practice. But this is not all you are doing. You are also implying that *everyone* ought to disapprove of it—that it is a form of conduct *no one* should engage in. This explains why moral judgments, unlike judgments of taste, very often spark controversy. If they were simple expressions of interest or taste, they would not appear to be attempts to persuade others, nor would they so frequently elicit disagreement and debate.

Though the preference you are expressing is, of course, one of yours, it is impersonal in the sense that it is not intended to reflect the particular circumstances that bear upon you. It results from your attempt to take the moral point of view—a viewpoint from which you give yourself no special consideration, viewing your own interests and desires on a par with those of everyone else, as you contemplate how it would be if everyone were to act in accordance with a certain rule or principle. Though your interests, feelings, and desires are very important to you when you regard them from your own point of view (from the inside, so to speak), you are also capable of seeing them from a more general point of view in which you view yourself from the outside as just one particular person among others. From this general viewpoint, you see that your own interests, feelings, desires, etc. are no more and no less important than those of anyone else. When you take this point of view, employ it in an impartial survey of the human condition, and then express a preference as to the rules or principles you would like to see everyone follow in their treatment of one another, you are expressing a preference from the moral point of view. You are making a moral judgment. To make a moral judgment is to express a moral preference which, in turn, is to express a preference from the moral point of view.

Three important questions remain unanswered at this point in our study of moral value. First, what moral rules or principles might emerge from our taking the moral point of view? Does taking this point of view yield principles of conduct that not only coincide with our pre-philosophic intuitions about what is morally right but also fit well with our philosophic deliberations about the nature of value and morality — principles that give expression to those very general or fundamental moral preferences about which there is widespread agreement? If so, what are they? What principles have been offered by intelligent people who have thought carefully about this matter?

Secondly, do these moral principles have universal application? Is what is morally right and morally wrong the same for everyone regardless of time, place, society, or culture? Or, on the other hand, does what is morally right vary from culture to culture, or from one time to another within a given society or culture?

Thirdly, why should we take the moral point of view at all? Instead, why not simply focus exclusively on the satisfaction of our own needs and desires? Why should we concern ourselves with the feelings, desires, and preferences of others? Or, at any rate, what should we say to someone who seriously raises such questions?

UTILITARIANISM

With respect to our first question, we might begin by considering an extremely influential moral maxim. It has been called the "greatest happiness principle," and may be expressed as follows: Every morally relevant action, whether of a private individual or of a governing body, ought to be such as to promote the greatest happiness of the greatest number of people. The view embracing this principle has been termed utilitarianism, probably because its founder, Jeremy Bentham, referred to this principle as the principle of utility.[2]

It is not difficult to see why this principle is so appealing. Since happiness is clearly an intrinsic good, acting in accordance with this principle would maximize the production of something that we all vigorously, and sometimes desperately, seek—something that is undeniably of great value. Also, this principle embodies the impartiality central to the moral point of view. The individual who follows this principle when engaged in moral deliberation assesses the value of his own happiness from the outside, as having no more and no less importance than the happiness of any other person who may be affected by the outcome. The happiness of each is weighed on the same scale, as our moral intuitions require.

Unfortunately, there are serious difficulties standing in the way of accepting this principle. To begin with, there is the practical difficulty of applying it. Predicting what course of action will actually result in the greatest amount of happiness may be very difficult in many situations. Of course, what we are trying to apply is a very general principle, and a utilitarian may argue that we are merely referring to a problem inherent in the application of any general principle. Though the general principle doesn't tell us what to do in any particular instance, we may nevertheless be able to apply it to the case in question by acquiring sufficient information about the case and its context to know what the probable consequences of the various alternative courses of action will be. At any rate, the utilitarian can point out to us that this principle doesn't somehow guarantee our ability to do the right thing. Rather, it is a very general characterization of what right action *is*—a characterization which, when kept in mind and conscientiously employed, will help us do the right thing most of the time.

But another problem comes into view when we see that one may carry out his intention to fulfill the principle and yet fail to fulfill it. Contrary to his intention, his course of action turned out not to be the best one he could have taken. As things turned out, another would have resulted in more happiness for more people. This disparity could end up being extreme. The best of intentions could conceivably lead to disastrous consequences. And if this happened, there could be no escape from the conclusion that one's action was morally wrong. For utilitarianism is a *consequentialist* theory; and according to such theories, consequences are the only relevant factors to be considered in determining whether what one did was morally right. The intentions, motives, and feelings of the agent really make no difference, or at any rate, no difference that extends beyond the consequences of the action they prompt. And this may make us feel uncomfortable.

The Deontological Critique of Utilitarianism

Immanuel Kant, the great German philosopher who rejected all consequentialist theories, held that the only thing that is good without qualification is a good *will*. Other traits, such as intelligence and perseverance, are good only if they occur in conjunction with it. And it remains desirable even if it fails to yield actions having desirable consequences. Kant went on to argue that consequences are *not* what makes an action right or wrong; the morally decisive factor is the *principle* by which one acts. Since one's will or intention is reflected in this principle, one's intentions have moral significance independently of what actually happens. And they should have. If someone acts responsibly and with the best of intentions only to see that action lead to unintended results, we would certainly hold that the person's intentions should enter into, if not determine, our judgment as to the morality of the action.

Kant is regarded as a deontologist in moral philosophy. A deontologist maintains that what makes a right action right is not, or at least is not entirely, a function of the amount of good that would result from performing it. In this view, certain principles, notably of justice and honesty, prescribe actions that are right even if more evil than good would result from performing those actions. In accordance with the principle of justice or fairness, a deontologist may hold, as Kant did, that it is always wrong to treat people merely as a means to some end not involving them. The deontologist would argue that people have intrinsic value and should be regarded as intrinsically valuable ends in themselves. One should never use them as *means only*, even if doing so should result in more good than evil. Let us keep in mind these concerns of the deontologist as we proceed with our examination of utilitarianism.

Another problem with utilitarianism as we have formulated it, and as it is usually formulated, is its assumption that happiness is the only intrinsic good. But it is far from obvious that this is so. Perhaps knowledge, autonomy, dignity, liberty, the moral virtues, or all of these are good in themselves, independent of the happiness to which they may lead. However, we can be utilitarians without making this assumption; we can reformulate the utilitarian principle by saying simply that one should always act in such a way as to bring about the greatest *good* for the greatest number of people. Or, since our actions usually have better consequences for some people than for others, we might formulate it as follows: One should always do that which will bring about the greatest balance of good over bad consequences for the greatest number. In either case, we have formulated the principle without committing ourselves on the issue as to which consequences are to be considered intrinsically good. So this may not be a serious problem for the utilitarian.

A much more serious problem comes into view when we see that the utilitarian puts the emphasis on the greatest *good* rather than on the greatest *number*. For this commits him to approve of practices that strike us as profoundly unjust. Suppose that the overall balance of good over bad consequences could be increased in a certain society by taking some of the possessions of 5 percent of the population and giving them to the other 95 percent. Though the 5 percent are deserving of all the possessions that are to be taken and the 95 percent don't deserve to get them, the utilitarian nevertheless seems to be committed to the position that this redistribution should be done—that it is the morally right thing to do. But most of us would find this action morally offensive, thereby indicating that sometimes we value a practice, such as not taking things from people who deserve to have them, not because it maximizes happiness or other intrinsic goods, if there are any others, but simply because, as the deontologist would emphasize, it is *fair*. Can the utilitarian explain this?

Even this, however, does not portray the full depth of the utilitarian's problem. For he may be unable to avoid approving of actions that conflict with moral beliefs that seem absolutely fundamental. Some of the most detestable actions that we can imagine consist in deliberately sacrificing the liberty or even the lives of innocent members of a group to increase the happiness of the others. It is not difficult to imagine a scenario in which the general good of a society, at least when understood as happiness, is increased through the enslavement of a small minority. Though the slaves may be miserable, their labor allows a great many others to attain a higher level of happiness (or to possess other intrinsic goods, if there are any, to a greater degree) than would have been possible without their enslavement. The additional good thereby made possible outweighs the negative value of the suffering and/or deprivation experienced by the slaves, so that the overall balance of good over bad consequences is significantly greater than what it would have been in a slave-free society. If such a scenario is possible, as it surely seems to be, then the utilitarian seems forced to embrace the conclusion that, under some circumstances, slavery would be a morally acceptable practice. But it seems evident that slavery is morally unacceptable if anything is. What reply is the utilitarian able to give?

Perhaps a utilitarian who rejects the assumption that happiness is the only intrinsic good would argue that our scenario may seem to be a possible state of affairs but is really not. Slavery, human sacrifice, torture, and other equally repugnant practices generate so much of negative value that the balance of good over bad consequences could never be greater in a society that permitted such things than in a similar one that didn't. Perhaps so, but even if liberty is taken to be an intrinsic good, it is difficult to see how this could be shown without violating the utilitarian principle. Since happiness must be recognized as an intrinsic good in any account, the challenge is to show that the increased happiness of a great many people could not possibly outweigh the negative value of the unhappiness and loss of liberty suffered by a few. Besides, as the philosopher John Rawls has noted, there surely seems to be something wrong with a moral view that would have us *even consider* whether there are conditions under which slavery would be a morally acceptable practice, irrespective of what further examination would reveal about the matter.[3]

In any case, the mainstream utilitarian committed to the greatest happiness principle would apparently have to concede that there are conditions under which slavery and other less extreme breaches of justice would turn out to be morally acceptable practices. Then, to make such a position seem plausible, he would have no alternative but to try to dispel our powerful aversion to practices that strike us as radically unjust by arguing that we are confused about what is of fundamental value and the relation that the fundamentally valuable has to such practices. Treating people in a just and fair manner is indeed a valuable practice—one in which a morally enlightened society will engage. But this practice is not valuable in itself, for its own sake, as the deontologist maintains. Rather, its value consists in its tendency to maximize happiness. The utilitarian may emphasize this point by asking us what we would find so wrong about slavery, for example, if it made no one unhappy. He will also argue that when we take the long-range consequences of an unjust practice into account, considering such sources of unhappiness as the erosion of the respect for the rights of others and the worry of the morally sensitive in virtue of their awareness that they could just as well have been the ones unjustly treated, we come to see how unlikely it is that some particular unjust practice would in fact maximize happiness over the long term. Still, he must concede that there are circumstances in which justice will conflict with happiness. And so in the end he must also concede that in such circumstances, rare though they may be, his utilitarian commitment requires him to sacrifice justice for the sake of happiness. But this is a concession to be avoided if at all possible. Let us see if we can arrive at a position that allows us to avoid the need to make such a concession and to accommodate, as best we can, the moral insight of the deontologist.

A SYNTHESIS OF UTILITARIANISM AND DEONTOLOGY

The problem with utilitarianism is that it doesn't guarantee every individual the right to fair or just treatment. The utilitarian principle must be altered or supplemented in such a way as to guarantee this right. The right to fair treatment is violated when we treat others merely as a means to an end from which they derive no benefit, such as the greater good of others. It is surely violated in the case of someone who is enslaved, tortured, or treated in some other morally outrageous manner, supposedly for the sake of the common good. So in an attempt to guarantee that no one will be treated in such ways, we must take seriously the deontological maxim that we never treat others as means only, i.e., never violate their moral right to be treated as intrinsically valuable ends in themselves. We see that we would never wish to be treated merely as means to an end from which we would obtain no benefit. When we take note of our concern for our own welfare, we have no doubt that we regard ourselves as intrinsically valuable ends and that we have a moral right to be treated as such. And so we treat others as moral equals, refusing to treat them in those ways in which we would deem it immoral for them to treat us. Out of these considerations we can derive a principle or test for right action. To acknowledge the moral equality of others is to approve of their acting as we do when they are in a situation similar to our own. Not to do so is to give ourselves special status, and that is to violate the principle of the moral equality of all persons. Consequently, a test for right action is a universalizability test: Your action has passed the moral test if it is something you would judge to be right for anyone to perform in your circumstances. To paraphrase Kant, your action should be such that you could will the principle by which you act to become a universal law.

We would still take utilitarian concerns into account. But it appears that we should not be utilitarians if subscribing to the greatest happiness principle, or even the greatest *good* principle, does not allow us to respect the principle of the moral equality of all persons. Perhaps a utilitarian view that would allow this could be worked out, but it's difficult to see how. For if we share the deontologist's resolve never to treat others as means only, then we must acknowledge that the greatest happiness principle, and apparently the greatest good principle as well, will sometimes have to be overridden by other moral considerations—deontological concerns that appear to be incompatible with the utilitarian view that the morality of an action is to be determined solely by its consequences.

The problem before us now is how we might retain what is so appealing about utilitarianism without rejecting what is fundamental to the deontological view. Can what is most appealing in each view be fitted together into a single unified view? The problem would be diminished considerably if we were justified in simply taking the deontological principle (that we should never treat others as means only) as fundamental and the utilitarian principle as subordinate—as a principle of action that must be overridden if in conflict with a fundamental one. The difficulty with such an approach, however, is that the two principles seem to be on a par in that taking either as the one to be followed in all imaginable situations of moral significance sometimes leads to actions that may strike us as morally unacceptable, if not outrageous from a moral point of view

We have already noted how an exclusive focus on consequences and an allegiance to the greatest happiness principle may lead one to condone the sacrifice of innocent victims for the greater good of the many. What we should note now is that an unwavering allegiance to the deontological principle of justice leads to the judgment that it is morally correct for everyone in certain extreme situations to perish if the majority can be saved only by using someone merely as a means to the end of saving them. Lifeboat-type examples come to mind. Imagine that seven people are in a six-person lifeboat that is about to sink and drown all seven, but would take six to safety if one were sacrificed. Suppose that no one volunteers to be the one to die by jumping into the sea even though each person realizes that all will die if no one voluntarily jumps or is thrown overboard by the others. Suppose further that they cannot all agree on a process by which the person to be sacrificed is to be determined, with the result that whoever is selected will be an unwilling victim. Finally, suppose that there is no third alternative. For example, they cannot take turns in the water by swimming, using flotation devices, or clinging to the outside of the boat, since the water is too cold. Thus there are only two alternatives: either one person will involuntarily perish, or all will.

In such a dire, though unlikely, set of circumstances, the utilitarian position may well strike us, or most of us, as by far the more appealing one, as much more in accord with our intuitions about what the morally best course of action would be. For the utilitarian is able to sanction the saving of six people, whereas the deontologist's moral directive leads to the conclusion that the perishing of all seven is unavoidable if no one can be used as means only, regardless of the circumstances. The deontological position does have some appeal. An unwavering commitment to the high moral principle that people should never be used as means only is certainly worthy of respect, if not admiration. Nevertheless, our lifeboat case shows that the application of this principle is sometimes morally questionable at best. In this case, the utilitarian principle has the edge, if it is not the clear winner in the moral contest.

The main reason why the utilitarian position seems to so many to be the preferable one to take in the lifeboat case is not difficult to discern. It is difficult to consider this case without focusing on the *consequences* of the alternative courses of action; and if consequences are to be used to determine the morally right course of action in this case, then, of course, the utilitarian position is certainly the morally preferable one. For saving six is a much better consequence than saving no one. Moreover, a focus on the consequences seems quite appropriate, as they arguably have a moral significance that outweighs the other moral considerations. If this is so, we have reached the conclusion that the deontological position, like utilitarianism, fails to specify the morally correct course of action in every imaginable case.

The need to provide some sort of synthesis of utilitarianism and deontology should now be evident, if it was not so earlier. The extent to which a synthesis can be accomplished is limited, however, since the views yield conflicting results in a variety of situations; and so the realistic aim should be to capture in a single (internally consistent) view some of the most appealing aspects of both views while avoiding their extension to cases in which they would direct us to act in morally unacceptable ways.

Perhaps we can arrive at such a synthesis in the following way. Suppose that we retain the utilitarian principle but limit its scope. The morally right course of action in most situations is the one that has the best consequences—the one that brings about the greatest good for the greatest number. But we shall not be obliged to follow this principle in situations in which acting so as to bring about the best consequences will unnecessarily treat some as means only. For we also wish to retain the deontological principle, though in a restricted form. We will employ it to avoid the morally outrageous actions that would occasionally be sanctioned if the utilitarian principle were applied to all situations as the sole determiner of the right course of action. For, as we noted, a purely utilitarian approach, or more generally a purely *consequentialist* approach, untempered by a deontological respect for the moral rights of every individual and finding moral value only in consequences, would sometimes lead to an avoidable sacrifice of individuals for the sake of the common good. In a great many of the cases in which people are used as means only, such treatment of them is avoidable. If the overall good of a society could be increased by the enslavement of a small minority, then, as we noted earlier, one taking a purely utilitarian approach would be obliged to approve of their enslavement. But clearly their enslavement is avoidable. The overall good could be increased in other ways instead. Even if the overall good could not be maximized in any other way, its maximization is not necessary, and, indeed, as the deontologist would point out, *should not* be brought about if the cost of doing so is the violation of the moral rights of a few. Our deontological concerns should lead us to refuse to sanction any *avoidable* use of people as means only.

Still, there is a strong case for limiting the application of the deontological principle, despite the great importance of maintaining our deontological concerns. For, as we saw, there are life-threatening lifeboat-type cases in which the use of people as means only is unavoidable if a tragedy involving considerable loss of human life is to be prevented. Though we should experience a powerful moral reluctance to treat anyone in that way, this reluctance is decreased some by the realization that those who are sacrificed would have died anyway if no one had been treated as means only. In these (fortunately) rare cases we would allow, or at least appreciate the strong case for allowing, our utilitarian concern to cut the loss of human life override our deontological concerns.

To sum up, our attempt to synthesize these two sets of concerns will lead us to use the utilitarian principle as our guide in most of our ethical decision making, overriding it only in those situations in which it would violate unnecessarily the moral rights of others by using them as means only. In such situations, we need not violate anyone's moral right to be treated as an intrinsically valuable end, rather than as a mere means to some other end; and an appeal to the deontological principle will justify our refusal to violate the moral right of anyone, even when violating them would have better consequences than refusing to violate them. But in those rare situations in which the violation of someone's moral rights is unavoidable if an impending catastrophe is to be averted, we may allow our deontological concerns to be overridden by a concern to bring about the best possible consequences.

Of course, this very general description of a possible synthesis will not provide us with a clear directive as to what the morally best course of action would be in every imaginable situation. The goal of providing such a directive may prove to be simply unachievable, not so much because of the difficulties in formulating a synthesis of general principles that would have universal applicability, but because there may be situations in which there is no morally *best* course of action, or even a course of action that could not be shown to be morally unacceptable according to some defensible moral principle. Given the moral complexity of the situations that life sometimes presents, along with the apparent fact that matters of moral value are not matters of objective fact existing independently of our preferences, we should be prepared to acknowledge that we may encounter moral dilemmas that are irresolvable in that no matter what we do we end up violating a moral principle we would very much like to honor. Perhaps the best we can do to prepare ourselves for dealing with such morally problematic situations is to carefully think through our moral principles, focusing on the limits of their applicability and on how one might be weighed against another, while remaining open to new considerations that may lead us to re-think the matter. As always in philosophy, there is more to do. But we have pursued this matter far enough to get results that not only provide at least a tentative answer to our first question, about what moral principles should be recognized as fundamental (i.e., those which never, or hardly ever, may be justifiably overridden), but will be of help in answering our other two questions as well.

THE UNIVERSALITY OF MORAL PRINCIPLES

Our second question was about whether there are certain fundamental moral requirements that are universal, applying to all persons irrespective of culture, geographical location, or historical period. Are there fundamental (though, as we saw, perhaps not inviolable) moral principles that *everyone* is obliged to respect and follow? Our initial impression may be that there are not. Virtually all the ways of treating others that we may believe are profoundly wrong have been systematically practiced by some society or other in the past or present. Racial segregation, persecution for political or religious views, infanticide, torture, human sacrifice, and slavery have all been regularly practiced in the past. In the case of each, large numbers of people must have believed this practice to be morally justified, or at least not morally wrong. Furthermore, they may have believed this with as much conviction as we feel in holding these practices to be morally abhorrent.

Confronted with such facts, we may begin to wonder if the belief that there are fundamental moral values is only one more manifestation of the widespread tendency to impose one's own values on others. Can it be that the fundamental moral values or principles we are seeking are fundamental only to *us*—that is, only from our historical-cultural standpoint—and that there is no transcendent standpoint from which we are entitled to make a cross-cultural evaluation? The moral relativist would claim that there is not, maintaining that there are no universally applicable moral principles. Moral judgments and values are context-dependent, and thus relative to culture or historical period. Certain practices of other cultures, slavery, for example, may strike us as morally awful, and indeed it would be morally wrong for us to enslave anyone. But it may have been morally permissible for other cultures to have done this. For, the relativist may argue, what is morally wrong in one cultural-historical setting may have been right in another. Right and wrong are not the same for everyone, the relativist may remind us. There are no fundamental moral values that everyone is obliged to hold.

The relativist may seem to have a strong case not only because the moral judgments people make are profoundly influenced by their cultural-historical context but because moral value is rooted in preference, and preference typically varies with, and is thus relative to, the individual. As we noted earlier, to make a moral judgment is to express a preference from the moral point of view. But then we note that different individuals express apparently different preferences, especially if they have been influenced by very different cultural-historical circumstances. If the preferences expressed by others clash head-on with our own, we may make the moral judgment that if these are indeed their moral preferences, then they should not have them—that no one should. But in doing so we are only expressing what we prefer to see everyone prefer. And if that is what they too are doing, then we have merely countered one prefer-ence with another without providing any basis for endorsing one rather than the other. We have reached a stand-off, which is what relativism implies we would reach at some point. Fundamental moral disagreement would certainly not bode well for the non-relativist.

So what can we say in reply to the relativist? The fact that societies have engaged in practices that we consider morally atrocious does not by itself carry much weight. For this fact fails to show, or even indicate, that there is no culture-transcendent standpoint from which these practices may be morally evaluated and condemned as wrong. In brief, the fact that societies have engaged in certain practices doesn't make those practices morally right. Societies as well as individuals often do what is morally wrong. The relativist teaches us about the importance of context to the moral judg-ments we make, but he is not entitled to infer from this that one moral judgment may not be morally superior to another in some transcendent sense.

If, however, the cross-cultural differences that the relativist makes so much of do reveal the existence of substantial and fundamental moral disagree-ment, then the non-relativist has a serious problem, especially if he holds, as we do, that morality is grounded in preference. For in that case, fundamental moral disagreement would imply different moral preferences (preferences that differ even after full consideration of the moral point of view) and thus fundamentally different moralities. With the ground of morality in prefer-ence, there could be no higher moral court of appeal or transcendent stand-point from which the relative merits of these competing moralities could be measured. Thus moral relativism would be true.

But perhaps when we take a more careful look at just what fundamental moral disagreement *is* we will see that there is very little of it, or at any rate, not the substantial amount the relativist would have us believe exists. We have already taken note of the great amount of cross-cultural disagreement there seems to be when we acknowledged that societies have systematically engaged in practices that we find morally awful. But this in itself does not reveal fun-damental moral disagreement. For two individuals to exemplify such dis-agreement, they must find that they have genuinely different moral preferences, even after having taken seriously the moral point of view and hav-ing faithfully gone through the moral reasoning that a full understanding of that view requires. And this condition may be rarely if ever satisfied. We must bear in mind how easy it is for someone to claim to have a moral preference without fully understanding the moral implications of his claim, in particular, without having noticed that when universalized it could be used to justify a treatment of him that he would find morally unacceptable.

To illustrate this point, suppose that we encounter a white man who claims to believe that racial discrimination against black people is morally justifiable. Segregating them, depriving them of educational and employment opportunities enjoyed by whites, and generally treating them as inferior are all morally acceptable practices. Indeed, he tells us that even enslaving them would be all right as far as he is concerned. Unlike most other bigots, he doesn't base his position upon a theory that blacks differ from whites in intelligence, moral character, or in some other way. For then his position would be open to refutation by science. Instead, he claims that skin color alone is a morally sufficient reason for such discrimination.

We explain to him how any morally acceptable position must pass the "universalizability test," and his reply is that this presents no problem. He thinks all whites should oppress blacks and that everyone should feel as he does about this. Indeed, he is concerned because not everyone does. Have we here encountered someone with whom we have a fundamental moral disagreement?

In all likelihood we have not. Suppose that in addition to being very bigoted he is also very credulous, and that, in an attempt to determine what his fundamental moral preferences really are, we get him to believe the following story.[4] We tell him that the Association for the Improvement of Race Relations (AIRR) has through its research program discovered a very infectious virus which has a peculiar property: If it infects a white person it permanently blackens the person's skin, whereas it makes white the skin of an infected black person. We also tell him that because this infection is physically harmless and because bad race relations have been the cause of so much grief for so many people, the Association has managed to persuade our government to allow this infection to be spread throughout our population. Though this decision is not yet widely known, its effects will be apparent soon enough.

What reaction might we expect to his acceptance of this story? He is now forced to recognize that the principle he was expressing is one which when properly universalized would justify (formerly) black people oppressing *him.* His support of this principle was based all along on the privileged position he was bestowing on himself, as one of the oppressors. But now he has, in effect, been forced to see that he hadn't really been taking the moral point of view at all. The preference he had been expressing was never a *moral* preference because it was prejudiced in favor of his particular circumstances. To take the moral point of view he must free himself of such partiality toward himself. He must treat all others as moral equals, and that is to accept the role reversal dramatized in our story. But it seems very likely that he would reject his principle rather than accept this. Of course, it is logically possible that someone would accept this; but we must take that to be extremely unlikely, simply because virtually no one deliberately and freely wills unjust treatment upon himself.

We are now in a position to appreciate how very rare fundamental moral disagreement must be. For it must be grounded in conflicting *moral* preferences—preferences concerning how everyone, including oneself, should act and be treated. Since virtually no one genuinely desires to be enslaved, to be made a human sacrifice, to be used as a mere means to an end from which one derives no benefit, or even to be treated unjustly in some lesser way, virtually no one can truthfully express a moral preference for such practices. For anyone who did would be doing so with full awareness of the implication that these practices would remain morally justifiable even when *he* is the victim of injustice.

Without a significant amount of fundamental moral disagreement, the case for moral relativism breaks down. The relativist has failed to show that there is no transcendent standpoint from which the preferences of different individuals and the practices of different cultures can be morally evaluated. That there is such a standpoint now seems undeniable, and is, in any case, further supported by the fact that it is always possible for us to evaluate morally the accepted practices of our own society. For when we do so, we are surely not (at least in the typical case) appealing to the moral standards of some *other* society. We are viewing the matter from a standpoint that transcends the ways of any particular society and appealing to a conception of what is really right and wrong, i.e., of a universal morality, as contrasted with what most people happen to believe about the matter.

THE CASE FOR BEING MORAL

Let us now proceed to our third question: Why should we take the moral point of view at all? What should motivate us to do so?[5] It may seem only too obvious that many people fail to take it very commonly, if ever. Their actions seem to be guided only by their beliefs about what is in their own self-interest. But what, if anything, is wrong with that? So what should we say, or more generally, what important things have been said, to those who wonder why they should take the moral point of view, when acting out of self-interest alone is comparatively effortless and gratifying? Obviously, these questions are of central importance, for little is gained in showing that there are moral principles of universal application if the case for thinking that we are obliged to respect them is weak.

Many of the attempts to show that we should place value on being moral proceed by trying to convince us that by being moral we will be able to get something else that we already value. The religious argument that we should be moral because God commands it is of this type. God will (in the afterlife) reward us for being moral and will punish us for immorality. Some will say that this is a rather crass way of expressing the believer's position, though it very likely does accurately state the primary motivation of many religious people.

They would say that we should be moral not out of desire for reward or fear of punishment, but out of love of God. Since God loves us and gave us life, we should love Him. And since He desires or commands us to be moral, we should be so out of love for Him. This may seem to be a more attractive version, for our motivation is not portrayed as mere self-interest. But whatever form the religious argument takes, its core is that we should be moral because this is what God desires or commands. The implication is that religion is the foundation of morality.

This argument in one form or another has appealed to a great many people. Indeed, it has been claimed in great literary works and elsewhere that if God does not exist, then morality collapses—"then everything is permissible."[6] But despite its widespread appeal it cannot succeed in showing that morality has a religious foundation. The obvious objection is that it is launched from the controversial assumption that God exists. Morality seems to have a more secure place in the world than what the religious argument can give it. It would surely seem, especially to those who question God's existence, that right and wrong would remain and we would still have moral obligations to one another even if we should somehow discover that God had never existed.

Another problem comes into view when we see that we are assuming some prior knowledge of right and wrong in making the judgment that certain claims about how we should conduct ourselves express the commands of God. Even if we assume that we have knowledge of God's existence and of His having revealed His moral views to us at some place and time, we would still be unable to believe of some purported revelation that it really was a revelation from God unless it passed our moral tests. That is, it could not be in radical disagreement with what we already believe to be right and wrong. To illustrate, suppose that the commandments, which according to scripture Moses brought down from Mt. Sinai, had made such assertions as: Steal from the poor and downtrodden; Covet your neighbor's possessions and take them if you can; Sacrifice young maidens in honor of Me; Betray your parents and friends for My sake, etc. Few could believe that such assertions are the commands of God. It is conceivable that God might have revealed Himself in such a definitive and unmistakable manner that virtually all doubt would be out of the question. In that event we wouldn't need to apply a moral test. But no such event has occurred.

A more serious objection to any argument of this type is that it treats moral action as something not worth doing for its own sake. We are urged to be moral in order to receive a reward or avoid punishment, or, perhaps, to express our love for God or to avoid disappointing Him. But this gets the motivation wrong. We should be motivated to act in a moral way simply because it is the right thing to do. Some would argue that the moral way is the right way because it brings about what is intrinsically good, viz., happiness. But even this fails to express our intuition that we should be motivated to act in a moral way because we see it to be the *right* way, and not for some other reason.

This difficulty is closely related to another that is by itself fatal to the religious argument. It appears when we inquire into the relationship between the morality of an action and God's commanding it. There are two possibilities: either (1) an action is moral because God commands it, or (2) God commands it because it is moral. The first alternative turns out to be totally unacceptable; for, on this alternative, what it means to say that something is right or good is that God commands it. God's commanding it is what *makes* it good. But this implies that if God commanded us to do something silly, or at least without any moral significance, such as putting our right shoe on before our left, then this procedure would be, by definition, the morally right course of action. Worse yet, God could command us to spend our time trying to cheat, torture, and kill one another; and if He did so, then these actions would be morally right. It is of no help to reply that God would not command such things, even though He could, for He could have a reason not to command them only if they were morally wrong independent of His commands. But to concede that actions are right or wrong independent of His commands is, in effect, to reject the first alternative and embrace the second one: God commands us to do certain things *because* they are morally right. That is why we should do them and why God commands them.

So the second alternative is the only acceptable one. The problem for the defender of the religious argument is that this alternative seems ruled out for him. For he has told us that we should be moral not simply because it is the right thing to do but because being moral will enable us to gain a reward, or avoid punishment, or please God. If he were to say that he was merely giving us additional reasons for being moral—that he was all along endorsing the position that we should be moral because it is right for us independent of theological considerations—then he would be conceding that the fundamental reasons for being moral are not theological. And that would be to reject the view that religion is the foundation of morality. Of course, that view must be rejected anyway in accepting the second alternative. So two conclusions have emerged: (1) the foundation of morality (if it has one) is not constituted by theology or religion, and (2) the religious argument fails to provide a satisfactory account of why we should be moral.

We have been considering a view that would motivate us to be moral by appealing to our concern about how God will eventually treat us or about how our behavior will affect Him. But this view also has a secular form, which we arrive at simply by substituting *other people* for *God*. It is a familiar view. We are told that if we treat others in a moral way, then they will, or more likely will, treat us in a similar fashion. This is undoubtedly good advice, but we should nevertheless have doubts about whether it constitutes an adequate answer to our third question (about why we should be moral). Like other answers of this type, it tries to show that by being moral we can get something else that we value, viz., moral treatment from others. In other words, it makes an appeal to our self-interest. Perhaps this will turn out to be unavoidable—perhaps self-interest is our only fundamental source of motivation. Yet at the same time we should not ignore our impulse to say that we should do what is morally right, even if doing so is not in our self-interest, simply because it is the right thing to do. It still seems that this impulse expresses the true source of morality.

Another problem with this view is that it provides motivation for us to be moral only in those circumstances in which we believe that our behavior will affect how others treat us. Consequently, it wouldn't motivate us to be moral when we believe that others will not find out what we do. But those are the occasions when many people apparently have a great need for such motivation. What again becomes apparent is that this motivation will be found only by appealing to a concern for the welfare of others that is not rooted entirely in self-interest. Our concern for that which is in our own self-interest will prompt us to act morally on some occasions, but the only unwavering source of moral action is a direct concern for the welfare of others.

Harm is clearly bad for the one who suffers it. But in what sense can it be bad for the rest of us? Why should *we* be concerned with it? The foundation of morality is the conviction that harm is bad for each sentient creature, not merely from its own standpoint but also from a more general standpoint which is accessible to all persons capable of imaginatively projecting themselves into the circumstances of another. Our interests, our desires, and our sufferings are of great importance to us, but they are also important in a transcendent way—in a way that transcends what they are to us and that obliges others to be concerned about them too. So what do we say to someone who doubts that we have such an obligation, that is, someone who wonders why we should have a concern for others that is not ultimately rooted in self-interest? This is a difficult question, but perhaps at least part of the answer consists in attempting to show him that when he thinks through his concerns in a *consistent* way he will find either that he already has such a concern or that he *should* have it if in fact he does not. We might speak to him in the following way.

You have no difficulty appreciating the harm that comes about when you are treated unjustly and caused to suffer. Nor do you have any difficulty seeing that others have a moral reason for not treating you in that way. You would also agree that this reason is not one that applies only to some particular person or other: It is one that anyone would have for not harming you. But to agree that there is such a reason is to agree that your welfare is important not only to you but in a way that should concern everyone in a position to affect it.

The next step is to acknowledge that there is nothing special about you, that this reason would be a reason for refraining from harming not only you, but everyone else (in similar circumstances) as well. And since this is a reason everyone would have, it is a reason that you too would have for not harming another, or more generally, for being concerned about the welfare of others. Thus you see that to be consistent you must acknowledge that you too have it. Your motivation for respecting it is based not only in your desire to be treated in a moral way but in your awareness that it is a requirement of reason—to respect it is to act in a rationally consistent manner.

Of course, the person we are trying to convince may see that he has such a reason and still not care to act in accordance with it. He may not care much about consistency. In any event, a concern about consistency and respect for the principle we want others to follow in their treatment of us is not a substitute for a direct concern for the welfare of others. Nothing can take the place of *that*. It is the core of the motivation to be moral. For those who have it, nothing more is needed. But for those in whom it is easily overridden by other concerns, a consideration of these other reasons for being moral may be of help.

We have now completed our study of moral value. We have located it within the larger realm of value, offered a conception of morally right action, discussed what it is to take the moral point of view, and tried to specify what moral judgments are. We have examined principles for determining whether an action is morally right, addressed the question of whether there is a universal morality, and considered what might or should motivate us to be moral. Yet we have offered only a sketch of the territory with little attention to the detail of the terrain. As always, many questions remain unanswered. We have discussed the importance of a direct concern for others, but we have said little about how the interests and desires of others are to be balanced out in relation to our own. We are morally obliged to be concerned about them, but are we obliged to have as *much* concern for their welfare as we have for our own? Should we care about others as much as we care about ourselves? And speaking of others, are we obliged to have concern for everyone to the same degree, or is it quite justifiable to have special concern for the welfare of our friends and family members. Obviously, there is much more to be said about these matters. Also, we have not addressed ourselves to such important ethical issues as those concerning the morality of abortion, suicide, euthanasia, and capital punishment. Still, we have managed to articulate the framework within which these issues are to be settled, if indeed they ever are.

QUESTIONS FOR FURTHER THOUGHT

1. Is it obvious that, as stated in the text, "nothing can be of value without being of value *to* someone"? What might one say to someone who insists that value exists in and of itself, independent of anyone's experience of it?

2. Are there other moral principles as fundamental as the greatest happiness (or greatest good) principle and the principle of the moral equality of all persons? If so, what are they?

3.   Is it true that morality has no deeper ground than preference? If this is true, can our moral judgments still have the fundamental importance that we believe them to have?

4.   Consider the following claim: If morality is founded on religion, then moral action is not something worth doing for its own sake. Is this claim true? Would its truth show that morality is *not* founded on religion?

5.   Is there a universal morality? If not, why not? If there is, how might we describe it?

6.   Is direct concern for the welfare of others the highest and best motivation for moral action? If it is, how might we foster its development in people who lack it? How might we convince them by reason and argument that they should be moral?

7.   Is a universal morality possible if morality has no deeper ground than preference? If not, would there be any moral principle to which one might appeal in trying to resolve fundamental moral disputes? If so, what makes such a morality possible?

9

DEATH

We all live in the shadow of death. The inevitability of death is one of the most prominent and sobering features of our human condition. No strategy, however clever, and no struggle, however intense, passionate, or heroic, can keep it at bay indefinitely. What gives us inner strength and ennobles us—such traits as determination, endurance, courage, and wisdom—may serve us well while we live, but cannot enable us to prevail in a contest with death. It will ultimately defeat us all. Perhaps we could gain some small measure of power over it if we could just put it out of our minds. But try as we may, we cannot shut it out for very long. The unmistakable signs of our mortality are not only all around us but within us as well.

DEATH AND THE POSSIBILITY OF EXTINCTION

We can hardly think about death without wondering whether it constitutes the absolute end to our existence. Perhaps what lies beyond it is only an everlasting nothingness—the infinite void on the other end of life. Before our entrance into this world, there was only an empty void insofar as our experience is concerned. As we think about that immense amount of time that elapsed before we came into existence, we realize that much must have been going on; but for us, subjectively speaking, there was only a total blank. From the inside, there was nothing. And so, if our existence comes to an absolute end when we die, we might think of it as bounded on each end by nothingness—a nothingness that on the death end extends infinitely far into the future. In that case, death would be annihilation and extinction from the universe forevermore.

The view that death results in our permanent extinction receives powerful support from what we see happening to the bodies of people when they die. We know that death will result in the complete destruction of our bodies. Consequently, if we are identical with our bodies, then, of course, *we* are completely destroyed as well. Indeed, if your body is even an essential *part* of what you are, then *you* could not survive its destruction. For you must survive in your entirety if you are to survive at all. Our earlier reflections on the nature of the self revealed that no one can be only *partly* you. Thus if a self or person were to survive the destruction of your body, that person would be either you in your entirety or not you at all.

Given that your continued existence after biological death is an "all or nothing" matter, we must wonder if your continuing to exist after death is even conceivable. Can we even *conceive* of what you would have to be for you to continue on existing after the death of your body? Here again our earlier reflections on the self come to our aid, this time with an affirmative answer to our question. Those reflections indicated that what you essentially are (as contrasted with what you *have*, such as a mind and a body) is a subject of conscious states. Thus they indicate that we are conceiving of your continued existence after biological death when we conceive of the subject of the conscious states or experiences that you are having now (i.e., yourself) continuing to have experiences after the death of your body. Given that you *are* that subject, we are conceiving of *your* continued existence. Though we are no longer conceiving of you in association with your physical body, our conception is not thereby rendered incoherent if that body is only something that you *have*, not something that you *are*. We need not try to conceive of you as no longer having any experience of a body; for you might seem to yourself to be in a body and having various sensory experiences associated with it, much as you now do when you have a vivid dream in which you seem to yourself to be engaged in various body-involving activities (e.g., hiking, playing tennis, walking by a mirror in which you see what you take to be your body), even though your physical body is lying motionless in bed.

Any remaining doubt that we can conceive of our continued existence after death should disappear when we consider the dream hypothesis again. If the dream hypothesis is conceivable or coherent (i.e., describes a logical possibility), then so is the hypothesis that we will continue to exist after biological death. When you conceive or imagine that the dream hypothesis is true, you imagine that your body is merely part of the content of your dream and thus not a physical organism existing independently of your consciousness. Since this "dream body" would be a phenomenal body rather than a physical one, you are imagining yourself to exist in a phenomenal world without a physical body when you imagine that the dream hypothesis is true. But to imagine yourself no longer in association with your (deceased) physical body and experiencing a purely phenomenal world is to imagine or conceive of what it might be for you to continue existing after biological death.

These considerations, along with our earlier reflections on the nature of the self, indicate that we are conscious subjects distinct from our bodies and logically separable from them. But even if we are logically separable from our bodies, our existence may well depend upon their continuing to function, in which case we will perish when they do. In view of this, we might wonder if we have *any* evidence or reason to believe that we continue to exist after death. Perhaps the widespread belief in an afterlife is nothing more than a blind faith, prompted by the paralyzing fear of annihilation and permanent nonexistence.

What is central to our present inquiry then is the question of what happens to us when we die. It is a question of ultimate concern. Indeed, we might wonder how anyone could *fail* to find it interesting and of fundamental importance. Perhaps some are not interested in trying to answer it because they suppose that they already have the answer. That is, they suppose that the question is to be decided simply on the basis of faith, and they believe on faith alone that there is an afterlife. But we have already witnessed the barrenness of this approach when we were wondering whether we have any basis for believing that God exists. As we noted then, people who take this approach are suggesting, at least in an implicit way, that the *truth* of the matter is of no concern to them.

Others may claim to find the question uninteresting, or at least not worthy of serious attention, because they suppose that no one can come to *know* what the answer is. Since we apparently lack the means to unravel in any absolutely conclusive way a mystery of this depth, we will utilize our time and energy more productively by directing our attention elsewhere. But this view too is based on a confusion. It places the standard for knowledge too high, a mistake we have already discussed in another context. Of course we should not expect to find conclusive evidence—a *guarantee* that we will, or will not, survive death. But we may be able to find evidence or good reasons for believing one way or the other; and these reasons may even be strong enough to justify the claim that we *know* what will happen to us, at least in the weaker sense of what it is to know.

Another concern about our central question is a worry about whether thought about one's own nonexistence is even meaningful. The question we have posed assumes that we can conceive of our own nonexistence. But some would maintain that we cannot do this. For what we must do is conceive of conditions under which we would be unable to conceive of anything—conditions that lie beyond the bounds of any possible experience. We must attempt to become aware of conditions under which no awareness is possible.

Though this concern suggests that we are trying to acquire knowledge of the unknowable, there really isn't any serious problem here. Of course we cannot conceive of *experiencing* these conditions, for we cannot conceive of having experiences at a time when we no longer exist. But our inability to conceive of experiencing them is no ground for supposing that we cannot conceive of them at all. Our inability to conceive of our nonexistence at a time when we no longer exist does nothing to show, or even suggest, that we cannot conceive of it *now*. We can conceive of it as a condition under which we would be unable to have any experience or conceive of anything. There is no reason to doubt that we can do this. The fact that we cannot experience such a condition makes no difference. From the external standpoint we have on it now, we might think of it as like the nothingness of deep, dreamless sleep. Upon awakening from such sleep we realize that time has elapsed, but it was nothing for us—a total blank. Obviously, the fact that we cannot experience being in such a state doesn't prevent our viewing it from a standpoint external to it. After all, that is the standpoint to which we are limited whenever we direct our attention to anything lying beyond our own experiential world.

Another important factor to consider before focusing on our central question is the possible influence of our feelings upon the answer we may eventually accept. Our desires and fears take on an especially important role as we approach this subject, for they may make it difficult to maintain the level of open-mindedness and impartiality needed in a search for objective truth. Detachment or even a respectable emotional distance from the subject matter seems very difficult here. After all, we are dying. Still, a reminder of the power of our desires to pull us in the direction of their satisfaction may help us maintain the intellectual honesty and courage needed to follow our reason wherever it may lead, even if that should be to a conclusion that crushes our hopes.

This concern is founded upon the assumption that if death is annihilation, then it is a bad thing—something difficult if not psychologically impossible to embrace. We have been implicitly assuming this; but now we must ask if we are justified in doing so. Some would argue that though a premature death or a painful dying process would be bad, death in itself is not a bad thing. Since death, if it is annihilation, cannot be anything at all for the person who is dead, it can have neither positive nor negative value. That person is no longer in existence, and so there is no one for whom it could be good or bad. To paraphrase the ancient Greek philosopher Epicurus, death is not bad for the living because they are not dead, and not bad for the dead because they do not exist.[1] It can be very bad for others of course, but the issue here is one of whether it can be bad for the person whose death it is. Should we agree that it cannot?

This challenge to our assumption points to a truth we must acknowledge: If our future nonexistence is a bad thing for us, it is so not because of any positive features this state may have. It cannot be painful or demeaning or unpleasant in any way. We must also admit that our feelings about our own nonexistence are not as clear-cut as we may be led to suppose when we think about death. There are conditions under which our nonexistence does not strike us as troubling. Our (apparent) nonexistence prior to our coming about in this world is not troubling to us at all. Moreover, our future nonexistence if known to be temporary would not be of great concern to us. For even though this period of nonexistence might be lengthy, from the viewpoint of a subject returning to conscious existence with vivid memory of his past, it may be comparable to awakening from a night of dreamless sleep. That is, the actual length of the period of nonexistence need not make any difference to how the matter seems to the subject upon regaining consciousness. A long period could seem like a moment. Of course, there would be other concerns arising from the fact that the world may have changed a great deal since the time of one's death. This would surely be of some concern to those who plan to have their bodies preserved by freezing with the hope that an advanced technology of the future will enable them to be revived. The concern here, however, is not about one's future nonexistence itself, but about a *consequence* of temporary nonexistence. The state of nonexistence itself would be of relatively little concern.

But we can acknowledge all of this and yet remain convinced that death (conceived as permanent future nonexistence) is a bad thing. Someone may say that what is really (or at any rate, all that *should be*) bothering us is the dying process, but that, it seems, would not bother us nearly so much if it didn't end in death. Again we confront our conviction that death is bad for us quite independently of the circumstances in which it occurs. And so our challenge is to show that we have a basis for this conviction—that it is not to be simply dismissed as arising from a confusion. Let us see if we can meet this challenge.

If death is indeed bad for us, it is so not because it is a state in which we could suffer in any way, or because it has features that have negative value for us, but because it deprives us of a great good, namely, our existence. In doing so it deprives us of everything we find enjoyable—the beauty of nature, art and music, association with friends and family, the discovery of truth, the satisfaction of coming to know and understand, the possibility of further moral and intellectual development, the opportunity to achieve a higher level of creativity and self-actualization, and, more generally, the freedom to pursue what is of value to us. Against this, death looms as the final defeat of all our hopes and aspirations, the ultimate negation of all our possibilities.

This explanation of why death is so commonly taken to be a bad thing does not assume that existence is unqualifiably good under all circumstances. We must acknowledge that there are conditions under which one's existence may not be good enough to be worth having—that one's life may have become so painful or so impoverished, as in the case of extreme debilitation and helplessness, that death may seem preferable. And perhaps it is preferable, at least under the worst conditions we may encounter. But even then there is value in simply having experience, quite apart from the quality or content of that experience. If this content (i.e., *what* one is experiencing) is so unbearable as to outweigh that value, then we may be led, however reluctantly, to the conclusion that one is better off dead. But the point is that if there is some value in just having experience, however bad the experience may be, then we have the makings of an explanation of our feeling that death always brings some loss, even when the conditions under which it occurs are so awful that, under those conditions, it seems preferable to life. Perhaps the feeling of loss is partially explained by the thought of the value that this life could have had under other conditions. But such an explanation, unlike the one we have given, involves a value that the life in question doesn't actually have.

Perhaps more needs to be said about why our past nonexistence does not trouble us. Since we seem to assume that we could have been born much earlier, it may seem peculiar, if not inexplicable, why, if our nonexistence deprives us of a great good, we are not troubled by our nonexistence in the past. For a consequence of our past nonexistence is that we had no opportunity to enjoy existence then. Why don't we take this to be a deprivation, or at any rate, one that troubles us? Does the fact that we are not troubled undermine our explanation of why we consider, or should consider, death to be bad for us? In other words, if our "deprivation theory" is true, then shouldn't we expect to find that our feelings about our past nonexistence are similar to those about our possible nonexistence in the future?

This is a puzzle that should not be ignored, even though we may be unable to provide a completely satisfactory solution to it. If our deprivation theory is to retain its appeal, then we must offer a plausible explanation of why we fail to find our past nonexistence to be a troubling deprivation. But perhaps we can do just that, for these two periods of nonexistence seem to differ in at least two important respects.

First, we know that our past nonexistence was not a permanent state, and we see this to be important when we remind ourselves that temporary future nonexistence does not bother us nearly as much as the permanent version. As we noted, we can conceive of a lengthy, but temporary, period of future nonexistence as appearing, from the viewpoint of the subject who is regaining conscious existence, to be but a moment of unconsciousness. Similarly, our past nonexistence appears, subjectively speaking, to have been but a moment, or at least of insignificant length, even though we realize that from an objective point of view it may have been unimaginably long. The fact that we had no consciousness of its passing makes a great deal of difference from the subjective point of view.

Secondly, we tend to focus on the future when we think about our possibilities; for unlike the past, it is still open. Because the past is fixed, possibility can no longer be actualized in it; and because it is over it is no longer something to anticipate. These facts prevent it from having the sort of value we implicitly attribute to the future. If we could in some way remove ten years of our past, that, it would seem, would not trouble us nearly as much as would removing ten years of our future. Perhaps this is so not primarily because we remain secure in our knowledge that the past cannot be removed or because such a suggestion about the past is not sufficiently intelligible for us to make a value judgment in relation to it, but because the past ten years, though lived through, is not now experientially accessible to us—it cannot be something to anticipate. There are now no possibilities to actualize in it. It may have been of great value in many respects, but the fact that it is now over diminishes considerably the value it has for us now. So we look at our past nonexistence and find ourselves quite untroubled by it, perhaps because (or partly because) we see that even if we had existed then, that portion of our existence would now be over and gone. Since in being over it would have lost much of its value—namely, the experiential value it would have had while taking place—its not having occurred at all fails to strike us as a significant loss.

Perhaps this is an adequate explanation. In any case, let us suppose that it is, and that we are quite justified in assuming that death (conceived as permanent future nonexistence) is bad for us. If this is what death is, then inevitably something bad awaits us all. But maybe this is not what death is. Great numbers of people have rejected this view of death. Let us see if there are any good reasons for agreeing with them.

RELIGIOUS TEACHINGS ABOUT DEATH

Many people are led by religious teachings to believe that we will continue to exist after death. But we must ask whether these teachings point to any evidence that such belief is true. This question cannot be avoided by saying that this belief rests entirely on faith. As we have seen, a faith that is not even concerned with evidence (and thus not concerned with truth) is not a genuine alternative for us. Such faith may offer comfort and consolation, but we come to see that it is not worthy of us, and that we should demand more of ourselves when we are reminded that we possess a rational intelligence enabling us to weigh evidence, to evaluate truth claims, and to reach conclusions based on reason. To refuse to consider the question of evidence certainly appears motivated by a lack of courage to confront the truth.

So our reason for taking religious claims seriously must ultimately rest on the grounds for thinking that they are true. But these grounds seem unsatisfactory in two respects. First, when we consider in an objective and impartial manner the afterlife claims made in a particular religion such as Christianity or Islam, or in some religious movement within them, we see how difficult it is to find good reason to believe that they are true, even when we consider them without regard to the conflicting afterlife claims made in other religions. Consider, for example, the afterlife claims made within the Christian religion. They are centered around the deeds and statements attributed to Christ. In addition to making statements about an afterlife, Christ is claimed to have performed various miracles and to have risen from the dead. But we have reason to believe these claims only if we have reason to believe that the accounts we have of the life and teachings of Christ are historically accurate. Here, however, lies the problem. Though one may believe with great conviction in the truthfulness of these accounts, a sober and impartial examination of them reveals that doubts about their historical accuracy are very well founded. The Gospel accounts available to us are not the originals, not the so-called autographs. At best, they are copies of copies. The originals perished long ago. Moreover, the process by which they were generated does not inspire confidence. New Testament scholars agree that even the earliest of the Gospels, the Gospel according to St. Mark, was not written until approximately forty years after the death of Christ. Then too, they contradict each other at various points; and they, along with other books in the Christian Bible, show ample evidence of tampering and forgery. Of course, these concerns do not show that no Gospel account is a historically accurate record of what actually happened. But they certainly stand in the way of accepting the claim that these accounts provide a rational basis for belief in an afterlife. And it is just such a basis that we have been trying to find.

Afterlife beliefs found in other religious traditions suffer from similar verification problems. We have grounds for accepting them only if we have grounds for believing that we have a historically accurate record of the events and circumstances out of which they arose or on which they are based. Since we lack the latter, we lack the former as well. But even if we were to overlook the lack of evidential support provided by individual religions for their afterlife claims, we must still confront a formidable obstacle to believing them to be true—namely, the fact that the afterlife claims of one religion, or tradition within it, are contradicted by those of another. We are told that we will continue to exist immediately after death, and also that we will cease to exist until our resurrection at the end of history. We are told that we live on this earth only once, and also that we are born back into an earthly existence time after time. We are told that we will survive in a material body, and also that our afterlife body will be spiritual rather than material. We find that according to some accounts we will survive as individuals, but that according to others there is no individual survival of death.

This list of contradictory claims could be continued to great lengths. One gets the impression that every afterlife claim we encounter within a religion is contradicted, explicitly or implicitly, by claims made in some other religion. The problem that this spectacle presents is grave indeed. Unless we have good rational grounds for preferring one religious teaching over another—something we apparently do not have—whatever we might take to be evidence supporting the afterlife claims of one is canceled out by the "evidence" supporting the contradictory afterlife claims of another. But canceled evidence is no evidence at all. And so the prospects of finding support for afterlife claims by appeal to religious teachings seem very dim.

It is true that in the great majority of religious traditions we find belief in some form of afterlife, even though there is widespread and fundamental disagreement about what form that is. And it may seem that this truth should not be ignored. But whatever significance we may be inclined to give it certainly diminishes when we reflect upon the fact that fear of death is almost universal, as is the desire to go on having experience and, in particular, to be reunited with departed loved ones. What people hope the truth to be tends to affect their beliefs, as do their fears and what they find painful to contemplate. In this case at least, their hopes and their fears push in the same direction—toward a belief in an afterlife. Perhaps this widespread belief is nothing more than a manifestation of the instinctual drive toward self-preservation. In any case, a purely psychological explanation along these lines seems quite adequate to account for this belief. And, of course, the adequacy of such an explanation removes any reason we might otherwise have had for supposing that the great popularity of this belief provides some basis for believing that it is true.

DEATH AND THE PARANORMAL

Though the evidence for an afterlife that is found within religious teachings seems too flimsy to support a rational belief in existence after death, we should not be led to conclude from this fact alone that evidence supporting such belief simply does not exist. For such evidence may lie in areas we have not yet considered. In particular, we should not overlook the fact that there are numerous reports on record of extraordinary occurrences that appear to show that at least some persons have survived bodily death. They come to us from a great variety of places and times. Unlike the events attested to in religious teachings, many of these alleged occurrences have been so thoroughly investigated and documented that we can have little doubt about their actually having taken place as reported.

The extraordinary occurrences, or psychic phenomena, attested to in the reports may be categorized into several groups. We will look at three: (1) apparitions of the dead, (2) reincarnation cases, and (3) mediumship phenomena. Unfortunately, a detailed examination of any of the important cases would become far too lengthy for us to engage in here.[2] So we will have to be content with a rather general characterization, not only of the important cases themselves, but of how they might be interpreted and of what significance they have in supporting the belief that some persons have survived bodily death. Before we begin, however, we should note that though these cases appear to show that at least some persons have continued to exist after bodily death, other interpretations of these cases are possible as well—alternative interpretations that we should keep in mind as we examine the cases.

All told, there are three possible interpretations of the phenomena to be considered. No fourth interpretation has ever been suggested. Let us call them (1) the fraud hypothesis, (2) the ESP hypothesis, and (3) the survival hypothesis. The survival hypothesis is the interpretation we have already mentioned—that at least some of these reports of extraordinary occurrences are best interpreted as showing that some people have survived death. According to the fraud hypothesis, none of these reports should be given *that* interpretation. All of them can be explained in a normal fashion, that is, without appealing to anything beyond what we already know to occur. More specifically, we know that sometimes people try to deceive us, and sometimes they are themselves deceived. In this hypothesis, all of these reports are expressions of fraud or deception. They are made either by people who are trying to deceive us or by people who are themselves deceived in thinking that they have encountered deceased people still in existence.

The ESP (extra-sensory perception) hypothesis is the view that though the fraud hypothesis provides an adequate explanation of many of the reports in question, there are others which cannot be adequately explained unless we suppose that some (living) persons have displayed extra-sensory powers of perception. More precisely, the events described in some of these reports can be adequately explained only if we acknowledge that some persons can sometimes employ "mental telepathy" to "read" the minds of other living persons, or can "clairvoyantly" apprehend presently existing objects and events that are not at the time accessible to their sense organs, or can "retrocognitively" apprehend past events that they did not witness at the time of occurrence, or can "precognitively" apprehend the future, or can employ all or some combination of these powers. Since such powers are, at least in the opinion of most scientists and other scholars, unknown to science and cannot be fit into the prevailing conception of the natural world, we might call an explanation that appeals to them a *paranormal* explanation. For such an explanation goes beyond what is generally thought to be "normal" or in accord with the laws of nature. What these ESP powers amount to and how the ESP hypothesis appeals to them will become clearer when we look at the reports themselves. For the moment, let us note that according to the ESP hypothesis all of the reported occurrences that cannot be explained by the fraud hypothesis *can* be explained by appeal to the ESP powers of certain living persons. In other words, *none* of the occurrences attested to in the reports should lead us to believe that some people have survived bodily death.

We are now in a position to state the survival hypothesis with more precision. It is in agreement with the claim that many of the reports are fraudulent. It also allows the possibility that some of the extraordinary occurrences attested to in the non-fraudulent reports are best explained by the ESP hypothesis. In addition, and most importantly, it includes the claim that there have been some extraordinary occurrences that *cannot* be explained by either of the other hypotheses, or, at the very least, are *best* explained by acknowledging that some persons have continued to exist after bodily death. Let us now focus on some of the main kinds of phenomena that seem to support this hypothesis.

Apparitions of the Dead

If people did survive death, we might expect to find that they occasionally appear to the living. This is what seems to occur when someone experiences an apparition of a deceased person. Sometimes an apparition of a deceased parent will be experienced by a son or daughter. Our initial response may well be to suppose that such an experience is nothing but an internally generated hallucination, perhaps caused by feelings of grief, remorse, or loneliness, but which provides no evidence of an objective encounter with another person. No doubt that supposition is quite justified in most cases. But in some cases the apparition supplies the experiencer, or percipient, with information that at the time was unknown to her, and to every other living person. The well-documented Chaffin will case was of this sort. An apparition of James Chaffin, a North Carolina farmer, appeared, some four years after his death, to one of his adult sons, informing the son of the existence and location of a second will unknown to everyone alive at the time. The new will required a major redistribution of property, and so was an item of considerable legal importance. Though it was not witnessed, it was agreed by everyone concerned, including experts in handwriting analysis, to be in Chaffin's handwriting, and, consequently, was deemed valid by the Superior Court of Davie County, North Carolina. Here then is a case of an apparition of a deceased person providing information that was known to only that person and that resulted in the alteration of the official records of a court of law.

Though the extremely thorough investigation of the Chaffin will case seems to rule out the possibility of Chaffin's son acquiring knowledge of the will in a normal or fraudulent manner, the case may seem to suffer somewhat from the fact that the Chaffin apparition was experienced only a few times and only by a single person. But there are well-documented cases of apparitions that appeared on numerous occasions over a period of several months, or even several years in some cases, and that appeared to sizable groups of people on several of these occasions. The apparition of a deceased woman, a Mrs. George Butler, repeatedly appeared in a Maine village to as many as forty people at a time. It appeared both indoors and out of doors, moved freely among the people gathered to witness it, spoke at length on various topics, accurately predicted births and deaths, and revealed knowledge of some of the most private details of the lives of those present. Sworn affidavits testifying to what they had witnessed were obtained at the time from thirty of the more than one hundred people who, in the company of others, had experienced the apparition.

Another intriguing case is that of the apparitions of the pilot and second officer of Eastern Airlines flight 401, which crashed in 1972 killing both these men. Two months later, apparitions of these two men began to appear on other Eastern Airlines flights that were using or carrying salvaged parts from the plane that had crashed. The presence of the pilot's apparition was first noted when the crew of plane 318 was checking to see why the head count was off by one passenger too many. The apparition appeared to be dressed in a pilot's uniform and seated in the first-class section. It was seen by many but it spoke to no one, despite efforts made to communicate with it. After some time the pilot came to investigate and recognized the apparition as that of the pilot of flight 401. At that moment, the apparition simply disappeared before the eyes of all watching.

Though the appearances of the pilot were confined to plane 318 and soon ceased to occur, the appearances of the second officer continued for over two years after the crash. This apparition was friendly, frequently engaging in conversation with various people around it. It was also helpful, assisting crew members with minor repairs and warning them of potential mechanical problems. On one occasion it accurately predicted a potential electrical failure, and on another it warned of a fire which occurred as predicted later that day. Like the other apparition, it sometimes disappeared before the eyes of those around it.

What should we make of such phenomena? We have been looking at cases so impressively documented that the fraud hypothesis is virtually ruled out. Perhaps the Chaffin will case can be plausibly explained by the hypothesis that Chaffin's son clairvoyantly obtained knowledge of the hidden will—knowledge that by hypothesis was received subconsciously and then revealed to his conscious mind as he hallucinated an apparition of his deceased father. But even if the ESP hypothesis does provide the most plausible explanation of this case and others like it, we must wonder if that hypothesis stands any chance of providing the *best* explanation of those apparitions that repeatedly appeared before sizable groups of people. If living persons were the sources of those apparitions, then some people must possess ESP powers much greater than any independently known to occur. But let us postpone further consideration of the ESP hypothesis until we have looked at some cases of apparent reincarnation and communication through mediums.

Reincarnation Cases

The cases suggestive of reincarnation usually center around the recollections of young children. In the typical case, a young child, usually between two and five years old, begins to talk about the details of a previous life that he or she claims to have lived. In many cases, the child begins spontaneously to talk about a previous life as soon as she is able to speak. She may give a remarkably detailed description of that life, mentioning such details as the name she had, where and when she lived, the names and characteristics of her family members and relatives, the kind of life she led, and the specific circumstances under which she died. Along with details about her personal life, she may provide a rather full description of the environment in which she lived and of the events that were occurring then.

These claims about a prior life are often accompanied by various kinds of behavior that are unusual for a member of the child's family but quite in agreement with her claims about a prior life and often in harmony with what others say about the life and character of the person she claims to have been.

The child frequently exhibits adult behavior and acts toward other children as an adult would. Apparently, the child's memories of a prior life as an adult are so vivid and captivating that, though physically a child, she regards herself as an adult.

These prior-life claims are usually ignored, if not discouraged, by parents and other relatives. It seems that even in Asia these reports are met with disapproval. The fact that some children persist in making them, despite a largely unsympathetic audience, attests to the strength of their conviction that they are remembering a previous life. Some repeatedly request to be taken to their former home and family; and when this request is granted, the child's apparent familiarity with the new surroundings and people may be quite astounding. She may correctly anticipate what will appear around the next corner and comment on changes that have taken place since she lived there. When she encounters the relatives of the person she claims to have been, she may recognize them without any introductions, calling them by name and displaying the appropriate emotions. Indeed, there were cases in which the investigators tested the child by attempting to mislead and confuse her about these matters; but those attempts failed. Not only are the prior-life claims she had been making now confirmed by prior-life family members, but in the course of conversing with them she may remind them of nonpublic and even intimate details concerning the life they had spent together. In response to questions from them, she may reveal information that could have been known only by the person she claims to have been—for example, the exact location of a set of rings she had secretly hidden in the house before she died.[3]

In addition to possessing knowledge that could not have been acquired in any normal manner, the child may also display skills that seem equally astonishing. If the members of her prior-life family speak a dialect foreign to her, she may begin to converse with them in their language even though she had not been exposed to it in her natural life. Or she may play in their presence a musical instrument played by the person she claims to have been, though again without any normal exposure to that instrument.

In these cases, as in the cases of apparitions that we examined, the fraud hypothesis seems completely ruled out. Very careful and comprehensive investigations failed to reveal any normal means by which these children could have acquired their extraordinary knowledge and skills. So apparently no explanation is possible without conceding that something paranormal has occurred. But in these cases the ESP hypothesis appears to get stretched even further than in the apparition cases. If the children involved acquired their extraordinary knowledge through ESP, perhaps by telepathy and clairvoyance, one would expect them to exhibit ESP capacities in a more general way. But they do not; their knowledge seems to be confined to what would have been known by the deceased persons they claim to have been. Also, if these children had acquired their knowledge via ESP, one would think that they would give evidence of an ESP capacity in other contexts. But they do not.

And if ESP is the source of their knowledge instead of prior-life experiences, then we must ask why memory is the form in which this knowledge is revealed to them.

The ESP hypothesis provides no reason to expect that a child's ESP-acquired information should be both confined to what some deceased person would have known and also so well camouflaged as memories of that person's experiences that the child falsely believes herself to have been that person. All this must seem very peculiar, if not incredible. But perhaps what puts the most strain on the credibility of the ESP hypothesis is the difficulty in seeing how the *skills* that the child exhibits could have been acquired through ESP. If the ability to, say, converse in a language to which one has never been exposed in one's natural life is ESP-acquired, then the ESP involved must be truly a Super-ESP. For it would seem that skills can be acquired only through practice, and thus are something that even a Super-ESP would be unable to provide. At any rate, the need for a Super-ESP hypothesis again becomes apparent as we look at mediumship phenomena.

Mediumship Phenomena

Perhaps the most impressive empirical evidence that we survive bodily death is that which is provided by cases in which the deceased appear to be communicating with us through persons called "mediums"—persons who, according to the survival hypothesis, act as communication links between our world and the world of those who have died. And the most impressive cases of mediumship are those in which the medium goes into a trance state before such communications begin. In most of these cases, when the communications are taking place it is as though a different person is temporarily using the body of the medium to express herself. For, at least in the best of these cases, the handwriting, the voice, the verbal mannerisms, the ways in which ideas are associated, and the fund of information displayed are remarkably different from those of the medium in her normal state. Even more remarkable, the communications are characteristic of and are claimed to emanate from a deceased relative or friend of the person who is currently sitting with the medium, viz., the "sitter." But what is of the highest significance for the survival hypothesis is that in some of these cases the communications received appear to be such that they could not have had their source in the medium, or indeed in anyone other than the deceased person whom the communicating personality claims to be. In other words, the *source* of the communications, i.e, the *communicator,* appears to be just what it claims to be—a deceased person who has survived bodily death. Let us look at some highlights of one of these cases—the mediumship of Mrs. Willett.[4]

One of the main communicators in the Willett mediumship claimed to be Edmund Gurney, a classical scholar who at the time of the communications had been dead for several years. Let us call it the "Gurney-communicator," so as to avoid suggesting at the outset that it really was the person it claimed to be and that therefore the deceased Edmund Gurney had survived bodily death. It proved to be a highly important communicator not only because it seemed very familiar with the thought and work of Edmund Gurney, who had devoted much of his life to the study of mediumship and other phenomena suggestive of an afterlife, but because it engaged in extensive, high-level dialogue with Lord Balfour, one of Edmund Gurney's close friends who was very familiar with Gurney's thought and who himself had a keen philosophical mind.

These dialogues came about at the request of the Gurney-communicator. It wanted Balfour to serve as Mrs. Willett's sitter, claiming that he would be interested in discussing the nature of the processes by which the deceased are able to communicate with the living. As things turned out, the Balfour sittings did deal mainly with the nature of the processes involved in communication. But the discussions that ensued are of great importance to our inquiry primarily for two other reasons: First, they involved rather esoteric philosophical and psychological thought of a sort to which Mrs. Willett had never been exposed in her natural life, and secondly, the interaction between communicator and sitter was characterized by a conversational give-and-take which stretches the ESP hypothesis to the breaking point.

The fact that Mrs. Willett had had no exposure to the subject matter of the discussions is significant, for it indicates that the real identity of the Gurney-communicator could not have been the normal mind of Mrs. Willett. It indicates, in other words, that something paranormal was occurring here. But this fact is consistent with the ESP hypothesis, more specifically, with the hypothesis that Mrs. Willett's entranced mind was in telepathic contact with the mind of Balfour, who was knowledgeable of the subject matter of the discussions.

It was the conversational form in which this subject matter was expressed that presents the greatest problem for the ESP hypothesis. The dramatic form of the conversations was such as to suggest that Balfour was in telephone conversation (in which Mrs. Willett's body functioned as the telephone) about philosophical and psychological topics with a very intelligent and learned friend who had traveled to a distant land where the conditions of existence were strange and difficult to describe. According to the ESP hypothesis, the entranced mind of Mrs. Willett uses ESP (probably by telepathically accessing the mind of Balfour) to acquire the informational content of the Gurney-communicator's speech and then, like a person in hypnotic trance, weaves that information into a dramatic and highly authentic imitation of Edmund Gurney in animated conversation with a friend. Given the evidence for the existence of telepathy and the ability of a hypnotized person to provide a dramatic subconscious imitation of someone known to him and who he now, under hypnosis, believes himself to be, the ESP hypothesis may seem quite plausible. But a closer look reveals that it is not. First, we note that Mrs. Willett had *never* met Edmund Gurney. More important, however, if the Gurney-communicator was really nothing but the entranced mind of Mrs. Willett, then Mrs. Willett must have had an ESP-acquired *skill*—namely, the skill of philosophizing well.

Here again we see how the ESP hypothesis gets pressed into the hypothesis that some people have Super-ESP. To accept the ESP hypothesis is to believe that high-level skills have been acquired through ESP. That may be hard enough to believe. But the full extent of the difficulty for the ESP hypothesis does not come into view until we focus on the distinction between the dramatic imitation of a personality and the dramatic interplay between different personalities. As we noted, a hypnotized person may be remarkably adept at imitating the personality of a person whom she is hypnotized to believe herself to be. But mere imitation, even if done very well, is very different from and much easier to simulate than the interaction that occurs when two intelligent people who are long-time friends as well as colleagues engage in high-level animated conversation about a complex subject that is very familiar and interesting to both.

Such interaction is the phenomenon to be explained in the Willett communications when Balfour was the sitter. For they exhibit all the dynamics of animated conversation between two friends who had shared various experiences and were familiar with each other's thought. The Gurney-communicator displayed, with remarkable precision, the temperament, the memories, the emotional sensitivity, and the manner of associating ideas that were characteristic of Edmund Gurney as he would have engaged in lively conversation with his long-time friend and associate, Lord Balfour. To account for this on the ESP hypothesis, we would have to suppose that the telepathically acquired item must be instantly translated into the dramatic form it would have taken if uttered in that conversational context by Edmund Gurney. We would have to suppose that when certain information is needed in the conversation, a telepathic rapport with the mind of the person who has it is instantly established, and the information is instantly acquired. But then the rapport must be instantly relinquished so that the information can be translated, instantly again, into a dramatic, highly authentic impersonation of Edmund Gurney as he would have acted in conversational give-and-take. If ESP on the part of the entranced mind of Mrs. Willett is what is behind all this, then the power she was wielding was truly a *Super*-ESP.

Super-ESP or Survival?

We are now in a position to draw a tentative conclusion about how these cases of psychic phenomena should be interpreted, even though we have done little more than scratch the surface in our study of them. Though the fraud hypothesis can never be absolutely ruled out, for all practical purposes it is not a real option in the best cases. Thus we are left with only the ESP and survival hypotheses. The ESP hypothesis may seem to have the edge until we see that it must be stretched into a Super-ESP hypothesis to accommodate the best cases of psychic phenomena. For having to postulate the existence of Super-ESP may give us pause for at least two reasons. First, our postulation that Super-ESP occurs in the best cases must stand completely on its own, for we have no independent evidence that such ESP ever occurs. Secondly, if we are willing to postulate that some persons have a superpower to acquire not only knowledge but complex skills as well, then we must ask ourselves where we *would* draw the line and concede that the phenomena are beyond the explanatory scope of the ESP hypothesis. What astounding things that someone may know or do could *not* be "explained" by postulating even more marvelous ESP powers? We may think that a Super-Super-ESP hypothesis that would not be falsified by anything we can conceive a person knowing or doing would explain everything, but in fact it would explain nothing. It must have limits and be falsifiable. Considerations such as these may lead us to the conclusion that the survival hypothesis has the edge.

It appears, then, that in the best cases of psychic phenomena, the survival hypothesis is the most plausible one. In other words, the most plausible interpretation of those cases is that some deceased persons have survived bodily death and have managed to reveal the fact of their continuing existence to the living. This is, of course, of the highest significance to us because there is, apparently, nothing special about these persons: What is true of them is very likely to be true of us as well. Still, in the final analysis it may be difficult to accept the survival interpretation, despite the apparent evidence for it, simply because of the difficulty in accepting the implication that persons are logically distinct from their bodies and logically capable of existing independently of them. But, in our deliberations concerning the nature of the self, we have already seen reason to accept this implication. What we will now examine is an argument which, if sound, would not only show that this implication is true but that you existed prior to your biological conception. In other words, it would show that you are not identical to your body, that you are capable of existing without it, and that your survival of death is highly probable. For if you did not come into existence with your biological conception, then it is quite unlikely that you will go out of existence with your biological death. Let us look at this argument.[5]

AN ARGUMENT FOR ETERNAL EXISTENCE

The argument depends upon a rather weak form of the principle of sufficient reason (PSR)—a principle whose plausibility we have already noted. We appealed to it earlier to justify the claim that even if the world is infinitely old, the positive fact that there are and always have been dependent beings is a fact that stands in need of explanation. Now we appeal to it not to support a claim about the world considered in its entirety, but more modestly, to argue only that in the case of each person or thing that comes into existence at some moment in time (other than the first moment if there was a first moment), there must be some explanation of why that person or thing came into existence then, rather than some other person or thing or nothing at all. We are now appealing to a weaker or less extravagant form of the PSR; for we are claiming only that *the coming into existence of every person or thing* must admit of explanation, and not that there must be an explanation of every positive fact and of every person or thing that has existed eternally, if there are any such persons or things. And this weaker claim surely seems plausible. To deny it is, in effect, to claim that there simply is no explanation as to why some particular person or thing came into existence at the time that it did. Certainly the scientist routinely assumes that such an explanation exists and, indeed, is often able to provide it.

Perhaps it is already fairly clear as to how the argument will proceed. If we accept the PSR in at least its weak form and then come to see how, in the case of some presently existing person or thing, there could be no explanation of its coming into existence, then we should be led to the conclusion that it never did come into existence, i.e., that it has always existed (or at any rate, has been in existence as long as time itself). The central part of the argument will consist in an attempt to show that there really is some presently existing person or thing that is such that no explanation of its coming into existence is possible. The challenge is to show not merely that we are unable to provide any such explanation but that none exists (at least so far as we can tell).

This challenge, however, may seem impossible to meet, especially if we ignore the possibility that matter is infinitely old and that there are some fundamental material elements that are essential to its existence. For when we consider some ordinary material thing such as a stone or a tree, we see not only that there is an explanation of its coming into existence but that this is something that science can actually provide. Human beings, of course, are much more complicated than these things; they have a complex array of both mental and physical properties. But there is no good reason to doubt that a much more advanced science would be able to explain by appeal to natural laws why some human being with certain mental and physical characteristics should exist at a certain time and place. For even the mental properties are scientifically accessible properties in virtue of their association with the physical properties (more specifically, the brain properties) studied in science. Is there anything here which is beyond the reach of scientific explanation?

Scientific Explanation and the Self

The answer to this question comes into view when we remind ourselves of a truth about persons, more specifically, of the truth that someone exactly like you might have existed *in your place*. The possibility expressed by this truth seems easy to imagine. We can easily imagine your having had an identical twin, and then we imagine this person existing *not with you* as your twin but *instead of you.* In this way we imagine a person distinct from you but nevertheless qualitatively and relationally identical to you. This person is qualitatively identical to you in virtue of having exactly the mental and physical characteristics that you have, and relationally identical to you in virtue of occupying your place in the world; for to occupy your place is to stand in relation to all other things in exactly the ways in which you are related to them.

Since this person (your possible-world twin, T) would be exactly similar to you, the question of who is actually in the world—you or T—would be utterly beyond the power of science to answer. Indeed, from the "outside" or third-person viewpoint to which science is confined, the question couldn't even be raised, for it wouldn't make any sense. Obviously, from the third-person viewpoint, a world containing T would be absolutely indistinguishable from the actual world—the world containing you. And if each of us didn't have an "inside" or first-person viewpoint on reality we would be utterly unable to make such a distinction in the first place. But, of course, we do have; and from your inside viewpoint our question about who actually inhabits this world is not only meaningful but is of the highest significance; for if T were the one who exists, then you would not be in the world at all.

Since science lacks the power even to raise this question, it would surely be unable to explain why you are in the world instead of T, or any other person qualitatively and relationally identical to you. From its view there would be nothing to explain. As we noted, an advanced science may be able to explain the presence of that complex set of mental and physical properties which in fact belongs to you. And if the presence of a mental state of a certain kind implies the existence of a person who is in that state, then science could infer the presence of a person as well. But all that it could infer is the presence of someone or other. It could not know that these states belong to *you*, much less explain why they belong to you rather than to someone else.

It seems clear then that even a completed science could offer no explanation of your presence in the world. Yet, given the acceptability of the PSR in at least its weak form, if there were an event that consisted in your coming into existence, then that event must be explicable. Since such an event could hardly be self-explanatory, it would seem that any possible explanation must involve reference to the creative activity of God. What possibility is left if the event in question is neither self-explanatory nor explainable even with complete scientific knowledge of the natural world?

At this point it may seem that your presence in the world points to the existence of a supernatural order. Perhaps it does, but not in the decisive way we might have expected. If we were to go on assuming that you came into existence a relatively short time ago, then, for the reasons already considered, we would appear to have very good grounds for believing that your existence is the result of the intentional activity of a supernatural agent, viz., God. But then we see that we have no grounds for reasoning in this way when we see that even a supernatural agent of great knowledge and power could not have intentionally brought you about. We reach this conclusion by once again employing the distinction between you and your possible-world twin. Though we cannot exclude the possibility that God created you, what our previous reflections indicate is that if He did create you, He did so without knowing who He was creating and thus could not have been intending to create *you* in particular.

God may have the power to create persons, but not with knowledge of *who* He is creating. Why this is so becomes clear when we reflect upon what distinguishes you from your possible-world twin T. From the outside you are absolutely indistinguishable from T. From your first-person viewpoint, however, the difference is unmistakable and profound. It is a difference between existence and nonexistence. But every other viewpoint, including God's (if God is distinct from you), is a third-person viewpoint. God may know much more about you than anyone else. Perhaps God knows exactly what kinds of thoughts, feelings, and sensations you are having at any given time. But not even God can share the viewpoint from which you are able to view yourself as just the person that you are—the only viewpoint from which you can be distinguished from T, who does not actually exist. Thus not even God can distinguish you from T, your possible-world twin.

Perhaps this conclusion about the limits of God's knowledge and power seems very difficult to accept. So let us look at it more closely. We realize that other human beings have access to you only through perception, and thus only from the outside—they see your body, they take note of your gestures and other behavioral expressions, and they listen to what you say. They may regard you as the person connected to these outward expressions and come to know much about you in this indirect manner. Nevertheless, their access to you—their *only* access to you—is indirect. It is not an access to you as precisely the person that you are, and thus not the direct access that you yourself have. Your access enables you to take the first-person viewpoint with respect to yourself, a viewpoint from which any confusion about who is in the world—you or T—would be unthinkable.

But why should we conclude that even the knowledge of God reaches a limit here? God is not conceived as a being who shares our limitations. In particular, we should not assume that God's epistemic access to us is confined to the perceptual modes to which other human beings are restricted. So what, if anything, is wrong with claiming that God may know us as directly and as individually as we know ourselves? Why can't God share with you your first-person viewpoint?

The answer comes into view when we focus our attention on the sharp, apparently absolute distinction between persons. We might give expression to this distinction by pointing out that no one can be partly you and partly another. You are you, and every other person, including T, is someone else. There is no blending or merging of persons. But God, though not a human being, is a personal being distinct from you. Thus God, in relation to you, is clearly *someone else*, someone as distinct from you as any other person. That absolute, though indescribable, difference between persons remains undiminished.

Now, the absolute distinction between persons implies that there is an absolute distinction between first-person viewpoints or perspectives. Just as it is impossible for two people to blend or merge, so it is impossible for two people to share a single first-person perspective. Put somewhat differently, a single first-person perspective cannot be shared by two persons any more than a single experience can belong both to you and to someone else. First-person perspectives are as closely tied to individual persons as the experiences in which they are rooted. You have a first-person access to yourself in virtue of having experiences that belong to you. But no one else, including God, can have that access to you without having your experiential states, and no one can have *them* without *being you*. Since no one else can *be you*, we are led once more to the conclusion that no other person whatsoever can somehow assume your first-person viewpoint and come to know you as just the person that you are.

We conclude, then, that even God's knowledge of you is limited to what can be known from an outside or third-person viewpoint. This is to conclude that there are first-person truths that you can know, but God cannot, e.g., that you are in the world rather than one of your possible-world twins. Moreover, these are significant truths, for God's failure to know them would have prevented Him from knowingly or intentionally creating you. To create you, He must, of course, create you as precisely the person that you are. Clearly, creating one of your possible-world twins would not suffice. But God cannot know you as precisely the person that you are. Consequently, He could not have knowingly or intentionally created you.

To accept this consequence, however, is to concede that we cannot make reference to God's intentions in an attempt to explain your (alleged) coming into existence. We should no longer attempt to explain this by saying such things as "God created you so that you might enjoy existing in this world," "God saw that the world would be better if you were in it," or "God created you to fulfill some purpose." For all these attempts falsely assume that God could have intentionally created you. On the other hand, to suggest that God unintentionally or accidentally created you seems almost on a par with the suggestion that your coming into existence was a chance or random occurrence and so not something that can be explained. Thus we reach the conclusion that your (alleged) coming into existence cannot be plausibly explained by making reference to God's creative activity.

When we combine this conclusion with our previous ones (viz., that such an event would be neither self-explanatory nor scientifically explainable), we end up concluding that an event which consisted in your coming into existence is not explainable at all. But the PSR, even in its weak form, states that no such event is possible. You did not come into existence at some moment in time, other than the first moment, if there was one. Since your existence at this moment is undeniable, it must be true that you have always existed!

Of course, this conclusion will strike us as implausible, if not simply incredible. At any rate, that is likely to be our initial reaction. Perhaps with time we will react differently. But let us ignore for the moment this credibility problem and focus on the implications this conclusion would have on the issue of whether we survive bodily death. Our first thought may be that if we have always existed, then our continuing to exist after bodily death is guaranteed. But we are not entitled to draw that inference. Our reasons for thinking that your inception would be inexplicable seem not to apply to your ceasing to exist, i.e., your extinction. This is because an explanation of your inception must make reference to your elusive individuality, while an explanation of your extinction need not. As we saw, an explanation of your inception must uniquely pick you out from all other beings like you, but an explanation of your extinction need not do that simply because the conditions under which you would be extinguished are very likely conditions under which all other beings like you would be extinguished as well. Thus if we knew that such conditions did obtain we would have an explanation of your ceasing to exist which did not pick you out from all other beings like you. And, of course, without a guarantee that those conditions will not obtain, we would have no guarantee that you would continue to exist indefinitely.

Nevertheless, the argument we have been considering is certainly relevant to the *likelihood* of your surviving bodily death. If it is sound, then your survival, although not guaranteed, would be highly probable. For if you have always been in existence, then you have existed independently of your body for a very long time, as it is only a few years old. And this bodes very well for your survival of bodily death. If, on the one hand, you have already been embodied many times prior to acquiring your present body, then you must have survived the death of each of these earlier bodies. In that case, surviving bodily death is something you have undergone numerous times. On the other hand, if this is your first embodiment (or one of just a few), then the conclusion must be that existence without a physical body is your normal state and thus the one to which you are likely to return after bodily death. In either case we should conclude that your existence very likely depends upon something other than the life of your present physical body and so will very likely continue after that body dies.

But can we really believe that you, and everyone else, have always existed? Can we even take this suggestion seriously? There are two obstacles standing in the way of our doing so. One has its source in religious concern. A line of reasoning which would have us conclude that God could not have intentionally created us may seem very uncongenial to a religious view of the world. It may seem so to a great many religious people, primarily because they have always thought of God as a creator of persons. But these people could accept the argument we have considered and nevertheless maintain that God is needed as our *sustainer*. They could maintain that we have always existed only because God has always been sustaining us, and in so doing retain a concept of God which is not diminished in any important way. With respect to this matter, then, our argument neither supports nor undermines a religious view that places God at the center of reality.

In another respect, however, our argument *supports* a religious interpretation of the world. If persons have always existed, then they do not fit well into a natural order where everything (with the possible exception of physical items of the most fundamental kind) comes and goes. Moreover, as we noted in an earlier chapter, persons appear to be curiously disconnected from all of the other items in the natural realm. What we should note now is that our argument is, in part, a development of this idea of an apparent disconnection—a disconnection that indicates the presence of a realm beyond the natural world. Thus our argument is certainly not hostile to a religious interpretation of the world, and so its implications for religion should not pose as any obstacle to accepting it.

Consciousness and the Self

The other obstacle in the way of accepting the view that persons have always existed is much more serious. We might indicate what this obstacle is with a question: What could you be, i.e., how are you to be conceived, if you are something that has always existed? Of course, the question of what you ultimately are is very difficult to answer, perhaps so difficult that we would be wise to leave it alone. But we cannot avoid it altogether, for we cannot consider the proposition that you have always existed without inquiring into the relation you have to your conscious states. If you have always existed, then before your present biological life began you were either having states of consciousness or you were not having any. These are the only alternatives. But each is open to serious objections and consequently is very difficult to accept.

Let us first consider the alternative that you did not have any conscious states before your present life. This may seem to you to be the more plausible of the two, especially if you (like the great majority of people) have no prior-life memories or any other evidence indicating that you were conscious prior to your present life. The lack of such evidence supports this alternative. But this alternative implies that consciousness is not necessary to your existence—that you are not essentially a conscious being. It also implies that you are not essentially a physical being. Yet there must be something which is essential to your existence for you to exist at all. What then can you be?

It may seem that prior to your present life you could have existed as a mere *capacity* for conscious states, and perhaps, for biological life. But this we must reject, for capacities are "ontological parasites"—they cannot exist without something to have them. The suggestion that you are something that *has* such a capacity (and retains it when you are not conscious) is more plausible. But if only your own conscious states are directly known to you and if this capacity-bearing entity which you supposedly are does not enter into any of your conscious states, then it is not directly known to you, or of course, to anyone else. We must then wonder if it can be known at all. If, as it seems, this view implies that the self is only indirectly known if not completely unknowable, then it is exposed to a variety of objections that make it very difficult to accept.

So let us consider the other alternative—the possibility that you have been having conscious states prior to this life. The absence of prior-life memories weighs *against* this alternative, but surely not decisively against it. Indeed, this fact may carry rather little evidential weight. For though you do not remember having had any conscious states prior to your present biological life, it may be that you had a great many but that they are now dissociated from you, analogous to the way in which your waking life is dissociated from you while you are experiencing a non-lucid dream. During such a dream you have no awareness of your waking life—a fact that becomes clear to you upon awakening. The dream not only seems real but seems to be reality in its entirety, for you have no awareness of anything else. Your waking life is not accessible to, i.e., is dissociated from, the awareness to which you are restricted during the dream. But upon awakening you attain a viewpoint from which you see the non-lucid dream taking its place among all the other experiences you are then having or remember having had. Similarly, upon biological death you may have an awakeninglike experience in which you attain a viewpoint from which you see your entire biological life to have been a non-lucid episode in an enormously long series of experiences that you now remember having had.

It seems, then, that your inability to remember any prior-life experiences does not weigh heavily against the view that you had a great many of them. Of course, the first view—that you didn't have any experiences prior to your present life—has the advantage with respect to this matter. But the second view has a great advantage with respect to a different matter: One who subscribes to it is able to reject the implication that the self is known only indirectly, if known at all. And, as we noted earlier, accepting that implication leads to great difficulties. Let us see what this advantage comes to.

If we accept the second view we need not concede that the self exists when it is not having experience, and so we have no temptation to place the self entirely outside its experience. If it does exist entirely outside its experiences or conscious states, then it can be known only indirectly, perhaps as the possessor of a certain set of those states, if indeed its existence can be known at all. But in accepting the second view we are free to maintain that the self, though something in addition to its conscious states, is not beyond them but enters into them in such a manner that direct knowledge of it by way of them is possible. Perhaps a defender of the first view is not excluded from saying something such as this. It is not clear that he is. What is clear is that if he maintains that the self may be directly known in its experience, then we are entitled to expect him to be able to specify some positive feature (other than a mere capacity) which the self is directly known to have—a feature which, on his view, it must retain even when it is not conscious. Perhaps that can be done, but it is difficult to see how.

In accepting the second view, however, we are able to maintain that the positive feature in question is *consciousness*—the self is a conscious being. Perhaps this is not to say much about the self. Perhaps in this case, much of what can be known cannot be *said*.[6] But how do we know that we can truthfully say even this much, and what exactly do we mean in saying it?

How do you know that you are conscious? You know this not merely by having conscious states but by becoming conscious of yourself having them. You become aware of yourself as a subject of conscious states. But what could a subject of conscious states be if it is not a physical body and yet is sometimes without consciousness? Perhaps nothing at all. It seems that a subject of conscious states needs to have conscious states in order to exist, just as conscious states need something to have them, i.e., something whose states they are. This line of reasoning drives us to the conclusion that the self is a conscious being *essentially*; consciousness is essential to its existence.

If this is a truth about what you are, then it is surely an important one. But one of its implications may be difficult to accept. If you are a conscious being essentially, then you exist only when you are conscious. But if you have always existed, then you have always been conscious. And if you have always been conscious, then virtually all of the conscious states you have had are presently dissociated from you. Furthermore, you must have been continuously conscious throughout your present life, even during those times when we would have commonsensically assumed that you were not, e.g., during deep dreamless sleep.

These conclusions follow from the claim that the self is essentially a conscious being that has always existed, but they may seem impossible to accept. Perhaps we should simply reject them without further consideration. But instead let us see what might be said in their defense. The conclusion that virtually all the conscious states we have had are presently dissociated from us is not, upon reflection, so difficult to accept, especially when we remind ourselves that we have forgotten the great majority of the experiences we have had since birth. Though there can be no question of our having had them, they are surely dissociated, perhaps permanently, from us now. Perhaps many of the experiences we had prior to this life are only temporarily dissociated from us, in which case this truth might become apparent to us in an awakeninglike experience occurring after biological death. But it may also be true that a great many are permanently dissociated and thus irretrievable by any means. This possibility is much easier to reconcile with our ordinary experience of a very limited memory. But even the possibility of a greatly expanded memory presents no real difficulty. So the conclusion that presently we must be witnessing the effect of a great deal of dissociation is not so implausible.

However, the other conclusion, that we have been continuously conscious throughout this life, seems obviously false. But even this cannot be rejected with utter confidence. For if, as it seems, consciousness is something that obtains in levels or degrees, then we may have or acquire some grounds for believing that during the periods when, to all appearances, we were unconscious, we were actually having low-level conscious states, all of which are permanently dissociated from our normal waking consciousness. An advanced science of mind-brain relations might even be able to support this belief by detecting in the brain, during times of apparent unconsciousness, an activity of a kind usually in association with low-level conscious states. At any rate, this belief is not preposterous or known to be false.

It seems, then, that the view that you have always existed does not break down under critical scrutiny. The obstacles in the way of accepting it are not insurmountable. Still, in the end it may not seem very plausible either. So what should we conclude as we bring to an end our deliberations about death? First, as always in philosophical inquiry, much remains to be considered. We have barely touched upon the vast area of psychical research. Secondly, there is a case, though perhaps a weak one, for thinking that we will survive biological death. Is this case strong enough to support *rational* belief in existence beyond death? This is difficult to answer, not only because the factors to be taken into account in assessing the strength of this case are numerous and complex, but because the standard to be satisfied for a belief to be rational is difficult to specify. Belief in survival would be irrational if we were to hold it in the face of knowledge that we are identical to our bodies, or that, though distinct from them, we cannot exist without them. For there is no question about what happens to *them*. But our investigations have at least shown that we do not have such knowledge, even if they have failed to show that there is a powerful case for thinking that we will survive bodily death. Perhaps this is all we should have expected, given the scope and the depth of the questions we have been attempting to answer.

QUESTIONS FOR FURTHER THOUGHT

1. Should we accept the view that death is bad for us if it results in our permanent nonexistence? Will we be better off if we can reject that view?

2. Many people find their apparent past nonexistence untroubling and yet are quite disturbed by the prospect of future nonexistence. Are such feelings irrational?

3. How strong is the evidence provided by religion for the existence of an afterlife? Is it stronger than the text suggests?

4. Is the survival hypothesis the most plausible explanation of the reports of paranormal occurrences? If so, is it more probable than not that you will survive bodily death? Is this more probable than not, *all things considered?* Or should we conclude that surviving death is highly unlikely?

5. Does it make sense to suggest that someone exactly like you could have been in your place? If so, what distinguishes you from that person? Can this difference be described?

6. Is the suggestion that you have always existed one we should take seriously? Would the truth of this suggestion imply that you have always been conscious?

7. Is your self-knowledge only indirect? What might it mean to assert that it is?

8. Does it make sense to suggest that you might survive bodily death as someone who is only partly you in relation to who you are now? Could you be what survives in virtue of the survival of some of your parts (assuming that you have parts)? Should we conclude that you must survive in your entirety if you are to survive at all?

9. Is there great difficulty in conceiving of what you would have to be for you to continue existing after the death of your body? Is the difficulty diminished if what we are trying to conceive is your continued existence in some other physical body? Must you be something essentially non-physical in either case?

10. What would have to be true of you for you to be such that you could be reincarnated in some other body? Would you have to be something distinct from and separable from either body?

11. Does the fact (if it is a fact) that you cannot exist independently of all physical bodies imply that you cannot conceive of yourself as an essentially non-physical being? *Can* you conceive of yourself as such a being?

12. If you can conceive of yourself existing independently of all physical bodies (and thereby conceive of yourself as an essentially non-physical being), would your having such a conception establish the *possibility* that what you are is an essentially non-physical being?

10

The MEANING of LIFE

What is the meaning of existence? Why do we exist? What is the point of it all? The joys of life may seem altogether too fleeting, the disappointments too numerous, the struggle often too wearisome, and the specter of unavoidable suffering, loss, and eventual death too foreboding for us to remain blissfully insensitive to such questions.

Is the point of it all, if there is one, to be found in our day-to-day activities? Or is there some higher destiny that awaits us, some higher purpose that our lives may serve, or some final goal that, if achieved, makes them worthwhile? What, we might wonder, is the point in striving as we do, despite the suffering that we must endure, and the death and destruction we cannot avoid, if there is not something of great value that awaits us or that even now infuses our lives?

Almost all of us have raised questions of this sort at some time, perhaps when grieving the loss of a loved one or contemplating our own mortality. They tend to be somber questions that press upon us when we momentarily step back from our ordinary activities and immediate concerns, take a survey of our human condition from an outside standpoint, and see how our lives as a whole appear from that view. These questions about the meaning of our lives seem to be of the highest importance, even though we may be at a loss to explain precisely what is troubling us when we raise them. We may find ourselves wondering about what makes a life meaningful, or even about whether a truly meaningful life is possible. When we come to feel that our lives cannot culminate in anything lasting—that the march of time eventually erases through death and destruction anything that we may manage to achieve—then we may feel the specter of meaninglessness hovering over us. Does it really matter *what* we do if, in the end, everything comes to the same, namely, to nothingness? This may be, for many, the tormenting question that prompts them to wonder about the meaning of human existence. Perhaps the widespread assumption that our lives can be meaningful is incompatible with the conditions under which we must live. In any case, it is not difficult to understand how we might be led to raise questions about meaning.

CONDITIONS AFFECTING THE QUEST FOR MEANING

A sensible first step to take in our attempt to answer such questions is to determine how they may be affected by our previous reflections on the other fundamental questions. There are certain conditions whose satisfaction, if not essential for one's life to be meaningful, make success in the search for meaning much easier to achieve, at least for people whose search for meaning is tied to their search for truth — people unwilling to make their quest for meaning easier by allowing themselves to be deceived about the character of human existence. Perhaps the most fundamental of them is that there is objective truth to be known and that some knowledge of it is not impossible for us. Though we did not argue in a direct and sustained way for the fundamental assumption that there is objective truth to be known, it seems clear that the burden of proof must be borne by the one who denies this assumption, and also that the burden would be exceedingly difficult to bear. Even an otherwise successful denial would seem to imply, inconsistently, its own objective truthfulness. With respect to our capacity to acquire knowledge, we saw how that would become considerable if knowledge were not limited to what can be directly known.

Hardly less fundamental is the condition that there is something for us to be, that is, something whose identity through time is determinate and which persists long enough to be the possessor of a meaningful life. Another is that we have genuine alternative courses of action open to us as we try to direct our lives in one way rather than another. Stated negatively, the condition is that our (apparent) decisions are not causally necessitated, not items in causal chains of events extending infinitely, or at least indefinitely, far into the past. If this condition were not satisfied, any sense of meaningfulness we could attain in virtue of our conviction that we play a role in the shaping of our lives—a conviction without which any sense of meaningfulness would be peculiar if not impossible—would be founded upon an illusion. A further condition whose satisfaction may be found by many to be extremely beneficial, if not essential, to living a meaningful life is the existence of some basis for believing that reality includes a spiritual (or non-natural) dimension, that the natural order is not the only (concrete) reality that there is. Others may feel that a basis for belief in an afterlife, either in conjunction with a spiritual dimension or as an extension of the natural order, is a condition which, if not essential, renders the quest for meaning much more likely to be successful. One thinks of the tragic sense of life expressed by Unamuno when he exclaims, "If consciousness is, as some inhuman thinker has said, nothing more than a flash of light between two eternities of darkness, then there is nothing more execrable than existence."[1]

The fulfillment of these conditions is not, of course, something we are in a position to demand. But we might consider ourselves to be fortunate if, as our previous reflections indicate, at least some of them are met. With respect to the second, and crucially important, condition, we would not have doubted that we are beings who retain a determinate identity as we persist through time until we probed rather deeply into the issue of whether selves exist and saw what might lead many to believe that the notion of a self is an illusion. Clearly, the concession that we are *not* selves, that what we have implicitly supposed to be true of us on the most fundamental level is utterly mistaken, would make questions about meaning more difficult to address. Indeed, it might strike many as a concession that renders meaning-nihilism unavoidable. But, as we noted, the case for concluding that we are not selves is unconvincing. Much more convincing is the view that we *are* selves, whatever else is true of us. We are selves in virtue of persisting through time as the selfsame subject of conscious states. It is in virtue of our being subjects that our identity through time cannot fail to be determinate and that there is a deep difference between any two of us.

The third condition would be met if the agency theory is true. If it *is* true, the problem of finding meaning in a world in which all of our decisions and actions are causally necessitated to occur just as they do occur would not arise. We would not have to wonder whether our lives should matter to anyone if whatever we do or however we live is a causally necessitated result of events occurring long before we were born. Thus the evidence we have for believing that, essentially, we are not only subjects of conscious states but also subject-*agents*, able to act freely in virtue of initiating causal chains, might be taken to be a great boon to our quest for meaning.

With respect to the question of whether an afterlife awaits us or of whether there is a non-natural realm, the evidence yielded by our study may have seemed quite weak, or at least not as strong as we might have hoped. We can see how such an epistemic situation might prompt the response that any intellectually honest search for meaning should not go beyond a consideration of our lives as we presently live them in the natural world. Still, such an appraisal of our situation seems too dim. The proper appraisal may well be that we do not know, in anything approaching a conclusive sense, the answers to these questions, and so they may be legitimately regarded as open questions in relation to our search for meaning.

As we proceed to deal with our questions about the meaningfulness of our lives, we should note at the outset that we cannot provide a satisfactory answer to them without knowing precisely what we are asking when we ask them. But just clarifying these large questions will prove to be no easy task. For despite the depth and significance they seem to have, they are plagued with vagueness and ambiguity.

THE SOURCE OF MEANING

When we wonder about the meaning of life, we are probably assuming, unreflectively, that its meaning depends upon something external to or beyond it—perhaps an afterlife or a divine plan in which we have a place. That is, we may be assuming that life has meaning to the extent that it prepares us for an afterlife, perhaps in the company of God. In any case, let us begin with an investigation into why it is so tempting to think of the question of life's meaning in this way. One source of this temptation is linguistic. We commonly speak of the meaning *of* our lives, as opposed to meaning *in* them, thus suggesting that their meaning lies beyond them. Furthermore, when we think about meaning, we may be thinking of the kind of meaning that words and other symbols have; and this is a meaning that goes *beyond* the symbol. The word *dog*, for example, is in itself nothing more than a mark on paper, or a noise if spoken. Its meaning consists in what it refers to, and thus in something beyond the word itself. So if we are thinking of this kind of meaning when pondering the meaning of life, we will be led quite naturally to suppose that life's meaning is external to it. Of course, a moment's reflection should lead us to see that the meaning of life must be quite different in kind from the meaning of a word.

A much more important source of the temptation to think of life's meaning as something external is the feeling we get when we view our lives in a much larger context. We are able to step back and view our lives as a whole from a standpoint outside them—a cosmic standpoint. From that standpoint, they appear momentary, minute, and insignificant—hardly a ripple in that enormous sea of matter and space-time that we know as the physical universe. The picture that emerges is certainly not uplifting. It may leave us with the conviction that if this is all our lives come to, then it would not have mattered in the least if we had never existed. Let us look at this matter more carefully to see precisely what sort of obstacle it poses in our quest for meaning.

Though we have not yet attempted to specify what it is for a life, or any activity, to be fully meaningful, we can say with confidence that a meaningful activity must be one that matters; it has significance or importance. We might also point out that if an activity is not pointless—if it is directed toward some end that has significance—then the activity itself has significance. But if this is so, then what is the problem about meaning? Our lives seem to be filled with meaningful activities. At this moment, you may have an approaching test to prepare for, groceries to buy this afternoon, a party to attend this weekend, and an interesting job interview in two weeks, among countless other goal-directed concerns and expectations that keep you occupied almost continuously. But you would not cite them as constituting the meaning of your life. That must involve something of greater significance, perhaps such great goods as self-actualization, love, or overall happiness. But even these seem to miss the mark when we go on to ask whether your life *as a whole* has some point to it. If we step back and view your life from the outside as one item among the others that appear from the cosmic standpoint we are now taking, there seems to be no point to it at all. In a few decades you will be dead and then eventually, if not soon, forgotten. Even if you should manage to create something of such great value that you will be remembered for hundreds of years, it can have no permanent significance; for eventually all human life and achievements will be obliterated if, as physicists predict, the universe will return to a state in which life is impossible. At that point, if not much sooner, it will not have mattered if you or I had never existed. Of course, our existence matters to those who care about us, but from this broad outside standpoint, their existence doesn't matter either. So it doesn't matter that we matter to them, or that they matter to us. There is no point to any of our individual lives.[2]

This feeling that our lives may be devoid of ultimate meaning—that ultimately it will not matter what we do or that we ever existed—is encouraged by the picture of the world that science presents to us. In this picture, the natural world is a world of matter in motion governed by blind, unconscious forces, incapable of caring about what happens or of intending one result rather than another. It is a world without purpose, without meaning. To predict or explain an event we look to its causes and not for any purpose its occurrence might serve. Of course, we have *our* purposes, but the natural world in which we live is entirely indifferent to them. It is indifferent to our ideals, our achievements, our values, our very existence. It is a vast spiritual emptiness. There is no cosmic plan in which our lives have a permanent place. The landscape of the natural world disclosed to us by science may strike us as distressingly bleak and alien to everything we value, and on the horizon lies only a cosmic darkness that holds no hope for anything better for us and our accomplishments than total annihilation followed by permanent nonexistence.

We see, then, why we might feel pressure to look for the meaning of our lives in a realm beyond them, and why questions about meaning are so frequently tied to concerns about the existence of God and an afterlife. We see why many people have felt that without the existence of God, or at least without faith that God exists, life is deprived of all meaning. Unfortunately, the theistic answer to the problem of meaning must fail as a completely satisfactory answer, not primarily because of difficulties in establishing a rational basis for belief in God but because it merely pushes the problem back a step.

The theist will say that we exist because God created us. But this answer only raises a further question: why did God create us? The reply may be that God created us for a purpose and that our lives are meaningful if they fulfill this purpose. Without that they would be pointless. But aren't we entitled to ask what point there is in fulfilling God's purpose? How can fulfilling *God's* purpose be what makes *our* lives meaningful? If these questions are legitimate, as they seem to be, then clearly the problem of meaning has been merely pushed back a step. A theist may suggest that these questions are not legitimate by claiming that our questions about meaning simply come to an end with this answer. But this seems quite unacceptable. Perhaps our questions about meaning must eventually come to an end; but if so, they must end in a purpose of our own making, or at least in one that we can make our own. This becomes clear when we see that we cannot find it meaningful to fulfill God's purpose unless we can embrace that purpose as our own as well. After all, a purpose for our lives is supposed to make them meaningful to *us*, not to God. In other words, if there can be some "question-terminating" purpose that makes our lives meaningful, it must come from *within* us; it cannot be imposed from without. And so our search for meaning should be primarily, if not exclusively, a search for something we might find here and now, internal to our lives.

A similar difficulty arises for the attempt to find the meaning of this life in an afterlife beyond it: Again the problem of meaning is simply pushed back a step. Unless we can embrace the afterlife as a meaningful one, its existence cannot give meaning to this one. We obviously cannot say that the afterlife gets its meaning from something else, perhaps something to which it leads, for that only takes us back a further step. Rather, it must be such that we can find it meaningful in itself, i.e., *intrinsically* meaningful. But *if* we can, then why shouldn't we believe that we can find *this* life meaningful in itself, without having to look beyond it for its meaning? Why should we believe that our present life differs from the afterlife, if there is one, in this respect? The afterlife may be much longer, perhaps even unending, but additional life by itself cannot transform a meaningless life into one with meaning. If a life is meaningless, then merely extending it will result in nothing better than a *longer* meaningless life. Unless life itself, even if short, can have intrinsic meaning, there can be no meaning either in this life or in another. Thus again we are led to the conclusion that the meaning of life must be found within it, if found at all.

It becomes clear why meaning is not something that can be conferred upon our lives from without or consist entirely in something beyond them when we consider more carefully how finding meaning in life should be understood. A meaningful activity is one that has significance. But to have significance is to have value, and value, as we have seen, does not exist apart from beings capable of making value judgments. Value is not an objective feature of the world that exists independently of all human subjective evaluation. Consequently, neither is the meaning of life. Thus we see in a somewhat different way why the meaning of our lives cannot be bestowed upon them from without. For their meaning must be something that makes them meaningful to *us*, or, more generally, *valuable* to us, and thus must involve a contribution on our part. The meaning of our lives is something that *we* must provide.

Still, whatever success we manage to achieve in making our lives meaningful does not depend entirely upon us. It also depends upon the conditions under which we must live, that is, upon our own given nature in conjunction with the laws that determine the course of all things in the natural world. And so, if our quest for meaning yields less than we would have hoped, that shortcoming may not be entirely our fault, even though the meaning we seek must spring forth from us. Let us see why this is so.

We have noted that life, or some activity within one's life, has meaning if it has significance or importance, and that to be significant is to have value. And though the world as it is in itself, independently of us, is value-neutral, our value judgments about it are *not independent* of its nature. They are surely affected by what we find it to be, or at any rate, by what we believe it to be. If the significance of an activity depended only on whether that activity had intrinsic value (i.e., value in itself, independently of its relation to other things), then the objective features of the world would have little, if any, impact upon our ability to view our lives as meaningful. We would have to admit that any doubts about the meaningfulness of our lives would be nothing more than a display of confusion. For we have no doubt that our lives have some intrinsic value, even when they are not going well. Indeed, the will to go on living remains strong in the great majority of us despite the adversity we may be enduring.

This resolve is not adequately explained by pointing to the widespread, and often paralyzing, fear of death. There is more to it than that. We seem convinced that to be alive and to have experience is a state that has intrinsic value even if that value is outweighed by the burden our lives may have become. Thus our questions about meaning cannot simply be questions about the intrinsic value of being alive. They are primarily questions about whether our lives can be of value in some *further* respect—a respect that, as we shall see, *is* affected by what is true of the world, independently of us and our efforts to see our lives as meaningful.

THE ELEMENTS OF MEANING

It appears that meaningfulness, of a life or an activity within one, is a complex feature made up of a number of elements. Since a life may be compared to an activity and since the meaning of an activity is a matter of degree, let us proceed by trying to determine what features an activity must have to be meaningful in the fullest sense. We think of various kinds of activity as having value. Consider a game you play solely for amusement: solitaire, for example. It has value in itself (intrinsic value) simply because it is pleasurable, even though it is pointless in the sense that it is not goal-directed. Other activities have little or no value in themselves but are carried out anyway because of the anticipated outcome. Here we might think of a certain kind of work that in itself is nothing but drudgery but is nevertheless deemed valuable or worthwhile because of the value of that to which it ordinarily leads.

Such work would have only *derivative* value. But it would have enough value to be worth doing if its aim could be achieved and the achievement of its aim would be worthwhile.

We are now in a position to specify the features an activity must have to be fully meaningful.[3] It must have enough intrinsic value to be worthwhile in itself; it must also have derivative value in virtue of being directed toward a goal; and this goal must be important and achievable. An activity would be meaningless if it lacked all of these features. And though it may still have meaning, it would be meaning-deficient to some degree if it lacked at least one of them.

An activity would be meaning-deficient if it were worthless in itself, i.e., without intrinsic value, independently of any benefit that might result from its performance. Lack of derivative value would be another deficiency. An activity would lack such value if it were pointless—if there were no goal or end to which it is directed. However, even if an activity is not pointless, the goal or end to which it is directed may be so insignificant or trivial as to be not worth seeking. The goal may not have enough value to justify the performance of the activity. Again, derivative value would be lacking. But an activity could be meaning-deficient even if it were worthwhile in itself in addition to being directed toward a significant end. For the end could be unattainable, thus rendering the activity futile.

THE THREAT OF FUTILITY

Futility is the sort of deficiency that threatens to cast a shadow of meaninglessness over our lives, despite our best efforts to make them meaningful. For it is a source of meaninglessness that is not under our control, at least not if there are unattainable goals we find ourselves virtually compelled to pursue. No matter how vigorously, persistently, and skillfully we may seek the goals we consider to be of ultimate importance, they may remain forever beyond our reach, not because we failed to do something we could have done, but because of the nature of the world itself. We may have no doubt that our lives have intrinsic value, at least under all but the most unfortunate of conditions, and that our goals are well worth seeking. But if the world is such that we cannot attain them, then our efforts will be futile, whether or not their futility is something we ever discover.

How seriously should we take this threat of futility—the possibility that the goals we regard as crucially important, indeed, the goals to which we may be directing our lives, are *unattainable*? Of course, we often fail to reach our short-term goals or objectives, not because we could not have done so, but for some other reason, perhaps lack of effort. On the other hand, there are times when we fail to reach such goals because under the prevailing conditions we could not have succeeded. Our efforts turned out to be futile, though this fact was unknown to us at the time. But can our *lives* turn out to be like this? Success in some short-term endeavor, such as landing an attractive job you were striving to get, may seem crucially important at the time, but it probably isn't. The meaningfulness of your life does not hinge upon getting it. This is not to suggest that numerous unsuccessful efforts of this sort, whether futile or not, have no impact on meaning. But the threat of futility which is of primary concern to us here is that which arises in relation to our most fundamental goals—those of ultimate importance to us, or which, if attained, prevent our lives from being pointless.

Perhaps it is possible to live well without such goals, without assuring ourselves that our lives have derivative value in addition to the intrinsic value involved in simply living them. In any case, most of us apparently assume, or at least hope, that there is some point to our lives which adds significantly to their value. But if the world renders our efforts futile, then our lives are not genuinely enriched, even if we manage to maintain the illusion that they are. For then the reality would be that those efforts are wasted. They would be like those of Sisyphus who, according to an ancient Greek myth, was condemned to an eternity of futile activity, forced to roll a stone to the top of a hill, only to have it roll down again so that his labor might be endlessly repeated. Sisyphus, however, had no illusion about the futility of his labor. Perhaps he understood his condition better than we understand our own. Could it be that we are in the grip of such an illusion? Let us see what reason we have to believe that we are.

We have been trying to determine the truth about a variety of important matters in our quest to "make sense of it all." In so doing, we have been implicitly assuming that there are objective truths about the world—truths that obtain independently of what we conceive the world to be and of what we say about it. We might give expression to this fundamental assumption by stating that there is an independently existing world that *is what it is*, whatever it is—irrespective of whether we can discover *what* it is—that is, what is *true* of it. But now suppose that an extreme relativism is true—a relativism that maintains not only that no such truths can ever be known but that they do not exist. The implication would be that all claims about a reality that exists independently of all human language and belief are false, if not meaningless. Thus our quest for objective truth would be futile. Reality would be such that our best efforts must fail; and if we were to discover their futility, the purpose of our quest would lose its power to imbue them with meaning and to spur us on. We could continue to find our efforts meaningful only if we remained blissfully unaware of their futility.

An extreme relativism of this sort may seem so implausible as to be difficult to take seriously. How could it be that there is no objectively existing reality about which there are objective truths, whether or not we can ever find out what they are? Besides, when we try to imagine that this view is true, we see that its own truth would be an objective truth about the world that would be incompatible with its being true. Thus the view that there is no objective truth whatsoever is self-contradictory. So perhaps we need not worry that all of our truth-seeking efforts may be futile, even if many are, in fact, unsuccessful. Still, there is a form of relativism that may strike us as a cause for worry about futility: relativism with respect to moral value.

We have already noted that value, unlike truth, is apparently not a part of the world as it is independent of us and other sentient creatures. In other words, moral value exists only in relation to beings such as ourselves (and God, if God exists) who are capable of making moral judgments. As we have noted, our views about what is morally right or wrong apparently have no deeper basis than our own feelings, sentiments, and preferences. And our awareness of this fact (assuming, of course, that it *is* a fact) may strike many of us as diminishing the significance of our moral judgments—even those that we would otherwise take to be of the greatest importance.

We commonly take certain moral values to be sacrosanct. What is morally right, we may feel, is right not merely in relation to our preferences (which, after all, could have been other than they in fact are) but right, *period!* Its moral rightness is *absolute*, we may claim, and not merely relative to us. In any case, it is easy to imagine someone who suffers in vain for his morality, largely because he believes that his moral imperative is absolute—that moral *truth*, as well as moral principle, is at stake. He would not have suffered, or not have suffered so much, if his morality had been different. Perhaps some of the great martyrs who gave their lives for hopeless causes were motivated by an absolutist view of morality. If this were so, then even though they may have had no doubts about the meaningfulness of their lives, the morality for which they sacrificed themselves lacked the deep significance they thought it had. Their ultimate desire was to bring about something of absolute value. But such a desire cannot be satisfied, and so their efforts were destined to be futile. When viewed in this light, such people may strike us as more misguided than heroic—victims of a peculiar kind of illusion. It may be said that this evaluation is too harsh, that there can be no legitimate concern about the meaning of the lives of those who focused all their energy on doing what it was their ultimate desire to do. But on the other hand, though they may have displayed great conviction, confidence, and vigor in pursuing their goals, one can't help but think that they would have been better off if their ultimate desires had been other than they were.

Still, we need not find the subjectivity of moral value to be a serious threat to meaning. For we are free to embrace the view that there is no absolute moral value without undermining our conviction that morality is of fundamental importance. If, as we have argued, there is on the most fundamental level a nearly universal agreement about what is morally right, then we have an anchor for our moral judgments—an anchor within our own common nature. And we don't need a moral ground more substantial than this to justify the great importance we take moral matters to have. We often seem to assume, unreflectively, that there must be something beyond us that makes our moral judgments right or wrong—something that does not depend upon the contingency of our human nature. But we need not; we don't have to maintain the illusion that our moral values need an objective ground for them to contribute to the meaningfulness of our lives.

THEISM AND MEANING

However, the threat of futility, and thus the threat to meaning, seems quite serious when we consider the relationship between meaning and the theistic view of the world. For the threat that appears in this context is one which bears upon the meaningfulness of the lives of a great many people. Though we have seen that belief in the existence of an afterlife and a divine plan for us cannot by itself fill our lives with meaning, the loss of this belief would nevertheless profoundly affect the ability of many to find their lives meaningful, at least in the fullest sense. We have already noted how enormously appealing to us this belief can be. It is a belief held by great numbers of people, and, in the case of many, it deeply affects their lives. The point of much of their activity, as they would interpret it, is to win divine approval and to prepare themselves for an afterlife in the company of God. If successful in this, their lives would take on derivative value in addition to the intrinsic value they already have. Success might well be regarded by these people as what gives point to their lives. If they are right, then there is an outside standpoint from which our existence *does* matter.

But there is another respect in which the truth of theism would favorably affect the problem of meaning. The existence of a divine plan for us would indicate that the powers that control our ultimate destiny are not indifferent to our welfare. If the world was designed by a rational being and we have a place in that design, we could then have assurance that the world is not such that our efforts to fully actualize ourselves will inevitably prove to be futile.

Of course, many if not most of us fail to actualize ourselves to an extent that even approaches the limits of our capacities, often because of lack of opportunity or the brevity of life. One of the most sobering aspects of human life becomes conspicuous when we witness someone dying early in life without having had the opportunity to actualize her potentialities. Others die as they are just beginning to reach the height of their intellectual and creative powers. It seems impossible to look upon such apparently senseless events and remain unconcerned about the possible futility of human life. The truth of theism, however, would provide reason to believe that efforts which prove to be futile in this life are not futile in the long run.

We are now in a position to appreciate fully the impact that the falsity of theism could have on our quest for meaning. Efforts directed toward obtaining divine approval and an afterlife in the presence of God would, of course, be futile. Since they would be founded upon an entirely false belief, their futility would be guaranteed. And those who became aware of this unfortunate fact—that the goals to which they have been directing their lives are unattainable—might well feel, at least for some time, that the meaning had been sucked out of their lives. Such awareness could be devastating for those who had been counting on the truth of theism.

Meaning is also affected in a more general way. If the powers that control the world are indifferent to our welfare, we would have less reason to believe that our potentialities can be realized in it or that our fundamental desires are in accord with it. We would have to acknowledge that what appears to be futile effort on our part is not *mere* appearance. For what we fail to accomplish in our natural lives we fail to accomplish, period. Without a transcendent or supernatural dimension, the world would be roughly as it is known to science, at least with respect to its value-neutrality. It would be a world without concerns and indifferent to everything we value. There would be no outside standpoint from which our individual lives or anything about us would matter—not our ultimate desires, not our greatest achievements, not even the existence of our species. The outlook for us, at least in the long term, would be bleak indeed.

But all this would merely make the quest for meaning more difficult. Success would certainly not be impossible. Many have found their lives to be meaningful within a purely naturalistic framework, convinced that their existence comes to an absolute end when they die. And we too have noted that our lives can be meaningful even if they have no derivative value—even if there is no point to our lives as a whole. Perhaps we should not only come to *accept* the possibility that they are pointless but to strive to *embrace* that possibility—to view it with approval, or at least with indifference. Maybe the intrinsic value of our lives is sufficient, and all we should have expected, or even desired. Perhaps we should be content to seize whatever opportunities or enjoyment the moment offers, and to regard our days as sufficient unto themselves. It may well be that, as Nagel suggests, we take ourselves too seriously when we suppose that our lives should matter from some broader standpoint.[4] Perhaps it should not matter to us that from a broad outside standpoint it would not have mattered if we had never existed.

Suppose that in a hundred years it will not matter that you or I ever existed. Suppose that in a billion years after all traces of the human race have disappeared it will not matter that any human being ever existed, perhaps because there is no one left to whom it could matter. Should this bother us? There is reason to think that it should not. Though (as we noted earlier in considering our attitudes toward death) future nonexistence seems more troubling to us than past nonexistence, it is not clear that a realization of future non-significance is or should be similarly troubling to us in our present quest for meaning. Concerns about nonexistence seem relevantly different from concerns about non-significance, partly because the future nonexistence that troubles us is our own, whereas our future non-significance consists in our having existed not mattering to *someone else,* or in there being no others to whom it could matter. In addition, our future nonexistence entails the absence of the intrinsic value of the life we would have experienced had we existed in the future, whereas future non-significance amounts to nothing more than the absence of a derivative value that our lives otherwise would have had. Also, our past nonexistence (prior to our conception) fails to trouble us, largely because we realize on some level that had we existed in the distant past, that existence would now be over and thus would be nothing to anticipate having. But past meaningfulness, consisting in our having found our lives meaningful in the past, is certainly relevant to our finding them meaningful now. Thus our quest for meaning and our concerns about nonexistence seem to run along different tracks, and we should keep this fact in mind as we return to our focus on meaning.

If the passage of time severs the meaning connection, with the result that what we do now will not matter in the distant future, then it seems reasonable to infer that the gap thereby created has implications in both directions: What happens at t_1 does not matter at t_2 *and* what happens at t_2 does not matter at t_1. More specifically, if in x number of years it will not matter that you or I ever existed, then the fact that this will not matter at that time should not matter to us now. Similarly, the possibility that our lives do not matter from a standpoint outside our own limited human one should not trouble us.

Still, the possibility that our lives as a whole are pointless may be quite difficult to accept. But we should be up to the task. If there is a transcendent power not indifferent to our concerns and more existence in store for us, we might find that to be enormously uplifting—something which, if known to us, could greatly enrich our lives. But if there is not, then so be it. We can brace ourselves to face our extinction and the eventual destruction of everything we value. It is unbecoming of us, indeed *unworthy* of us, to be unwilling or unable to face the truth, whatever that should turn out to be. If a more uplifting view of the world—one more in accord with our hopes—can be sustained only with a faith that has no concern for the truth, then it is not worth having; and we should have the intellectual courage to reject it.

MEANING AND THE SEARCH FOR TRUTH

The quest for meaning should be in large part a quest for truth and understanding. We make our lives meaningful as we realize our potentialities, and one of the most important of these is our potential for understanding, rooted in the apprehension of truth. It is a potentiality that renders us unique among the life forms known to us. To never engage in or to abandon a genuine search for truth and understanding—to go through life with very little understanding of what we are, of what is going on within and around us, and of the broad outline of the world—is to live in an impoverished manner, despite the other riches one may possess. The meaningfulness of such a life is surely diminished. However, we should note again, as we did at the very outset of our study, that this search cannot be done for us by others, however much they may be of help to us as we proceed. There are those who would feign to do the search for us and to have us accept, uncritically and unreflectively, what they claim to have found. Perhaps more significantly in the case of many of us, there are churches and other institutions or organizations that would have us passively accept, without critical reflection, the dogmas they foist upon us. But we must not succumb to this, even if what we hear from these sources is what we would very much like to believe. We must insist on thinking things out for ourselves and on having our beliefs reflect our understanding of *truth*, rather than our desires or the opinions of some self-proclaimed authority.

To see the world with our own eyes, and to see it clearly with eyes unclouded by fear or desire and unblinded by the dogmas pressed upon us by authority—that is an aspiration which reflects both courage and wisdom. But it also points the way to compassion—that magnanimous compassion which lifts us above our small, sometimes petty, concerns and our keeping track of the moral lapses and improprieties of one another, as it leads us to focus on our lot as human beings struggling to find meaning in our lives. Compassion of this kind enlarges our view by leading us to look unflinchingly at the large scene, at the plight of humankind, but without losing sight of the fact that suffering is always borne by individuals. It prevents us from being unmoved by the quiet desperation, the futile struggling, and the unspeakable suffering that we witness all around us, and it prompts us to do what we can to help. Such compassion, especially in conjunction with courage and wisdom, will help us to live so as to leave a good legacy, and to see that one's legacy is of great importance, despite the likelihood that it be short-lived.

The search for truth, then, is all-important, both to our quest for meaning and to our efforts to "make sense of it all." We have done a great deal of thinking and searching; and although we have come to the end of our study, our search itself should continue, and indeed should never end while we still live. Though a satisfactory end to it is very likely beyond our reach and may not be in our best interest in any case, we might expect to see some progress. That is what we seem to have accomplished. We have not only made some progress in "making sense of it all," but, just as important, have gained some insight into how to live with what we have found.

QUESTIONS FOR FURTHER THOUGHT

1. Does the fact that we sometimes wonder about the meaningfulness of our lives indicate that we find them troubling in some way? If not, how should this activity be understood? If so, does the text provide a satisfactory explanation of what may be troubling to us?

2. How are questions about meaning related to questions about value? Are they *nothing but* questions about value, or are they also questions about what is true of the world, independently of the value judgments we make about it?

3. Do we take our lives too seriously when we suppose that they should matter from some broader standpoint outside them? In doing so, do we expose ourselves to the threat of futility? *Can* we take them too seriously?

4. How might we persuade ourselves to take our lives less seriously than we do? Can we do so? Would it be in our interest to do so if we could?

5. Would we be justified in taking meaningfulness to be an entirely subjective matter? More specifically, if a person finds his or her life fulfilling, should we take it to be meaningful, irrespective of how deplorable it may appear when viewed from an external, more objective standpoint?

6. Would the quest for meaning be much less difficult in a world in which theism was known to be true and accepted as true by nearly everyone? Would this quest be considerably easier in the actual world if people suffered less?

7. Is having experienced growth in character and virtue as a result of having endured a considerable amount of suffering conducive to finding one's life to be meaningful? Is some suffering necessary for a meaningful life? Or is suffering usually just an obstacle to be surmounted or circumvented in one's quest for meaning?

NOTES

CHAPTER 2: KNOWLEDGE

1. See William James, *The Meaning of Truth* (New York: Longmans Green, 1909) and John Dewey, *The Quest for Certainty in John Dewey: The Later Works, 1925–1953*, vol. 4, 1929 (Carbondale: Southern Illinois University Press, 1984). For an influential defense of the coherence theory (as a theory of both the nature of truth and of justification) see Brand Blandshard, *The Nature of Thought*, 2 vols. (London: Allen and Unwin, 1939).

2. See Richard Rorty, *Philosophy and the Mirror of Nature* (Princeton, N.J.: Princeton University Press, 1979), *Consequences of Pragmatism* (Minneapolis: University of Minnesota Press, 1982), and *Objectivity, Relativism, and Truth* (Cambridge: Cambridge University Press, 1991).

3. See Edmund Gettier's famous article, "Is Justified True Belief Knowledge?" *Analysis*, 1963.

4. I owe the concept of relevant justification to Dale Jacquette. For more discussion and application of this concept, see his *Six Philosophical Appetizers* (New York: McGraw-Hill, 2001), pp. 32–35.

5. Of course, you need to possess the appropriate concepts and (probably) have knowledge of a language. But these are not known to you more directly than is your immediate experience.

6. Perhaps Immanuel Kant, the great German philosopher, is the most famous defender of this view. His *Critique of Pure Reason*, translated by Norman Kemp Smith (New York: St. Martin's Press, 1965, first published 1787), contains a detailed defense of it.

7. Descartes employed this speculation in a most engaging way to raise questions about the foundations of our knowledge claims. See his remarkable little book, *Meditations on First Philosophy* (Indianapolis, Ind.: Bobbs-Merrill, 1960, first published 1641). Though a very brief work, only 56 pages, it is one of the most important philosophy books ever written.

8. Such a skeptic need not be committed to the more general and much more implausible form of skepticism according to which we cannot be absolutely certain of the truth of any proposition. Some propositions (e.g., "2 + 3 = 5," "All bachelors are unmarried," and "All black dogs are dogs") are *necessarily* true and thus such that one's knowledge of their truth is unaffected by the possibility that one is dreaming. What could it be, we might ask, to dream that

"All black dogs are dogs" is *false*? Nor is this skeptic committed to the view that all propositions of the form "I (you, we, they, etc.) *know* that p" are false. You could be such a skeptic and yet maintain that you know that you are now having an experience of reading. For you could hold that even if you are dreaming that you are reading, you are nevertheless having an experience of reading. As such a skeptic, your doubt would not be about whether you are having sense experience, but about how your sense experience should be *interpreted* or *understood*.

CHAPTER 3: REALITY

1. The distinction that I am trying to draw between objects and other entities probably requires some explication. Even what I have classified as non-objects can be *objects of consciousness*, and thus may be considered objects in this broad sense. However, the distinction that I have in mind is rooted in the complexity of an entity. The non-objects have an internal structure giving them a complexity that objects lack. Objects, whether concrete or abstract, possess properties. But a fact is what is expressed by a true proposition and consists in an object's possession or instantiation of a property, relational or non-relational; an event is a happening—an instantiation of a property at a time; a state of affairs is an actuality, possibility, or impossibility expressed by a proposition and to which there corresponds a proposition, either true or false; a proposition is something expressed by an assertion and which gives expression to a state of affairs; and a state is the way an object or system of objects fundamentally *is*. Of course, the issues of precisely how these non-objects are to be characterized, of how they are interrelated, and, in the case of some, whether they should be accorded any ontological status are quite controversial. But we have pursued this matter far enough to see that none of these items seem properly characterized as objects.

2. Not surprisingly, many philosophers would disagree with this view of color. For a discussion of alternative views along with a more detailed defense of this view, see my *Perception, Mind and Personal Identity: A Critique of Materialism* (Lanham, Md.: University Press of America, 1994).

CHAPTER 4: THE MENTAL AND THE PHYSICAL

1. I am excluding certain subjective properties, or intentional properties as they are frequently called, that are attributable to an entity because of the way that entity is regarded under some designation or description. Suppose, for example, that Smith believes that the evening star is the brightest star in the evening sky but does not believe that the morning star is the brightest star in the evening sky because he does not know that the names "morning star" and "evening star" are names for the same object, namely, the planet Venus. So the evening star has the property of being believed by Smith to be the brightest star in the evening sky whereas the morning star does not. But we certainly should not infer from such a property difference that the evening star is not identical to the morning star. Thus "intentional properties" should not be considered as objective properties that may be used to establish non-

identity. We must, however, distinguish these properties from the property of *inten-tionality* (of being directed upon something), which is a property an item may objec-tively possess. Thus if X is directed upon something and Y is not, then X and Y cannot be identical.

2. Others will come into view later on when we turn our attention to issues con-cerning the existence and nature of the self. For an inference that we will then be able to draw is that if the self exists as a subject of conscious states, it has an indivisibility and an identity through time that no material object (other than, perhaps, an ultimate micro-particle, if there are any) could have. Moreover, we will be in a position to see that a self or person possesses a *unity of consciousness* that seems impossible to under-stand as a material phenomenon. We will also be able to conclude that even if we were otherwise justified in claiming that a subject of conscious states is identical to some material entity, our claim would be defeated by the fact that it would be *indeterminate* as to *which* material entity the subject would be.

3. The source of the interpretation that makes possible the having of a thought or a belief remains totally incomprehensible within the framework available to a defender of this view. Either the interpretation itself is to be analyzed like thoughts and beliefs as existing only in relation to some interpretation, or else it is not. If it is not, then either it is the result of an intrinsically intentional state of consciousness and thus pre-cisely what cannot be acknowledged to exist, or it is nothing more than an assembly of physical items. But if it is the latter, then there could be nothing that picks it out as an *interpretation*. For any such assembly of items needs interpreting if it is to be seen as an interpretation. Thus only the first alternative remains: The interpretation is to be ana-lyzed like thoughts and beliefs, as existing only in relation to some interpretation. In other words, that something is an interpretation is itself only a matter of interpreta-tion. But this alternative leads to a regress that renders interpretation impossible. If interpretation is to occur, it must be supplied by someone. But since its being an inter-pretation is itself a matter of interpretation, a prior interpretation is required for it to exist as an interpretation. Hence, no one can come to be the first to have the property of supplying an interpretation. For coming to have this property depends upon the interpretation of someone who already has it. Consequently, no one can have this property. (For more on this matter, see Chapter 8 of my book, *Perception, Mind, and Personal Identity*, 1994.)

4. For the purposes of this discussion, we should construe the notion of a mental event broadly enough to make it compatible with any form of dualism in which the existence of mental particulars is acknowledged. Accordingly, a mental event may be either the occurrence of a subjectless experience (as it would be in a dualism accord-ing to which the mind is a bundle of subjectless experiences unified by certain rela-tions holding among the experiences, each of which is a particular rather than a state or property of some other particular), or a subject's *having* an experience, i.e., its *being in* an experiential state.

5. In this account, causal direction is determined by the direction of time. But this seems to commit one to an absolute view of time according to which time is something over and above the structure of relations of events, i.e., time is not reducible to rela-tions among events. Though this view of time is not ruled out by the truth of the spe-cial and general theories of relativity (as some may think), many may find it difficult to accept.

6. Perhaps the regularity view of causation cannot be reconciled with our com-monsensical conviction that sometimes, at least, there are genuine alternative courses of action available to us and that the one we take may be the result of our free choice. For the regularity view may imply that there are sufficient causal conditions for an event caused by an agent (i.e., for the *agent's causing* of the event); and, if there are such conditions, then the agency theory that we shall later consider in our attempt to resolve the free-will issue becomes either incoherent or (even if coherent) unable to provide an understanding of how free will might be a reality. The issues are complex, however, and would require lengthy consideration. Thus we cannot pursue them here. For an argument for the view that there may be sufficient causal conditions for an agent-causal event, see Richard Taylor, *Action and Purpose* (Upper Saddle River, N.J.: Prentice-Hall, 1966), pp. 114–115. For an opposing argument, see Timothy O'Conner, "Agent Causation," in *Agents, Causes, and Events,* ed. by T. O'Conner (New York: Oxford University Press, 1995).

7. If causation *is* reducible to something else, e.g., regular successions of events or natural law, then we may well find it ultimately mysterious as to why the world includes precisely the fundamental natural laws that it does in fact include rather than others we can imagine it having.

8. Dualistic interactionism would still be a logical possibility even if a completed brain science revealed that only physical-physical causation need be involved in a com-plete explanation of the workings of the brain. For the thesis of causal overdetermi-nation by the mental would not be ruled out. More specifically, it would remain a logical possibility that some brain events are overdetermined in that they have both a mental and a physical cause, each of which is sufficient for their occurrence. Similarly, it would remain a logical possibility that some brain events cause both mental and physical events in such a way that no mental event need be invoked to explain what happens in the physical realm. But such a thesis, though possibly true, would not be very credible.

CHAPTER 5: SELF

1. I do not mean to distinguish the self from the person, though I will distinguish the person (and thus the self) from the human being (or human organism). Thus when we later raise questions about the persistence of the self through time, we are raising questions that are frequently called questions of personal identity. The techni-cal term that philosophers sometimes use to denote personal identity is *diachronic* iden-tity – the identity of the person through time.

2. The issue of what our power of imagination discloses to us about what is possi-ble is a controversial one. Some well-known philosophers (W. V. O. Quine, for exam-ple—see his article, "On What There Is," originally published in the *Review of Metaphysics* 2 [1948]) have apparently held, or have at least taken seriously, the view that there are no non-actual possibilities—that, to illustrate, it was not possible for you to have closed this book a moment ago instead of continuing to read it. But such wholesale denial of non-actual possibility seems impossible to accept. And if there are possibilities which are not actualized, our power to imagine them must be acknowl-edged to be a guide to what they are. At the same time, we must exercise our power to

imagine with care, to make sure that we are not employing assumptions that are incompatible with the imagined situation.

3. For a very different interpretation, along with a defense of the relational view, see Derek Parfit's well-known book, *Reasons and Persons* (New York: Oxford University Press, 1984).

CHAPTER 6: GOD

1. Though I follow a well-established tradition in referring to God with such pronouns as *He, His,* and *Him,* I do not intend to suggest that God should be thought of as a male, or as a female. Indeed, we should try to avoid thinking of God as having gender.

2. Still, we may have serious reservations about the claim that we really can conceive of either time or the world extending infinitely far into the past. If the world is eternal, then an infinite number of past events have occurred. Since the past is actualized and complete, this would imply that past events constitute an actual infinity. But, so the argument goes, an actual infinite cannot exist in the natural world of concrete things and events (even if it can exist in an abstract realm of numbers or sets). Hence, the world cannot be eternal. For more about this, see William Craig, "Philosophical and Scientific Pointers to *Creatio ex Nihilo,*" in *Contemporary Perspectives on Religious Epistemology,* eds. R. Douglas Geivett and Brendan Sweetman (New York: Oxford University Press, 1992), 185–200.

3. The argument in its modern form may be traced back to the eighteenth-century philosophers G. Leibniz and S. Clarke. For a more detailed yet very readable presentation, see William Rowe's *Philosophy of Religion,* 2nd ed. (Belmont, Calif.: Wadsworth, 1993), 16–28.

4. I have here employed a version of Taylor's striking example. For more on this see Richard Taylor, *Metaphysics* (Upper Saddle River, N.J.: Prentice Hall, 1992), 100–103.

5. I am thinking especially of the famous existentialist philosopher, Martin Heidegger, who takes this question to be "the broadest," "the deepest," and "the most fundamental" one we can ask. See his *An Introduction to Metaphysics* (New Haven and London: Yale University Press, 1959), 1–6.

6. For more on the view that the universe is balanced on a razor's edge, see B. J. Carr and M. J. Rees, "The Anthropic Principle and the Structure of the Physical World," *Nature* 278 (1979), 605–612; and J. J. Davis, "The Design Argument, Cosmic 'Fine-tuning,' and the Anthropic Principle," *International Journal Philosophy Religion* 22 (1987), 139–150.

7. William J. Wainwright provides a very helpful treatment of these issues. For a more extensive discussion of the problem of evil, along with a well-argued theistic response to this problem, see his book, *Philosophy of Religion* (Belmont, Calif.: Wadsworth, 1999).

8. The phrase in quotes, or some variant of it, is often used by Christian mystics to describe the emotional quality of the mystical consciousness. Sometimes the phrase used is "the peace of God that passes all understanding."

CHAPTER 7: FREE WILL

1. John Foster very persuasively argues that if it were legitimate to treat a physical object as a basic subject, then the question as to which physical objects qualified for that role would have an objective answer. He proceeds to show that no objective answer is possible if the subject of consciousness is taken to be a physical object. See his *The Immaterial Self* (London: Routledge, 1991), pp. 210–211.

2. It would seem that a dual-aspect theorist who maintains that what bears the dual aspects are some of the brain constituents or processes is also exposed to the difficulty that no physical element or process can be a basic subject.

CHAPTER 8: VALUE AND MORALITY

1. There are, not surprisingly, well-known contemporary philosophers who may be in disagreement with this. Thomas Nagel, for one, argues for the objectivity of value. But he agrees that value is not a feature of the external world. And it seems that the objectivity of value comes down to an intersubjective agreement about what we should do and want, based on the proper operation of a "common evaluative faculty." See his *The View From Nowhere* (New York: Oxford University Press, 1986), 138–148.

2. Bentham defines the principle of utility in his book, *An Introduction to the Principles of Morals and Legislation* (1823).

3. John Rawls, *A Theory of Justice* (Cambridge, Mass.: The Belknap Press of Harvard University Press, 1971).

4. See R. M. Hare, *Freedom and Reason* (New York: Oxford University Press, 1963), 113–117.

5. My attempt to answer this important question is heavily influenced by the thought of Thomas Nagel. I owe to him the insight that the only true foundation of morality, and thus the only unwavering motivation for moral behavior, is a direct concern for the well-being of others. See his remarkable little book, *What Does It All Mean?* (New York: Oxford University Press, 1987), 62–67.

6. This is a famous phrase uttered by the atheist brother, Ivan Karamazov, a character in Fyodor Dostoevsky's great novel, *The Brothers Karamazov*.

CHAPTER 9: DEATH

1. See the selection "Death is Nothing to Us" in Jacques Choron, *Death and Western Thought* (New York: Collier Books, 1963), 58–63.

2. For books providing a rather detailed examination of many of the important cases, see Robert Almeder, *Death and Personal Survival* (Lanham, Md.: Rowman and Littlefield, 1992); my own *Death and Consciousness* (Jefferson, N.C.: McFarland and Co., 1985); and Ian Stevenson, *Twenty Cases Suggestive of Reincarnation*, 2d ed. (Charlottesville, Va.: University Press of Virginia, 1974).

3. I am here referring to the famous case of Shanti Devi. For more information about this case, see Almeder, *Death and Personal Survival*, 19–21, and L. D. Gupta, N. R.

Sharms, and T. C. Mathur, *An Inquiry into the Case of Shanti Devi* (Delhi: International Aryan League, 1936).

4. "Mrs. Willett" is a pseudonym. The medium's real name was Mrs. Charles Coombe-Tennant. For more information about her remarkable mediumship, see my book, *Death and Consciousness,* and also C. D. Broad, *Lectures on Psychical Research* (London: Routledge & Kegan Paul, 1962).

5. I owe the inspiration for this argument as well as much of its development to John Knox, Jr. See his article, "Pre-Existence, Survival, and Sufficient Reason," *American Philosophical Quarterly* 32 (April 1995).

6. I have argued in another context that we have fundamental knowledge of ourselves that cannot be described. See my book, *Perception, Mind, and Personal Identity.*

CHAPTER 10: THE MEANING OF LIFE

1. Miguel De Unamuno, *The Tragic Sense of Life* (New York: Dover Publications, 1954), p. 13. English translation first published 1921.

2. I owe this way of putting the problem—that our lives as a whole may be pointless, even if they are quite meaningful in other respects—to Thomas Nagel.

3. I owe the essentials of this analysis of a meaningful activity to W. D. Joske. See his essay, "Philosophy and the Meaning of Life," in *The Meaning of Life,* ed. E. D. Klemke (New York: Oxford University Press, 1981).

4. Nagel, *What Does It All Mean?,* p. 101.

FURTHER READING

The various books and articles I have listed in the "Notes" section should, of course, be regarded as suggestions for further reading. Here I offer a few more.

INTRODUCTION

Bertrand Russell's classic, *Problems of Philosophy* (New York: Oxford University Press, 1968, first published 1912) provides an excellent problem-oriented access to philosophy. For more recent and very engaging introductions to philosophy, see Tom Davis, *Philosophy: An Introduction Through Original Fiction, Discussion, and Readings*, 3d ed. (New York: McGraw-Hill, 1993); and Daniel Kolak and Raymond Martin, *Wisdom Without Answers*, 5th ed. (Belmont, Calif.: Wadsworth, 2002). Other valuable introductions include John Hospers, *An Introduction to Philosophical Analysis*, 4th ed. (Upper Saddle River, N.J.: Prentice Hall, 1997); Robert Solomon, *The Big Questions: A Short Introduction to Philosophy*, 6th ed. (Fort Worth, Tex.: Harcourt Brace, 2002); Richard Double, *Beginning Philosophy* (New York: Oxford University Press, 1999); and Emmett Barcalow, *Open Questions: An Introduction to Philosophy*, 3rd ed. (Belmont, Calif.: Wadsworth, 2001).

KNOWLEDGE

Rene Descartes's *Meditations on First Philosophy* (cited in the "Notes" section) begins with a swift and engaging excursion into the foundations of knowledge. For a helpful commentary on it, see Fred Feldman, *A Cartesian Introduction to Philosophy* (New York: McGraw-Hill, 1986). More extensive discussion of skepticism may be found in Richard Popkin, *A History of Skepticism from Erasmus to Descartes* (New York: Harper & Row,

1964), and Barry Stroud, *The Significance of Philosophical Scepticism* (New York: Oxford University Press, 1984). For an anthology addressing some of the fundamental issues in contemporary epistemology, see Michael Goodman and Robert Snyder, *Contemporary Issues in Epistemology* (Upper Saddle River, N.J.: Prentice Hall, 1993). A clearly written and well-organized text on logic is Patrick Hurley, *A Concise Introduction to Logic*, 7th ed. (Belmont, Calif.: Wadsworth, 2000).

REALITY

A philosophical treatment of color perception that is well grounded in color science is C. L. Hardin, *Color for Philosophers: Unweaving the Rainbow* (Indianapolis, Ind.: Hackett, 1988). For a detailed account of the various forms of sensory awareness, see Moreland Perkins, *Sensing the World* (Indianapolis, Ind.: Hackett, 1983). A very accessible defense of the view that perception is indirect is D. L. C. Maclachlan, *Philosophy of Perception* ((Upper Saddle River, N.J.: Prentice Hall, 1989). A valuable (but less accessible) selection of readings on perception is Jonathan Dancy, ed., *Perceptual Knowledge* (New York: Oxford University Press, 1988). Anthologies that provide a treatment of a broad range of metaphysical issues are Peter Van Inwagen and Dean Zimmerman, eds., *Metaphysics: The Big Questions* (Malden, Mass.: Blackwell, 1998); and Jaegwon Kim and Ernest Sosa, eds., *Metaphysics: An Anthology* (Malden, Mass.: Blackwell, 1999).

THE MENTAL AND THE PHYSICAL

A brief introductory study of the concept of mind and the mind-body problem is Dale Jacquette, *Philosophy of Mind* ((Upper Saddle River, N.J.: Prentice Hall, 1994). A good selection of readings is David Rosenthal, ed., *Materialism and the Mind-Body Problem* (Indianapolis, Ind.: Hackett, 1987). Other helpful works include Keith Campbell, *Body and Mind* (Notre Dame, Ind.: University of Notre Dame, 1984); Daniel Dennett and Douglas Hofstadter, eds., *The Mind's I* (New York: Basic Books, 1981); Stephen Priest, *Theories of the Mind* (New York: Houghton Mifflin, 1991); and E.J. Lowe, *An Introduction to the Philosophy of Mind* (New York: Cambridge University Press, 2000). For a selection of readings on the nature of causation, see Ernest Sosa and Michael Tooley, eds., *Causation* (New York: Oxford University Press, 1993).

SELF

A very brief and engaging work on the self is John Perry, *A Dialogue on Personal Identity and Immortality* (Indianapolis, Ind.: Hackett, 1978). For a debate between two well-known philosophers on the subject of personal identity, see

Richard Swinburne and Sydney Shoemaker, *Personal Identity* (Oxford: Blackwell, 1984). A comprehensive selection of contemporary readings on the self, personal identity, and the unity of consciousness is Daniel Kolak and Raymond Martins, eds., *Self and Identity: Contemporary Philosophical Issues* (New York: Macmillan, 1991).

GOD

A brief and accessible work which argues for the existence of God is Richard Swinburne, *Is There A God?* (New York: Oxford University Press, 1997). A more comprehensive and very readable work is Yeager Hudson, *The Philosophy of Religion* (Mountain View, Calif.: Mayfield, 1991). There are numerous good anthologies in the area of philosophy of religion. For one that includes several selections from non-Western sources, see S. Phillips, ed., *Philosophy of Religion: A Global Approach* (Fort Worth, Tex.: Harcourt Brace, 1996). Other important anthologies include Baruch Brody, ed., *Readings in the Philosophy of Religion: An Analytic Approach*, 2d ed. ((Upper Saddle River, N.J.: Prentice Hall, 1992); William Rowe and William Wainwright, eds., *Philosophy of Religion: Selected Readings* (New York: Harcourt Brace Jovanovich, 1989); Louis Pojman, ed., *Philosophy of Religion: An Anthology*, 3d ed. (Belmont, Calif.: Wadsworth, 1998); and Michael Peterson, William Hasker, Bruce Reichenbach, and David Basinger, eds., *Philosophy of Religion: Selected Readings* (New York: Oxford University Press, 1996).

FREE WILL

Anthologies on the subject include Bernard Berofsky, ed., *Free Will and Determinism* (New York: Harper & Row, 1966); and Sidney Hook, ed., *Determinism and Freedom* (New York: Collier Books, 1961). A good selection of essays on the free will–determinism issue may be found in Paul Edwards and Arthur Pap, eds., *A Modern Introduction to Philosophy*, 3d ed. (New York: Macmillan/ The Free Press, 1973). Also see Part IV, "Freedom," in Ronald Hoy and L. Nathan Oaklander, eds., *Metaphysics: Classic and Contemporary Readings*, (Belmont, Calif.: Wadsworth, 1991). For a defense of agent causation, see Roderick Chisholm, *Person and Object: A Metaphysical Study* (La Salle, Ill.: Open Court, 1976). Recent and sophisticated treatments of the issue include Daniel Dennett, *Elbow Room: The Varieties of Free Will Worth Wanting* (Cambridge, Mass.: MIT Press, 1984); Richard Double, *Metaphilosophy and Free Will* (New York: Oxford University Press, 1996); Ted Honderich, *A Theory of Determinism*, 2 vols. (Oxford: Oxford University Press, 1988); and Robert Kane, *The Significance of Free Will* (New York: Oxford University Press, 1996).

VALUE AND MORALITY

A very good general anthology on ethics is Paul Taylor, ed., *Problems of Moral Philosophy* (Belmont, Calif.: Wadsworth, 1978). A more recent anthology of high quality is Louis Pojman, ed., *Ethical Theory* (Belmont, Calif.: Wadsworth, 1989). Another recent work on the various ethical theories is Robert Solomon, *A Handbook for Ethics* (Fort Worth, Tex.: Harcourt Brace, 1996). Other good introductory works include John Hospers, *Human Conduct: Problems of Ethics,* 2d ed. (New York: Harcourt Brace Jovanovich, 1982); and Jonathan Glover, ed., *Utilitarianism and Its Critics* (New York: Macmillan, 1990). The classic expression of the view that religious belief cannot be the foundation of morality is Plato's *Euthyphro.*

DEATH

For a well-chosen group of readings that addresses a variety of issues concerning human nature and the possibility of surviving death, see Paul Edwards, ed., *Immortality* (New York: Macmillan, 1992). For a study that focuses on a Christian understanding of how these issues are to be resolved, see John Cooper, *Body, Soul and Life Everlasting* (Grand Rapids, Mich.: Wm. B. Eerdmans, 1989). A treatment of several issues involving death, along with a materialist account of it, is Fred Feldman, *Confrontations with the Reaper* (New York: Oxford University Press, 1992). A careful evaluation of mediumistic communications is H. H. Price, "The Problem of Life After Death," *Religious Studies 3* (April 1968); and an outstanding study of reincarnation is Ian Stevenson, *Twenty Cases Suggestive of Reincarnation,* 2d ed. (Charlottesville, Va.: University Press of Virginia, 1974).

THE MEANING OF LIFE

A classic expression of the problem of finding meaning in life is Leo Tolstoy's *My Confession.* It may be found in E. D. Klemke, ed., *The Meaning of Life* (New York: Oxford University Press, 1981), 9–19. Another very nice essay on this subject is Richard Taylor's "The Meaning of Life" in his *Good and Evil* (New York: Macmillan, 1970). It is also reprinted in the Klemke anthology. Another good anthology is Steven Sanders and David Cheney, eds., *The Meaning of Life* (Upper Saddle River, N.J.: Prentice Hall, 1980). For a wide variety of selections, both classical and contemporary, see Jonathan Westphal and Carl Levenson, eds., *Life and Death* (Indianapolis, Ind.: Hackett, 1993).

INDEX